BHAGAVAD GITA

The Rhythm of Krishna

BHAGAVAD GITA
The Rhythm of Krishna

Sanskrit Shlokas into rhythmic
English verses with
Sanskrit text and transliteration

Sushrut A. Badhe

SECOND Edition: 2020

Published by Midam Charitable Trust
Midam Ashram, K.P. Natham
Pondicherry - 605102
India
midamtrust@gmail.com

FIRST Edition: 2015

Published by Sri Aurobindo's Action
Pondicherry - 605002
India
sriaurobindosaction@yahoo.com

Credits:- Cover: Enjo Mathew, Back Cover Art: Avanti Badhe,
Illustrations: Aroul Vendhan P.

ISBN: 978-81-943838-2-6

Typeset by **PAGE VIEW Book Designs**, pvbookdesign@gmail.com

In Ode to the Master

"Soon this darkness too shall part

The great One hath summoned a new start

Bursting through the clouds on destiny's morn

Naked earth-golden light shall adorn"

Acknowledgements

My first acknowledgements go to my father, Dr.Ashok Badhe and my mother Dr.Bhawana Badhe for allowing me to walk the path of the spirit. Without your loving support nothing was possible. I am indeed blessed to have you as my parents.

After my parents, I bow in gratitude to my Guru and God father- Sri Madhusudan Damleji -who gave me my second birth. My four years with you have passed like four seconds. My salutations again! Whatever light there is in me today-it is yours!

And to my *Krishna*- O beloved, I love you!

After bowing to my parents, my teacher and my God- I would like to say thanks

To Avanti- my sister who has chosen to walk the same path with me. It has always been wonderful to have your company.

To Dora Vandana- the victor who sent me a steady trickle of inspiration despite being engaged herself in a battle of life and death.

To Manju Bonkeji- without whose initiation the first edition of this book would not have seen the light of day. Thank you for the acceptance, guidance and support.

To Mr. P. Veerachandiran- for his patient and continued support in the content design.

सुश्रुत बढे

Contents

The Message of the Gita

The shlokas of the *Bhagavad Gita* are aimed at attaining a realization that will lead to the conscious evolution of an individual, a society, a nation and the world at large.

The *Bhagavad Gita* is essentially a spiritual book and not a religious text. It is universal in its perspective and all 18 chapters emphasize the need for action for the *Lokasangraha-* betterment of all peoples of the world.

It speaks not about a material asceticism but instead speaks about embracing every sphere of *karma* to lead a Divine life on earth.

Throughout the text we hear *Arjuna-* the chosen one- ask the questions that arise in almost every human heart.

And we also hear the words of *Krishna* –the manifesting god head-patiently answering all his queries on God, man, life, death, living and being with a love that is truly Divine.

The *Gita* is integral in all its principles, which can be imbibed by all sections of the society.

It teaches a sage to become a better sage, a warrior to become a better warrior, a businessman to become a better businessman, a doctor to be a better doctor, an engineer to be a better engineer, a scientist to be a better scientist, a politician to become a better politician, a teacher to become a better teacher and a student to become a better student.

Sri Madhusudan R. Damle

The Story of the Gita

The *Mahabharata* is one of the greatest epics of India and is supposed to have taken its present form between the fifth and the first centuries B.C. The authorship of the *Gita* is attributed to *Vyasa*, the legendary compiler of the *Mahabharata*. The eighteen chapters of the Gita form chapters XXIII to XL of the *Bhismaparva* of the epic.

Kuru is the name of the leading clan of that time, and *Kurukshetra* was a vast field near Hastinapur (modern Delhi) where the *Kurus* used to perform their religious sacrifices. It was there that the *Kauravas* and *Pandavas*, two sections of the *Kuru* Family, fought the great battle without parallel in the history of ancient India, all the princes of the land joining one side or the other.

When *Dritharashtra* the blind king of the *Kuru* became old, he decided to give his throne, not to his own son *Duryodhana*, a man of evil propensities, but to *Yudhishthira*, the eldest son of his deceased younger brother *Pandu* and an embodiment of virtue and purity, fit to be the ruler of a kingdom based on *Dharma,* law, righteousness and justice. But *Duryodhana* by cunning and treachery secured the throne for himself and tried every means to do away with *Yudhishthira* and his four brothers one of whom was *Arjuna*, foremost among archers.

Krishna, God incarnate, was the head of the *Yadava* clan and a friend and relative of the Kurus. He tried to bring about a reconciliation between the *Kauravas* and *Pandavas*; on behalf of the sons of *Pandu* he asked for only five villages, but *Duryodhana* refused to give without battle even a needle-point of earth. The grim combat became inevitable to establish right and justice.

Drona, the common military teacher of the sons of *Dhritarashtra* and the sons of *Pandu*, went to the side of *Duryodhana*; so also did the great celibate *Bhishma* the grandsire in the *Kuru* clan. *Krishna* as an impartial friend offered a choice to the rival parties. *Duryodhana* chose for himself the mighty army of *Krishna,* while *Arjuna* chose *Krishna* alone,-and *Krishna* would not fight, he would be the charioteer of *Arjuna.*

As the legend says, *Vyasa* saw *Dhritarashtra* before the outbreak of the war and asked him whether he wished to have his sight restored so that he could himself see the events happening. *Dhritarashtra* refused for he did not think that he could bear the sight of the apprehended carnage, but he asked *Vyasa* to arrange for correct reporting of the events to him. *Vyasa* approached *Sanjaya,* the charioteer of the old king, for the purpose. To *Sanjaya* he gave the supernormal vision, and to the blind king he said, "O King, this *Sanjaya* will tell you about this battle. *Sanjaya* will have the knowledge of all things open or secret, whatever happens at night or in the day; he will be able to read even mind's thought. The battle -arms will not hurt him nor will fatigue overtake him."

The Gita opens with the question of *Dhritarashtra* asking *Sanjaya* about the events on the battle-field. The two armies, marshalled by their able commanders, are about to start the fight when *Arjuna* wishes to have a look at the champions of the opposite camp. He advances into the thick of the strife with an easy confidence; like the mighty goddess he would say,

Aham rudrāya dhanurā tanomi brahmadviṣe śarave hantavā u
"I draw the bow of the *Rudra*, I hurl the arrow to slay the hater of the truth."[1]

But lo, a miraculous change comes over him at the sight of relatives and friends, his own kinsmen who have to be slain in the war. In a moment, he is besieged with the despondency and grief and the god-given bow *Gandiva* slips from his hands." I shall not fight" he announces.

---

[1] Rig Veda , X. 125.6
[2] Savitri ,II.11.

Krishna, the Blessed Lord, the Divine Charioteer, takes *Arjuna* by the hand in that hour of overwhelming crisis and unveils to him, step by step the meaning of life, the secret of Divine action and the supreme truth. The Master gives his assuring word to man.

Our souls can climb into the shining planes[2] and the God-lover, the God-knower, the God-doer who can live in God and for God and do for Him joyfully whatever be the work in the world, made God-like he would enjoy the supreme spiritual consciousness, here on earth.

This is the message of the *Bhagavad Gita*, literally "the Divine song", and this path, it declares, is open for the whole of mankind, for all, irrespective of their past, who have taken the decision to turn to the Divine and live in the Divine. When the soul says in surrender, as did *Arjuna* at the end, "I shall do Thy will, O God", God delivers him from all sin and evil; this is *Krishna*'s promise.

21-2-1974   Shyam Sunder Jhunjhunwala

MANOGAT

Manogat is a Marathi word derived from the Sanskrit words 'manah' (mind) and 'gat' (thought) and is widely used in books to showcase the musings and reflections of the author. I approached various editors before the publication of the second edition. Some who did not connect to this book, suggested I rewrite the entire Gita in free verse instead of rhymes, others who did appreciate it, told me to approach Sanskrit language experts who in turn advised me to re-approach those with a mastery over the English language. When I turned to a very experienced editor, who was familiar with editing my writing for the Sri Aurobindo's Action Journal, Mary Premila Boseman and got a similar response, I was disappointed. When I expressed the same to her, with the love of a grandmother she told me that she and I would have to sit together for months and have discussions on each verse to perfectly edit it and that this luxury of time was not something both she or I had due to our own various other commitments. Quoting her about this book from the editorial perspective,

"On the foundation of a very wide knowledge and a creative use of English you have built what might as well be another language as far as editing it is concerned, though not for the reader who is drawn into the rhythmic presentation. For me to change almost anything would require other changes in nearly every case, and once that happens the integrity of the text is lost. What you are doing is individual before anything else and it may well be that you weave a particular spell with your syntax and word juxtapositions that would be a magical, and highly devotional, introduction or rereading for many people, especially young people I think."

During this COVID -19 period, this book has become a reference book for the virtual free for all Gita classes under the "Krishna's Butter Project" organized by Midam Charitable Trust and the need for its re-publication has arisen. So, I will not wait anymore for the foreword for this edition and will be using this space to share my own *Manogat* and in the process share a portion of my mind to the readers

It is always a nice feeling to see one's book enter into its second edition. But when one's teacher publishes it, the nice feeling transforms into plain ecstasy. Though my first edition of Bhagavad Gita: Rhythm of Krishna set records in India Book of Records and Limca Book of Records for being a unique book having all 700 verses of the ancient and immortal scripture in English rhymes almost five years ago, I have not really been able to understand one thing – "why did I write it?". I had written an "Author's Foreword" in the first edition but somehow even after 5 years of its publication, I still feel the rationale I had attempted to explain why I really wrote it fails completely.

"Why did a mechanical engineer choose to render the Gita in rhymes?"- is one question that really is unanswerable to me. I don't know why on the auspicious day of Hanuman Jayanti, after listening to my teacher, Sri Madhusduan Damle read out a Hindi story of Gita for children-"Gita Uvacha", I found the inspiration to ask for his blessings to begin this endeavour. I also don't know why he said yes. Because had he said otherwise I would not have even dared to spend the next year and half in this attempt. Some things in life are beyond the realm of mental logic, as is said in the Gita, and this I believe is one of those mysterious life occurrences for me.

The Sanskrit verse goes, *mukam karoti vachalam. pangum langhayate girim. yat-kripa tam aham vande paramanada madhavam* The dumb begin to speak with eloquence, the crippled limp their way to cross the mountains,

Only by your Grace, O Lord, Madhava- the source of Ananda- the bliss supreme.

I believe it is only the grace that made it possible for a fool like myself to complete this attempt. However, I can definitely say that the "Essays on the Gita" by Sri Aurobindo offered me all the love and support in my attempt to limp across all the 700 verses of the Gita. Also the commentaries of the Four Authorized Vaishnava saints – Sri Vishnuswami, Sri Madhavacharya, Sri Keshava

Kashmiri and Sri Ramanuja were used for reference.

The numbers at the end of the four line verses are according to the numbers written in the original Sanskrit text. No alterations have been made in the numbering and also the verses have not been grouped purposefully so that each verse may be studied and compared individually.

Though Krishna and Arjuna have been glorified by a number of different names throughout the Bhagavad Gita, I have chosen to maintain homogeneity in their names throughout my rhythmic verses.

For the younger generation that does not have much free time, the verses have been grouped as per the subjects and the groupings are mentioned at the beginning of every Canto.

For those well versed in the Devanagari script –the original Shlokas in the Sanskrit language have been provided in this book for their reference and comparison.

For those who are unaware of the Devanagari script, an English transliteration has been provided. The Devanagari script and the transliterations have been adopted from the e-version of The Bhagavad Gita made freely available to all students of the Sanskrit language by U.Stiehl. The Internationational Alphabet of Sanskrit Transliteration (I.A.S.T.) scheme of transliteration has been followed and a table of the vowels, codas and consonants has been provided at the end of the book so that the transliteration may be read out in a phonetically accurate manner.

Also for the readers who are not very familiar with the Sanskrit terms, a glossary of important Sanskrit terms and characters mentioned in the English verses has been provided.

I end this *Manogat* with a poetic rendition of the Varhadi poem "Mazi Mai Sorosoti" written by the great illiterate poetess, Aai Bahinabai Chaudhary. She never wrote a single poem, but her son wrote all that she sang while doing her daily chores in the fields and at home and recorded it in a diary. In 1951, 732 of her poems that were recorded by her son were published under the title " Bahinabainnche Gane" or "The Songs of Bahinabai" after being discovered by the educationalist Acharya Atre who wrote the introduction for the book describing the first poem that he had heard as 'pure gold' and thus, the poems reached the rest of the world long after her departure. In the year 2012, Yeshwant Rao Chaohan Open University declared her work as a part of the University's curriculum.

"My Mother, Sorosoti,
Teaches me to speak the language
In her daughter Bahina's mind
So many secrets, she has inscribed!
Just for my sake O Panduranga
Has emerged your Bhagavad Gita,
Nourished and nurtured by the rain
On the soil it has emerged once again.
The Darshana / Vision of the God-Almighty,
Has taken place, O so easily
By My father Soorya and Lord Hari's blessing
The form of the formless One, I am witnessing.
The sound of your footsteps I am hearing
In every single leaf's rustling
Of the God's coming and going
The wind too in my ears is whispering."

— Aai Bahinabai

Without more ado, I present to you – The Bhagavad Gita. I hope you find this book worth your time.

Hare Krishna

Sushrut
6th August 2020, Puducherry.

Prologue

To *Vyasa's* poetic genius, I humbly bow

For penning this sacred text several thousand years ago

Under the leaves, composed this great mystic

In a Divine language- both rhythmic and cryptic

1,00,000 verses of *Mahabharata* for us he disclosed

Meditating on the first great war, this epic he composed

A mighty story of "The Empire" painted in esoteric hues

With king-secrets progressively cloaked by symbolic clues

Portraying the mighty battle of darkness & light,

Through the oracle's eyes we saw -the *Kuru* princes' fight

A stunning evolution of weaponry and technology was portrayed

To the world an ancient *Bhaarath* was grandiosely displayed

The high philosophy of *Dharma* recollected the sage,

When most spiritual traditions hadn't even come of age.

Unveiling the voice of the manifestation Divine- *Krishna*

Who taught the best amongst men the 'Law of *Karma*'

Revealing the secrets of what was before birth

And the occult knowledge of what transpires after death

Of the forces aiding/impairing the journey of the soul

Of the way of life to attain *moksha*- the final goal.

Of the ultimate realization possible in this birth itself

Of living a sorrow-free life –dwelling in the state of
the awakened "Self"

To awaken the Divine consciousness on the human side

To uphold all that is right and to once more turn the tide.

Resonating the promise of *Krishna* to the whole of mankind

Of returning in an age when those who see choose to be blind!

Invocation

I invoke the Mother- *Saraswati*, the source of *Vyasa*'s
inspiration

Guide my words too, help me fulfill my aspiration

The sacred *Sanskrit* text, I attempt to sincerely translate-
Krishna's voice in a foreign tongue I seek to replicate

I call upon *Sri Krishna*, the one with the bamboo flute

The dreamy eyed *Avatar*- a figure so Divine and yet so cute

Whose very thought set the *Gopikas* into an intoxicated dance,

Even to this day your name sends your countless lovers
into a trance

Several centuries ago were we graced by your golden aura,

So beautiful you are- your majesty- our usher of the future era.

Kaliyuga's darkest cloak our earth has now worn,

O Love, Will you not return once more as you had sworn?

Your sacred homeland is now no more the same-

Our brother's immoral actions make us bend down in shame

Man's greed and lust today reign supreme –

He has become too deaf to hear nature scream,

Exclusive religions and preachers are destroying spirituality

Fuelling hate, they are spreading discord and animosity

What were we once, and what have we become –

O *Krishna*, the time is now ripe for you to once more come.

Our world begs for a Divine teacher to once more descend

To turn the *Karmic* wheel for everyone to ascend.

With folded hands I bequeath our *Krishna*, our beloved, our God

With your resplendent words awaken us and reside within,
my Lord-
With these simple words the immortal epic's translation
I have now begun-

Its golden words shall breathe as long as the fire burns
in the Eye of the sun.

✳ ✳ ✳

अथ प्रथमोऽध्यायः ।
atha prathamodhyāyaḥ

धृतराष्ट्र उवाच
धर्मक्षेत्रे कुरुक्षेत्रे समवेता युयुत्सवः ।
मामकाः पाण्डवाश्चैव किमकुर्वत सञ्जय ॥ १-१॥
dhṛtarāṣṭra uvāca
dharmakṣetre kurukṣetre samavetā yuyutsavaḥ
māmakāḥ pāṇḍavāś caiva kim akurvata sañjaya 1.1

सञ्जय उवाच ।
दृष्ट्वा तु पाण्डवानीकं व्यूढं दुर्योधनस्तदा ।
आचार्यमुपसङ्गम्य राजा वचनमब्रवीत् ॥ १-२॥
sañjaya uvāca
dṛṣṭvā tu pāṇḍavānīkam vyūḍham duryodhanas tadā
ācāryam upasaṅgamya rājā vacanam abravīt 1.2

पश्यैतां पाण्डुपुत्राणामाचार्य महतीं चमूम् ।
व्यूढां द्रुपदपुत्रेण तव शिष्येण धीमता ॥ १-३॥
paśyaitām pāṇḍuputrāṇām ācārya mahatīm camūm
vyūḍhām drupadaputreṇa tava śiṣyeṇa dhīmatā 1.3

अत्र शूरा महेष्वासा भीमार्जुनसमा युधि ।
युयुधानो विराटश्च द्रुपदश्च महारथः ॥ १-४॥
atra śūrā maheṣvāsā bhīmārjunasamā yudhi
yuyudhāno virāṭaśca drupadaś ca mahārathaḥ 1.4

धृष्टकेतुश्चेकितानः काशिराजश्च वीर्यवान् ।
पुरुजित्कुन्तिभोजश्च शैब्यश्च नरपुङ्गवः ॥ १-५॥
dhṛṣṭaketuś cekitānaḥ kāśirājaś ca vīryavān
purujit kuntibhojaś ca śaibyaś ca narapu ṅgavaḥ 1.5

Canto I: *The Grief of Arjuna*

**(Verses 3-24: Introducing the *Pandava* and the *Kaurava* warriors assembled to battle; 25: First words of *Krishna*; 26-46: Depression overwhelms *Arjuna)*

The blind emperor Dhritarashtra asked the oracle:
"Gathered together in *Kurukshetra* to battle
Assembled eagerly to prove their mettle
The *Pandavas* and my *Kauravas* poised for a fight
O *Sanjaya*! What happened there? Share your Divine sight" |1|

Sanjaya replied:
"Seeing the *Pandavas'* army approaching
King *Duryodhana* then began speaking
His teacher's attention he sought to invoke
To *Dronacharya* the following words he spoke:|2|

"O *Acharya*! Behold and cast your glance,
At the *Pandavan* army's battle stance-
The sons of *Pandu* and *Drupad* have thus arrayed
See the battle formation that they have arranged. |3|

Here stand in the battle field the mighty warriors
The great military heroes and archers
To *Arjuna* and *Bhima* they are equal in skill and might
Yuyudhana, Virata and chief *Drupad* are all ready to fight. |4|

Along with them are also lined the valiant-
Dhristaketu, the King of *Kashi* and *Chekitan*
And the most brave amongst men
Purujit, Kuntibhoj & *Shaivya*- all warriors brilliant. |5|

युधामन्युश्च विक्रान्त उत्तमौजाश्च वीर्यवान् ।
सौभद्रो द्रौपदेयाश्च सर्व एव महारथाः ॥ १-६॥
yudhāmanyuś ca vikrānta uttamaujāś ca vīryavān
saubhadro draupadeyāś ca sarva eva mahārathāḥ 1.6

अस्माकं तु विशिष्टा ये तान्निबोध द्विजोत्तम ।
नायका मम सैन्यस्य संज्ञार्थं तान्ब्रवीमि ते ॥ १-७॥
asmākaṃ tu viśiṣṭā ye tān nibodha dvijottama
nāyakā mama sainyasya saṃjñārthaṃ tān bravīmi te1.7

भवान्भीष्मश्च कर्णश्च कृपश्च समितिञ्जयः ।
अश्वत्थामा विकर्णश्च सौमदत्तिस्तथैव च ॥ १-८॥
bhavān bhīṣmaś ca karṇaś ca kṛpaś ca samitiñjayaḥ
aśvatthāmā vikarṇaś ca saumadattis tathaiva ca 1.8

अन्ये च बहवः शूरा मदर्थे त्यक्तजीविताः ।
नानाशस्त्रप्रहरणाः सर्वे युद्धविशारदाः ॥ १-९॥
anye ca bahavaḥ śūrā madarthe tyaktajīvitāḥ
nānāśastrapraharaṇāḥ sarve yuddhaviśāradāḥ 1.9

अपर्याप्तं तदस्माकं बलं भीष्माभिरक्षितम् ।
पर्याप्तं त्विदमेतेषां बलं भीमाभिरक्षितम् ॥ १-१०॥
aparyāptaṃ tad asmākaṃ balaṃ bhīṣmābhirakṣitam
paryāptaṃ tvidam eteṣāṃ balaṃ bhīmābhirakṣitam1.10

अयनेषु च सर्वेषु यथाभागमवस्थिताः ।
भीष्ममेवाभिरक्षन्तु भवन्तः सर्व एव हि ॥ १-११॥
ayaneṣu ca sarveṣu yathābhāgam avasthitāḥ
bhīṣmam evābhirakṣantu bhavantaḥ sarva eva hi 1.11

तस्य सञ्जनयन्हर्षं कुरुवृद्धः पितामहः ।
सिंहनादं विनद्योच्चैः शङ्खं दध्मौ प्रतापवान् ॥ १-१२॥
tasya sañjanayan harṣaṃ kuruvṛddhaḥ pitāmahaḥ
siṃhanādaṃ vinadyocchaiḥ śaṅkhaṃ dadhmau pratāpavān 1.12

Uttamauja the strong and the achiever *Yudhamanyu*
The son of *Subhadra*-the young *Abhimanyu*
Also marshaled are *Draupadi's* five warrior sons,
All exemplary generals in their own bastions. |6|

O Best amongst *Brahmin's*, let me now confide
And introduce the great warriors standing on our side
The prominent amongst the generals and leaders
Who stand ground to lead our armed warriors.|7|

Yourself, the mighty Grandfather-*Bhishma*
Karna and the undefeated *Acharya Kripa*
Each greatest amongst masters matched by none
Also are *Ashwatthama, Vikarna* and *Somadatta's* son |8|

Many other great ones have come to partake
Sacrificing their lives to battle for my sake
The advanced specialists of all forms of weapons
Have come to battle- all of them victors and veterans.|9|

With *Bhishma* as guardian, our army is unmatchable
Peerless in combat and looks highly unbeatable
As against the army that *Bhima* has guarded,
His side appears less formidable and limited. |10|

And so to all of you I thus request and ask
To perform this singular and important task,
Stand your ground during the battle and protect
The revered *Bhishma* whom we so respect.|11|

Grandsire *Bhishma* – the *Kuru* clan's eldest
Whose very presence enthused even the strongest
Like a king lion he sent out the fiercest roar
And the sound of his battle conch sparked a furore|12|

ततः शङ्खाश्च भेर्यश्च पणवानकगोमुखाः ।
सहसैवाभ्यहन्यन्त स शब्दस्तुमुलोऽभवत् ॥ १-१३॥
tataḥ śaṅkhāś ca bheryaś ca paṇavānakagomukhāḥ
sahasaivābhyahanyanta sa śabdas tumulobhavat 1.13

ततः श्वेतैर्हयैर्युक्ते महति स्यन्दने स्थितौ ।
माधवः पाण्डवश्चैव दिव्यौ शङ्खौ प्रदध्मतुः ॥ १-१४॥
tataḥ śvetair hayair yukte mahati syandane sthitau
mādhavaḥ pāṇḍavaś caiva divyau śaṅkhau pradaghmatuḥ 1.14

पाञ्चजन्यं हृषीकेशो देवदत्तं धनञ्जयः ।
पौण्ड्रं दध्मौ महाशङ्खं भीमकर्मा वृकोदरः ॥ १-१५॥
pāñcajanyaṃ hṛṣīkeśo devadattaṃ dhanañjayaḥ
pauṇḍraṃ dadhmau mahāsaṅkham bhīmakarmā vṛkodaraḥ 1.15

अनन्तविजयं राजा कुन्तीपुत्रो युधिष्ठिरः ।
नकुलः सहदेवश्च सुघोषमणिपुष्पकौ ॥ १-१६॥
anañtavijayam rājā kuntīputro yudhiṣṭhiraḥ
nakulaḥ sahadevaś ca sughoṣamaṇipuṣpakau 1.16

काश्यश्च परमेष्वासः शिखण्डी च महारथः ।
धृष्टद्युम्नो विराटश्च सात्यकिश्चापराजितः ॥ १-१७॥
kāśyaś ca parameṣvāsaḥ śikhaṇḍī ca mahārathaḥ
dhṛṣṭadyumno virāṭaś ca sātyakiś cāparājitaḥ 1.17

द्रुपदो द्रौपदेयाश्च सर्वशः पृथिवीपते ।
सौभद्रश्च महाबाहुः शङ्खान्दध्मुः पृथक्पृथक् ॥ १-१८॥
drupado draupadeyāś ca sarvaśaḥ pṛthivīpate
saubhadraś ca mahābāhuḥ śaṅkhān dadhmuḥ pṛthakpṛthak 1.18

स घोषो धार्तराष्ट्राणां हृदयानि व्यदारयत् ।
नभश्च पृथिवीं चैव तुमुलोऽभ्यनुनादयन् ॥ १-१९॥
sa ghoṣo dhārtarāṣṭrāṇām hṛdayāni vyadārayat
nabhaś ca pṛthivīm caiva tumulobhyanunādayan 1.19

Next echoed cymbals, conches and kodo-drums
And all the horns, trumpets and kettle-drums,
All at once in a singular cohesive sound
And their noise proliferated a tumult around |13|

Then in a magnificent chariot drawn by horses white
Arjuna and *Krishna* came into my sight
Both sounded together their conches Divine;
Seated in their vehicle -splendid and fine|14|

Sri *Krishna* his god gifted – *Panchajanya*
And *Arjuna* -the Divine conch *Devadatta*
And then the most fearsome *Pandava-*
Bhima blew the mighty *Poundra*|15|

And then *Kunti's* son, King *Yudhishthira*
Sounded his conch- *Anantavijaya*
And the brothers *Nakul* and *Sahadeva*
Respectively - *Sughosha* and *Manipushpaka*|16|

King of *Kashi*- Master archer and war-chief *Shikhandi*
Dhristadhyumna, *Virat* and the undefeated *Saatyaki*|17|

Drupad, mighty *Abhimanyu* and *Draupadi's* all sons
O King! From all directions, their conches bellowed at once|18|

The call of the conches sunk deep into the *Kauravan* heart-
Sending a ripple of fear even in their greatest stalwarts.
So fearsome -a shudder spread through the ground,
Even the mighty skies reverberated with the terrible sound|19|

अथ व्यवस्थितान्दृष्ट्वा धार्तराष्ट्रान् कपिध्वजः ।
प्रवृत्ते शस्त्रसम्पाते धनुरुद्यम्य पाण्डवः ॥ १-२०॥
atha vyavasthitān d ṛṣṭvā dhārtarāṣṭrān.h kapidhvaja ḥ
pravṛtte śastrasa ṃpāte dhanur udyamya pā ṇḍavaḥ 1.20

हृषीकेशं तदा वाक्यमिदमाह महीपते ।
अर्जुन उवाच ।
सेनयोरुभयोर्मध्ये रथं स्थापय मेऽच्युत ॥ १-२१॥
hṛṣīkeśaṃ tadā vākyam idam āha mahīpate
arjuna uvāca senayor ubhayor madhye ratham
sthāpaya mecyuta 1.21

यावदेतान्निरीक्षेऽहं योद्धुकामानवस्थितान् ।
कैर्मया सह योद्धव्यमस्मिन् रणसमुद्यमे ॥ १-२२॥
yāvad etān nirikṣeham yoddhukāmān avasthitān
kair mayā saha yoddhavyam asmin raṇasamudyame 1.22

योत्स्यमानानवेक्षेऽहं य एतेऽत्र समागताः ।
धार्तराष्ट्रस्य दुर्बुद्धेर्युद्धे प्रियचिकीर्षवः ॥ १-२३॥
yotsyamānān avekṣeham ya etetra samāgatāḥ
dhārtarāṣṭrasya durbuddher yuddhe priyacikīrṣavaḥ 1.23

सञ्जय उवाच ।
एवमुक्तो हृषीकेशो गुडाकेशेन भारत ।
सेनयोरुभयोर्मध्ये स्थापयित्वा रथोत्तमम् ॥ १-२४॥
sañjaya uvāca
evam ukto hṛṣīkeśo guḍākeśena bhārata
senayor ubhayor madhye sthāpayitvā rathottamam 1.24

भीष्मद्रोणप्रमुखतः सर्वेषां च महीक्षिताम् ।
उवाच पार्थ पश्यैतान्समवेतान्कुरूनिति ॥ १-२५॥
bhīṣmadroṇapramukhataḥ sarveṣāṃ ca mahīkṣitām
uvāca pārtha paśyaitān samavetān kurūn iti 1.25

Observing the *Kauravan* combative stance, *Arjuna*
Whose chariot bore the flag of the legendary *Anjaneya*.
Readied to battle by raising and lifting his Divine bow
And equipped his quiver with deathly arrows to let go|20|

O King! Then to the Divine charioteer *Krishna*,
The following words were spoken by *Arjuna*
"Between the two armies, I request you to take
Our chariot, into the battlefield's center for my sake|21|

Unless this warfield, I closely observe and see
Those who desire to wage the battle against me,
I cannot assess the warriors' strength and might
And decide the opponents who are worthy to fight|22|

All those who have thus gathered here
I wish to see all the warriors from near
The Alliance of wellwishers that has combined
To support the cause of *Duryodhana*'s false mind"|23|

Sanjaya spoke:
O Emperor! As per the words of *Arjuna*-
That were uttered to the Divine *Krishna*
Who then drove their chariot magnificent
In between the two armies that were present.|24|

Facing *Bhishma* and *Dronacharya*- the commanders
And all the other kings and all the mighty leaders
The following words escaped the lips of *Krishna*
"These are the *Kurus* you seek to battle! See O *Arjuna*!" |25|

तत्रापश्यत्स्थितान्पार्थः पितॄनथ पितामहान् ।
आचार्यान्मातुलान्भ्रातॄन्पुत्रान्पौत्रान्सखींस्तथा ॥ १-२६॥

tatrāpaśyat sthitān pārthaḥ pitṛn atha pitāmahān
ācāryān mātulān bhrātṛn putrān pautrān sakhīṃs tathā 1.26

श्वशुरान्सुहृदश्चैव सेनयोरुभयोरपि ।
तान्समीक्ष्य स कौन्तेयः सर्वान्बन्धूनवस्थितान् ॥ १-२७॥

śvaśurān suhṛdaś caiva senayor ubhayor api
tān samīkṣya sa kaunteyaḥ sarvān bandhūn avasthitān 1.27

कृपया परयाविष्टो विषीदन्निदमब्रवीत् ।
अर्जुन उवाच ।
दृष्ट्वेमं स्वजनं कृष्ण युयुत्सुं समुपस्थितम् ॥ १-२८॥

kṛpayā parayāviṣṭo viṣīdann idamabravīt
arjuna uvāca dṛṣṭvemaṃ svajanaṃ kṛṣṇa yuyutsuṃ
samupasthitam 1.28

सीदन्ति मम गात्राणि मुखं च परिशुष्यति ।
वेपथुश्च शरीरे मे रोमहर्षश्च जायते ॥ १-२९॥

sīdanti mama gātrāṇi mukhañ ca pariśuṣyati
vepathuś ca śarīre me romaharṣaś ca jāyate 1.29

गाण्डीवं स्रंसते हस्तात्त्वक्चैव परिदह्यते ।
न च शक्नोम्यवस्थातुं भ्रमतीव च मे मनः ॥ १-३०॥

gāṇḍīvaṃ straṃsate hastāt tvak caiva paridahyate
na ca śaknomy avasthātuṃ bhramatīva ca me manaḥ 1.30

निमित्तानि च पश्यामि विपरीतानि केशव ।
न च श्रेयोऽनुपश्यामि हत्वा स्वजनमाहवे ॥ १-३१॥

nimittāni ca paśyāmi viparītāni keśava
na ca śreyonupaśyāmi hatvā svajanam āhave 1.31

न काङ्क्षे विजयं कृष्ण न च राज्यं सुखानि च ।
किं नो राज्येन गोविन्द किं भोगैर्जीवितेन वा ॥ १-३२॥

na kāṅkṣe vijayaṃ kṛṣṇa na ca rājyaṃ sukhāni ca
kiṃ no rājyena govinda kiṃ bhogair jīvitena vā 1.32

Thus present there, *Arjuna* watched all his foes,
His own uncles and grandfathers who were close
Teachers and relatives and his dearest brothers
Children, nephews and friends amongst elders|26|

And his most beloved ones and in-laws too
In both armies he saw as he stood between the two
Arjuna noticed all those gathered to war
Every one of them who had come to spar|27|

Despondent and overcome by compassion,
A distraught *Arjuna* spoke in this fashion
"O *Krishna*, My own kin stand here in my sight
All together and filled with a desire to fight|28|

Watching them, my heart gives a cold sigh-
And my throat feels all so parched and dry
Down my spine now runs a shiver
That makes my whole body shudder|29|

From my hands, slips the *Gandiva* bow
And my skin seems on fire now!
My mind and head are spinning round
Impossible it is for me to even stand ground!|30|

Even all the signs that I observe
O *Krishna,* they seem so obverse
I see absolutely no fame or pride
In killing anyone on either side.|31|

O *Krishna*, I desire not a victory
Nor the comforts of a territory
Any kingdom or lordship acquired in this way,
Would it not be a waste? What else of it can I say? |32|

येषामर्थे काङ्क्षितं नो राज्यं भोगाः सुखानि च ।
त इमेऽवस्थिता युद्धे प्राणांस्त्यक्त्वा धनानि च ॥ १-३३॥

yeṣām arthe kāṅkṣitaṃ no rājyaṃ bhogāḥ sukhāni ca
ta imevasthitā yuddhe prāṇāṃs tyaktvā dhanāni ca 1.33

आचार्याः पितरः पुत्रास्तथैव च पितामहाः ।
मातुलाः श्वशुराः पौत्राः श्यालाः सम्बन्धिनस्तथा ॥ १-३४॥

ācāryāḥ pitaraḥ putrās tathaiva ca pitāmahāḥ
mātulāḥ śvaśurāḥ pautrāḥ śyālāḥ sambandhinas tathā 1.34

एतान्न हन्तुमिच्छामि घ्नतोऽपि मधुसूदन ।
अपि त्रैलोक्यराज्यस्य हेतोः किं नु महीकृते ॥ १-३५॥

etān na hantum icchhāmi ghnatopi madhusūdana
api trailokyarājyasya hetoḥ kiṃ nu mahīkṛte 1.35

निहत्य धार्तराष्ट्रान्नः का प्रीतिः स्याज्जनार्दन ।
पापमेवाश्रयेदस्मान्हत्वैतानाततायिनः ॥ १-३६॥

nihatya dhārtarāṣṭrān naḥ kā prītiḥ syājanārdana
pāpam evāśrayed asmān hatvaitān ātatāyinaḥ 1.36

तस्मान्नार्हा वयं हन्तुं धार्तराष्ट्रान्स्वबान्धवान् ।
स्वजनं हि कथं हत्वा सुखिनः स्याम माधव ॥ १-३७॥

tasmān nārhā vayaṃ hantuṃ dhārtarāṣṭrān
svabāndhavān svajanaṃ hi kathaṃ hatvā sukhinaḥ syāma mādhava 1.37

यद्यप्येते न पश्यन्ति लोभोपहतचेतसः ।
कुलक्षयकृतं दोषं मित्रद्रोहे च पातकम् ॥ १-३८॥

yadyapyete na paśyanti lobhopahatacetasaḥ
kulakṣayakṛtaṃ doṣaṃ mitradrohe ca pātakam 1.38

कथं न ज्ञेयमस्माभिः पापादस्मान्निवर्तितुम् ।
कुलक्षयकृतं दोषं प्रपश्यद्भिर्जनार्दन ॥ १-३९॥

kathaṃ na jñeyam asmābhiḥ pāpād asmān nivartitum
kulakṣayakṛtaṃ doṣaṃ prapaśyadbhir janārdana 1.39

My dearest ones, for whose very sake-
These kingly comforts I desire,
With their lives and wealth at stake,
They stand here in the line of fire!|33|

My teachers, brothers and my children
Nephews, in-laws and grandchildren,
My Elders and likewise grandfathers
And many other family members|34|

O *Krishna,* To kill them I desire not
Such a crime in life, I have never sought
Not for ruling the three realms of the earth
Surely, Is such a lordship any worth?|35|

O *Krishna,* by killing *Dhritarashtra's* sons
What happiness is there for me to gain?
I will only suffer for my sins with pain
For murdering these impetuous ones|36|

O Krishna, It does not seem fit
What satisfaction will I thus merit?|
Waging war against them, what can I win
For I shall then be killing my own kin?|37|

Even if they don't in this way perceive or see
However corrupt their greedy minds may be
The worst of sins is incurred from this felony-
That is acquired from carnage of friends and family|38|

Why shouldn't I think in this manner?
To escape from a sin I wish not to incur.
For this terrible sin of killing one's own
To us, its consequences are already known|39|

कुलक्षये प्रणश्यन्ति कुलधर्माः सनातनाः ।
धर्मे नष्टे कुलं कृत्स्नमधर्मोऽभिभवत्युत ॥ १-४०॥

kulakṣaye praṇaśyanti kuladharmāḥ sanātanāḥ
dharme naṣṭe kulaṃ kṛtsnam adharmobhibhavaty uta 1.40

अधर्माभिभवात्कृष्ण प्रदुष्यन्ति कुलस्त्रियः ।
स्त्रीषु दुष्टासु वार्ष्णेय जायते वर्णसङ्करः ॥ १-४१॥

adharmābhibhavāt kṛṣṇa praduṣyanti kulastriyaḥ
strīṣu duṣṭāsu vārṣṇeya jāyate varṇasaṅkaraḥ 1.41

सङ्करो नरकायैव कुलघ्नानां कुलस्य च ।
पतन्ति पितरो ह्येषां लुप्तपिण्डोदकक्रियाः ॥ १-४२॥

saṅkaro narakāyaiva kulaghnānāṃ kulasya ca
patanti pitaro hy eṣāṃ luptapiṇḍodakakriyāḥ 1.42

दोषैरेतैः कुलघ्नानां वर्णसङ्करकारकैः ।
उत्साद्यन्ते जातिधर्माः कुलधर्माश्च शाश्वताः ॥ १-४३॥

doṣair etaiḥ kulaghnānāṃ varṇasaṅkarakārakaiḥ
utsādyante jātidharmāḥ kuladharmāś ca śāśvatāḥ 1.43

उत्सन्नकुलधर्माणां मनुष्याणां जनार्दन ।
नरके नियतं वासो भवतीत्यनुशुश्रुम ॥ १-४४॥

utsannakuladharmāṇām manuṣyāṇām janārdana
narake niyatam vāso bhavatīty anuśuśruma 1.44

नरकेऽनियतं अहो बत महत्पापं कर्तुं व्यवसिता वयम् ।
यद्राज्यसुखलोभेन हन्तुं स्वजनमुद्यताः ॥ १-४५॥

aho bata mahat pāpaṃ kartuṃ vyavasitā vayam
yad rājyasukhalobhena hantuṃ svajanam udyatāḥ 1.45

यदि मामप्रतीकारमशस्त्रं शस्त्रपाणयः ।
धार्तराष्ट्रा रणे हन्युस्तन्मे क्षेमतरं भवेत् ॥ १-४६॥

yadi mām apratīkāram aśastraṃ śastrapāṇayaḥ
dhārtarāṣṭrā raṇe hanyus tan me kṣemataraṃ bhavet 1.46

The act of killing of one's own clan
Destroys our ancient ethical code for man
And when ethics of man are annihilated
In His posterity the sin is proliferated|40|

And O *Krishna*, in a household that is sinned
The women members only suffering you find
And when the women are afflicted
The balance of society is affected|41|

In the lives of such sinners only hell descends
And to their families too it extends
Even those who received the libations and rice
The ancestors fall in stature, even after their demise|42|

These sinners and destroyers of families
Bring forth to the society loss and tragedies
By destroying the ancient code of the human race
They break families and spread disgrace|43|

Those whose code of duty is vanquished
The fates of such men are sealed and finished
They are doomed for eternity to dwell
And suffer for their actions in the realms of hell.|44|

How did we agree to commit this sin?
Just for the kingly comforts, we desired to win
Our own clan, Did we seek to kill?
Alas! This terrible feat, why did we will?|45|

If I face their armies unarmed
And by *Kauravan* weapons I am killed
I would still retain some glory
By allowing them to claim a victory|46|"

सञ्जय उवाच ।
एवमुक्त्वार्जुनः सङ्ख्ये रथोपस्थ उपाविशत् ।
विसृज्य सशरं चापं शोकसंविग्नमानसः ॥ १-४७॥

sañjaya uvāca
evam uktvārjunaḥ saṅkhye rathopastha upāviśat
visṛjya saśaraṃ cāpaṃ śokasaṃvignamānasaḥ 1.47

Sanjaya spoke:
"After saying so, *Arjuna,* amidst the war-field
His bow and arrows he refused to wield
He dropped down onto his chariot's seat
In delusion he had already accepted defeat.|47|"

(Thus ended the first Canto of the Bhagavad Gita where Arjuna confessed his grief to Sri Krishna after having decided to abstain from participating in the mighty battle of Kurukshetra)

❈ ❈ ❈

अथ द्वितीयोऽध्यायः ।

atha dvitīyodhyāyaḥ

सञ्जय उवाच ।

sañjaya uvāca

तं तथा कृपयाविष्टमश्रुपूर्णाकुलेक्षणम् ।
विषीदन्तमिदं वाक्यमुवाच मधुसूदनः ॥ २-१॥

taṃ tathā kṛpayāviṣṭam aśrupūrṇākulekṣaṇam
viṣīdantam idaṃ vākyam uvāca madhusūdanaḥ 2.1

श्रीभगवानुवाच ।

कुतस्त्वा कश्मलमिदं विषमे समुपस्थितम् ।
अनार्यजुष्टमस्वर्ग्यमकीर्तिकरमर्जुन ॥ २-२॥

śrībhagavān uvāca
kutas tvā kaśmalam idaṃ viṣame samupasthitam
anāryajuṣṭam asvargyam akīrtikaram arjuna 2.2

क्लैब्यं मा स्म गमः पार्थ नैतत्त्वय्युपपद्यते ।
क्षुद्रं हृदयदौर्बल्यं त्यक्त्वोत्तिष्ठ परन्तप ॥ २-३॥

klaibyaṃ mā sma gamaḥ pārtha

naitat tvayy upapadyate
kṣudraṃ hṛdayadaurbalyaṃ tyaktvottiṣṭha paraṃtapa 2.3

अर्जुन उवाच ।

कथं भीष्ममहं सङ्ख्ये द्रोणं च मधुसूदन ।
इषुभिः प्रतियोत्स्यामि पूजार्हावरिसूदन ॥ २-४॥

arjuna uvāca
kathaṃ bhīṣmam ahaṃ sāṅkhye droṇaṃ ca
madhusūdana iṣubhiḥ pratiyotsyāmi pūjārhāv arisūdana 2.4

Canto II: *Eternal Secrets revealed*

(Verses 2-3: *Krishna's* order; 4-10: *Arjuna's* refusal; 7: *Arjuna's* first action of surrender; 11-30: *Krishna* imparts the secret of the Self to *Arjuna*; 31-38: The meaning of *Dharma;* 38- 53: The *Yoga* of Knowledge to liberate *Karma's* bondage; 55-72: The method of uniting with the Supreme- the state of a living *Samadhi*)

Sanjaya spoke:
"To *Arjuna* who was thus depressed
Sorrowful, distraught and distressed,
Teary eyed, remorseful and devoid of hope -
The following words *Krishna* spoke: |1|

(Words of the Divine *Krishna)*
"*Arjuna*, From where hast this delusion
So untimely within you arisen?
This behavior doesn't behove brave hearts,
Seekers of heaven or fame nor stalwarts! |2|

Yield not to this impotence of action,
Not worthy of you is such a renunciation.
This base weak-heartedness has no relevance
Give this up, Stand up- O Warrior of eminence! |3|"

Arjuna replied:
"Tell me how, as with weapons equipped
Stand revered *Bhishma* and *Drona* in my sight
Both these great souls, I have always worshipped
Even in dreams, Them I cannot fight? |4|

गुरूनहत्वा हि महानुभावान् श्रेयो भोक्तुं भैक्ष्यमपीह लोके ।
हत्वार्थकामांस्तु गुरुनिहैव भुञ्जीय भोगान् रुधिरप्रदिग्धान् ॥ २-५॥

gurūn ahatvā hi mahānubhāvān śreyo bhoktum bhaikṣyam apīha
loke hatvārthakāmāmstu gurunihaiva bhuñjjīya bhogān
rudhirapradigdhān 2.5

न चैतद्विद्मः कतरन्नो गरीयो यद्वा जयेम यदि वा नो जयेयुः ।
यानेव हत्वा न जिजीविषामस्तेऽवस्थिताः प्रमुखे धार्तराष्ट्राः ॥ २-६॥

na caitad vidmaḥ kataran no garīyo yad vā jayema yadi vā no
jayeyuḥ yān eva hatvā na jijīvi ṣāmas tevasthitāḥ pramukhe
dhārtarāṣṭrāḥ 2.6

कार्पण्यदोषोपहतस्वभावः पृच्छामि त्वां धर्मसम्मूढचेताः ।
यच्छ्रेयः स्यान्निश्चितं ब्रूहि तन्मे शिष्यस्तेऽहं शाधि मां त्वां प्रपन्नम् ॥ २-७॥

kārpaṇyadoṣopahatasvabhāvaḥ pṛcchāmi tvāṃ
dharmasaṃmūḍhacetāḥ yac chreyaḥ syān niścitaṃ brūhi tan me
śiṣyasteham śādhi māṃ tvāṃ prapannam 2.7

न हि प्रपश्यामि ममापनुद्याद् यच्छोकमुच्छोषणमिन्द्रियाणाम् ।
अवाप्य भूमावसपत्नमृद्धं राज्यं सुराणामपि चाधिपत्यम् ॥ २-८॥

na hi prapaśyāmi mamāpanudyād yac chokam ucchoṣaṇam
indriyāṇām avāpya bhūmāv asapatnam ṛddhaṃ rājyaṃ surāṇām
api cādhipatyam 2.8

सञ्जय उवाच ।
एवमुक्त्वा हृषीकेशं गुडाकेशः परन्तप ।
न योत्स्य इति गोविन्दमुक्त्वा तूष्णीं बभूव ह ॥ २-९॥

sañjaya uvāca evam uktvā hṛṣīkeśam guḍākeśaḥ paramtapaḥ
na yotsya iti govindam uktvā tūṣṇīṃ babhūva ha 2.9

Instead of killing the experienced teachers mighty,
Even a life spent begging for alms is worthy
If for my desire of wealth, they are dead
The worst of dreaded sins will loom over my head |5|

Killing my foes, my *Kauravan* brothers I firmly refuse
From these two outcomes, How can one choose
Our defeating them or our being defeated?
As both ways my own life shall be desecrated |6|

I ask to you in this state of confusion-
Tell me my right course of action
Thus afflicted and infected by fear,
I seek your refuge; Show the way teacher! |7|

I am unable to see what will drive my numbness away
Overwhelming me this sorrow is here to stay,
No happiness will come from any earthly aristocracy
Neither Godhood nor by an absolute supremacy. |8|"

Sanjaya said:
"To *Arjuna*-the mighty who had even mastered sleep
To he, who was unstable and in darkness deep
O King! To him, *Sri Krishna* then spoke
The warrior within *Arjuna*, He sought to provoke.|9|

तमुवाच हृषीकेशः प्रहसन्निव भारत ।
सेनयोरुभयोर्मध्ये विषीदन्तमिदं वचः ॥ २-१०॥

tam uvāca hṛṣīkeśaḥ prahasann iva bhārata
senayor ubhayor madhye viṣīdantam idaṃ vacaḥ 2.10

श्रीभगवानुवाच ।
अशोच्यानन्वशोचस्त्वं प्रज्ञावादांश्र भाषसे ।
गतासूनगतासूंश्र नानुशोचन्ति पण्डिताः ॥ २-११॥

śrībhagavān uvāca
aśocyān anvaśocas tva ṃ prajñāvādāṃś ca bhāṣase
gatāsūn agatāsū ṃś ca nānuśocanti pa ṇḍitāḥ 2.11

नत्वेवाहं जातु नासं न त्वं नेमे जनाधिपाः ।
न चैव न भविष्यामः सर्वे वयमतः परम् ॥ २-१२॥

natvevāhaṃ jātu nāsaṃ na tvaṃ neme janādhipāḥ
na caiva na bhaviṣyāmaḥ sarve vayam ataḥ param 2.12

देहिनोऽस्मिन्यथा देहे कौमारं यौवनं जरा ।
तथा देहान्तरप्राप्तिर्धीरस्तत्र न मुह्यति ॥ २-१३॥

dehinosmin yathā dehe kaumāraṃ yauvanaṃ jarā
tathā dehāntaraprāptir dhīras tatra na muhyati 2.13

मात्रास्पर्शास्तु कौन्तेय शीतोष्णसुखदुःखदाः ।
आगमापायिनोऽनित्यास्तांस्तितिक्षस्व भारत ॥ २-१४॥

mātrāsparśās tu kaunteya śītoṣṇasukhaduḥkhadāḥ
āgamāpāyinonityās tāṃs titikṣasva bhārata 2.14

यं हि न व्यथयन्त्येते पुरुषं पुरुषर्षभ ।
समदुःखसुखं धीरं सोऽमृतत्वाय कल्पते ॥ २-१५॥

yaṃ hi na vyathayanty ete puruṣaṃ puruṣarṣabha
samaduḥkhasukhaṃ dhīraṃ somṛtatvāya kalpate 2.15

To him, the Divine *Krishna* thus exclaimed
Standing in the middle of the warfield he proclaimed
In a voice laced with a mild tinge of laughter
Between both armies, He spoke in this manner.|10|"

The Voice of *Krishna:*
"You weep for whom tears shouldn't be shed,
Yet you speak the language of the enlightened!
Over those who are or who are going to be dead,
One mustn't grieve, this the wise have clearly said.|11|

There was never a time when I existed not
Neither a time when you nor these kings were not
In the future too such a time the world won't see,
When every single one of us will not be.|12|

Just us our soul, when in this body silently resides
Childhood, youth and old-age it consensually abides
After leaving this body, another one it requires
The wise grieve not, knowing that the soul never expires.|13|

Arjuna, your physical body and senses suffer and wear-
Heat, cold, joy and misery's effects they have to bear.
Know them to be fleeting sensations of body and mind
They too shall pass, endure and you shall thus find|14|

Who, by these sensations are not imbalanced or affected,
Who, in happiness and pain remain poised and unaffected?
O *Arjuna,* Only such men with the strongest foundation
Are deep enough to attain the liberation.|15|

नासतो विद्यते भावो नाभावो विद्यते सतः ।
उभयोरपि दृष्टोऽन्तस्त्वनयोस्तत्त्वदर्शिभिः ॥ २-१६॥

nāsato vidyate bhāvo nābhāvo vidyate sataḥ
ubhayor api dṛṣṭo.antas tv anayos tattvadarśibhiḥ 2.16

अविनाशि तु तद्विद्धि येन सर्वमिदं ततम् ।
विनाशमव्ययस्यास्य न कश्चित्कर्तुमर्हति ॥ २-१७॥

avināśi tu tad viddhi yena sarvam idaṃ tatam
vināśam avyayasyāsya na kaścit kartum arhati 2.17

अन्तवन्त इमे देहा नित्यस्योक्ताः शरीरिणः ।
अनाशिनोऽप्रमेयस्य तस्माद्युध्यस्व भारत ॥ २-१८॥

antavanta ime dehā nityasyoktāḥ śarīriṇaḥ
anāśinoprameyasya tasmād yudhyasva bhārata 2.18

य एनं वेत्ति हन्तारं यश्चैनं मन्यते हतम् ।
उभौ तौ न विजानीतो नायं हन्ति न हन्यते ॥ २-१९॥

ya enaṃ vetti hantāraṃ yaś cainam manyate hatam
ubhau tau na vijānīto nāyaṃ hanti na hanyate 2.19

न जायते म्रियते वा कदाचिन् नायं भूत्वा भविता वा न भूयः ।
अजो नित्यः शाश्वतोऽयं पुराणो न हन्यते हन्यमाने शरीरे ॥ २-२०॥

na jāyate mriyate vā kadācin nāyambhūtvā bhavitā vā na bhūyaḥ
ajo nityaḥ śāśvatoyaṃ purāṇo na hanyate hanyamāne śarīre 2.20

वेदाविनाशिनं नित्यं य एनमजमव्ययम् ।
कथं स पुरुषः पार्थ कं घातयति हन्ति कम् ॥ २-२१॥

vedāvināśinam nityam ya enam ajam avyayam
kathaṃ sa puruṣaḥ pārtha kaṃ ghātayati hanti kam 2.21

वासांसि जीर्णानि यथा विहाय नवानि गृह्णाति नरोऽपराणि ।
तथा शरीराणि विहाय जीर्णान्यन्यानि संयाति नवानि देही ॥ २-२२॥

vāsāṃsi jīrṇāni yathā vihāya navāni gṛhṇāti naroparāṇi
tathā śarīrāṇi vihāya jīrṇāni anyāni saṃyāti navāni dehī 2.22

Falsehood is that which holds no authority
And truth is omnipresent in every territory.
The essence of both have been shown
By the wisest of seers to whom it was known|16|

This truth of the indestructible 'Self' you must see
From this same 'Self' the visible world came to be
And there is no one on earth who is so capable
Of destroying that 'Self'which is undestroyable |17|

This physical body is untrue and perishes
This has been known without doubt over the ages
It's proven mortality why do you question?
Brace yourself to fight -O *Bhaarath's* son! |18|

Those who think that they kill this "Self"
Or those who think that the 'Self'is dead
Are both in their ignorance only mislead,
As the 'Self'is neither the killer nor the killed |19|

Neither is the 'Self'born nor is it killed
Neither is it created nor will it ever be destroyed
The 'Self'is primeval and ancient and birth-less,
Deathless even when the physical body perishes.|20|

The knowledge of the 'Self'that is ageless
Is that it is true, indestructible and birth less
So again- "Who is the man who is the killer?
And, Who is the man who is killed?" |21|

Just like old garments are discarded when shoddy
And thus for newer clothes they make way
The old physical bodies too are cast away
By the 'Self'which then acquires a new body.|22|

नैनं छिन्दन्ति शस्त्राणि नैनं दहति पावकः ।
न चैनं क्लेदयन्त्यापो न शोषयति मारुतः ॥ २-२३॥

nainaṃ chindanti śastrāṇi nainaṃ dahati pāvakaḥ
na cainaṃ kledayanty āpo na śo ṣayati mārutaḥ 2.23

अच्छेद्योऽयमदाह्योऽयमक्लेद्योऽशोष्य एव च ।
नित्यः सर्वगतः स्थाणुरचलोऽयं सनातनः ॥ २-२४॥

acchedyoyam adāhyoyam akledyośoṣya eva ca
nityaḥ sarvagataḥ sthāṇur acaloyaṃ sanātanaḥ 2.24

अव्यक्तोऽयमचिन्त्योऽयमविकार्योऽयमुच्यते ।
तस्मादेवं विदित्वैनं नानुशोचितुमर्हसि ॥ २-२५॥

avyaktoyam acintyoyam avikaryoyam ucyate
tasmād evaṃ viditvainaṃ nānuśocitum arhasi 2.25

अथ चैनं नित्यजातं नित्यं वा मन्यसे मृतम् ।
तथापि त्वं महाबाहो नैवं शोचितुमर्हसि ॥ २-२६॥

atha cainaṃ nityajātaṃ nityaṃ vā manyase mṛtam
tathāpi tvaṃ mahābāho naivaṃ śocitum arhasi 2.26

जातस्य हि ध्रुवो मृत्युर्ध्रुवं जन्म मृतस्य च ।
तस्मादपरिहार्येऽर्थे न त्वं शोचितुमर्हसि ॥ २-२७॥

jātasya hi dhruvo mṛtyur dhruvaṃ janma mṛtasya ca
tasmād aparihāryerthe na tvaṃ śocitum arhasi 2.27

अव्यक्तादीनि भूतानि व्यक्तमध्यानि भारत ।
अव्यक्तनिधनान्येव तत्र का परिदेवना ॥ २-२८॥

avyaktādīni bhūtāni vyaktamadhyāni bhārata
avyaktanidhanāny eva tatra kā paridevanā 2.28

आश्चर्यवत्पश्यति कश्चिदेनमाश्चर्यवद्वदतितथैव चान्यः ।
आश्चर्यवच्चैनमन्यः शृणोति श्रुत्वाप्येनं वेद न चैव कश्चित् ॥ २-२९॥

āścaryavat paśyati kaścid enam āścaryavad vadati tathaiva cānyaḥ
āścaryavac cainam anyaḥ śṛṇoti śrutvāpy enaṃ veda na caiva
kaścit 2.29

That which no weapon can decapitate
That which no inferno can incinerate
That which even the waters can wet not
And which the mighty winds can dry not |23|

This 'Self' Indestructible and incombustible
Is immutable, imperishable and insoluble
In its inertial stillness it is omnipresent
Ageless and timeless, everywhere it is present |24|

This invisible '*Self*', by the mind cannot be conceived
About the blemish-less '*Self*' Thus is said and perceived
This knowledge of the '*Self*' you must realize and see
Indeed! How pointless it is for you to lament or grieve? |25|

If you think the '*Self*' is subject to birth
Or if you think that it is subject to death
Either way O mighty armed warrior
It is not right to grieve in this manner.|26|

For he who has taken birth, death is certain
And for he who has died, birth is certain
Death or Birth is but an inevitable situation
It is not proper to bemoan on any occasion. |27|

The beginning, before the birth is unknown
The middle life span of birth alone is known
What happens after death is also unknown,
Hence O *Arjuna*, what causes you to moan? |28|

Some people see the '*Self*' as surreal
While some call it surreal and acknowledge.
Some others hear about the '*Self*' as surreal
After hearing of it too, some have no knowledge |29|

देही नित्यमवध्योऽयं देहे सर्वस्य भारत ।
तस्मात्सर्वाणि भूतानि न त्वं शोचितुमर्हसि ॥ २-३०॥

dehī nityam avadhyoyaṃ dehe sarvasya bhārata
tasmāt sarvāṇi bhūtāni na tvaṃ śocitum arhasi 2.30

स्वधर्ममपि चावेक्ष्य न विकम्पितुमर्हसि ।
धर्म्याद्धि युद्धाच्छ्रेयोऽन्यत्क्षत्रियस्य न विद्यते ॥ २-३१॥

svadharmam api cāvekṣya na vikampitum arhasi
dharmyād dhi yuddhāc chreyonyat kṣatriyasya na vidyate 2.31

यदृच्छया चोपपन्नं स्वर्गद्वारमपावृतम् ।
सुखिनः क्षत्रियाः पार्थ लभन्ते युद्धमीदृशम् ॥ २-३२॥

yadṛcchayā copapannaṃ svargadvāram apāvṛtam
sukhinaḥ kṣatriyāḥ pārtha labhante yuddham īdṛśam 2.32

अथ चेत्त्वमिमं धर्म्यं सङ्ग्रामं न करिष्यसि ।
ततः स्वधर्मं कीर्तिं च हित्वा पापमवाप्स्यसि ॥ २-३३॥

atha cet tvam imaṃ dhārmyaṃ saṅgrāmaṃ na kariṣyasi
tataḥ svadharmaṃ kīrtiṃ ca hitvā pāpam avāpsyasi 2.33

अकीर्तिं चापि भूतानि कथयिष्यन्ति तेऽव्ययाम् ।
सम्भावितस्य चाकीर्तिर्मरणादतिरिच्यते ॥ २-३४॥

akīrtiṃ cāpi bhūtāni kathayiṣyanti tevyayām
sambhāvitasya cākīrtir maraṇād atiricyate 2.34

भयाद्रणादुपरतं मंस्यन्ते त्वां महारथाः ।
येषां च त्वं बहुमतो भूत्वा यास्यसि लाघवम् ॥ २-३५॥

bhayād raṇād uparataṃ maṃsyante tvāṃ mahārathāḥ
yeṣāṃ ca tvaṃ bahumato bhūtvā yāsyasi lāghavam 2.35

अवाच्यवादांश्च बहून्वदिष्यन्ति तवाहिताः ।
निन्दन्तस्तव सामर्थ्यं ततो दुःखतरं नु किम् ॥ २-३६॥

avācyavadāṃś ca bahūn vadiṣyanti tavāhitāḥ
nindantas tava sāmarthyaṃ tato duḥkhataraṃ nu kim 2.36

Seated within the bodies of every being physical
O *Arjuna*, The 'Self'is invincible and eternal
And thus for the sake of every individual being
It is improper and incorrect for you to be grieving.|30|

Your *Dharma* moral duty you must consider
And from it you most definitely mustn't falter
For the warriors who to uphold the truth fight
Nothing is most appropriate but to defend the right! |31|

When such a bellicose moment abruptly presents
Of its own accord, it opens the doors of heaven
The Warrior, O *Arjuna*, only joyfully consents
For they consider this chance sacred and God-given.|32|

But if you, in this battle for justice do not participate
And from your duties you verily deviate
You'll gain no fame for this sin of inaction
But instead bear the consequences of abstention.|33|

And also all the people shall speak for eternity
Of this ill-action harboring only disrespect
For those who by their deeds have earned respect,
Even Death is far more glorious than notoriety.|34|

"Out of fear, you have deserted the war"
So of you the greatest of warriors shall think.
The esteem that you have earned, you'll scar
From your stature and grace you'll fall and sink.|35|

Your enemies shall insult your adeptness
Ridiculing your prowess as ineptness
Alas! How painfully agonizing this shall be
Anything worse than this, do you see? |36|

हतो वा प्राप्स्यसि स्वर्गं जित्वा वा भोक्ष्यसे महीम् ।
तस्मादुत्तिष्ठ कौन्तेय युद्धाय कृतनिश्चयः ॥ २-३७॥

hato vā prāpsyasi svargaṃ jitvā vā bhokṣyase mahīm
tasmād uttiṣṭha kaunteya yuddhāya kṛtaniścayaḥ 2.37

सुखदुःखे समे कृत्वा लाभालाभौ जयाजयौ ।
ततो युद्धाय युज्यस्व नैवं पापमवाप्स्यसि ॥ २-३८॥

sukhaduḥkhe same kṛtvā lābhālābhau jayājayau
tato yuddhāya yujyasva naivaṃ pāpam avāpsyasi 2.38

एषा तेऽभिहिता साङ्ख्ये बुद्धिर्योगे त्विमां शृणु ।
बुद्ध्या युक्तो यया पार्थ कर्मबन्धं प्रहास्यसि ॥ २-३९॥

eṣā tebhihitā sāṅkhye buddhir yoge tv imāṃ śṛṇu
buddhyā yukto yayā pārtha karmaba ndhaṃ prahāsyasi 2.39

नेहाभिक्रमनाशोऽस्ति प्रत्यवायो न विद्यते ।
स्वल्पमप्यस्य धर्मस्य त्रायते महतो भयात् ॥ २-४०॥

nehābhikramanāśosti pratyavāyo na vidyate
svalpam apy asya dharmasya trāyate mahato bhayāt 2.40

व्यवसायात्मिका बुद्धिरेकेह कुरुनन्दन ।
बहुशाखा ह्यनन्ताश्च बुद्धयोऽव्यवसायिनाम् ॥ २-४१॥

vyavasāyātmikā buddhir ekeha kurunandana
bahuśākhā hy anantāś ca buddhayovyavasāyinām 2.41

यामिमां पुष्पितां वाचं प्रवदन्त्यविपश्चितः ।
वेदवादरताः पार्थ नान्यदस्तीति वादिनः ॥ २-४२॥

yām imāṃ puṣpitāṃ vācaṃ pravadanty avipaścitaḥ
vedavādaratāḥ pārtha nānyad astīti vādinaḥ 2.42

कामात्मानः स्वर्गपरा जन्मकर्मफलप्रदाम् ।
क्रियाविशेषबहुलां भोगैश्वर्यगतिं प्रति ॥ २-४३॥

kāmātmānaḥ svargaparā janmakarmaphalapradām
kriyāviśeṣabahulāṃ bhogaiśvaryagatiṃ prati 2.43

In this mighty battle to uphold the right
Either the Heaven's doors shall open on defeat
Or your victory the whole earth shall joyously greet,
Success is certain *Arjuna,* Rise up and fight! |37|

In both sorrow and joy, if you hold your poise
In either profit or loss, by not seeking a choice
If you wage this war with this state of mind
Certainly there is no sin that you'll incur or find. |38|

Listen to what now I am going to reveal
That knowledge O *Arjuna,* that lifts the veil
That most ancient *Yoga of Knowledge-*
Which liberates one from *Karma*'s bondage. |39|

Here, the actions once begun bring no losses
Or any negative results or consequences
Even the smallest action done in the right manner
Can protect one from the greatest danger|40|

The decisive selfless intelligence all as one perceives
And is unifying-O beloved Son of the *Kuru* clan
But the divisive intelligence of desirers has a wide span
That splits like a tree's countless branches and leaves |41|

With eloquence and flowery language, men orate
Despite limited intelligence when they narrate
Quoting the *Vedas* with their pseudo interpretation
They dismiss the Divine origin of the world's creation.|42|

Desiring deeply the fruits of worldly wealth
Lustfully they seek the heavens and good birth
Ritual like their actions further merely one motive-
To achieve through every sacrifice a material objective.|43|

भोगैश्वर्यप्रसक्तानां तयापहृतचेतसाम् ।
व्यवसायात्मिका बुद्धिः समाधौ न विधीयते ॥ २-४४॥

bhogaiśvaryaprasaktānāṃ tayāpahṛtacetasām
vyavasāyātmikā buddhiḥ samādhau na vidhīyate 2.44

त्रैगुण्यविषया वेदा निस्त्रैगुण्यो भवार्जुन ।
निर्द्वन्द्वो नित्यसत्त्वस्थो निर्योगक्षेम आत्मवान् ॥ २-४५॥

traiguṇyaviṣayā vedā nistraiguṇyo bhavārjuna
nirdvandvo nityasatvastho niryogakṣema ātmavān 2.45

यावानर्थ उदपाने सर्वतः सम्प्लुतोदके ।
तावान्सर्वेषु वेदेषु ब्राह्मणस्य विजानतः ॥ २-४६॥

yāvān artha udapāne sarvataḥ samplutodake
tāvān sarveṣu vedeṣu brāhmaṇasya vijānataḥ 2.46

कर्मण्येवाधिकारस्ते मा फलेषु कदाचन ।
मा कर्मफलहेतुर्भूर्मा ते सङ्गोऽस्त्वकर्मणि ॥ २-४७॥

karmaṇy evādhikāras te mā phaleṣu kadācana
mā karmaphalahetur bhūr mā te saṅgostv akarmaṇi 2.47

योगस्थः कुरु कर्माणि सङ्गं त्यक्त्वा धनञ्जय ।
सिद्ध्यसिद्ध्योः समो भूत्वा समत्वं योग उच्यते ॥ २-४८॥

yogasthaḥ kuru karmāṇi saṅgam tyaktvā dhanañjaya
siddhyasiddhyoḥ samo bhūtvā samatvam yoga ucyate 2.48

दूरेण ह्यवरं कर्म बुद्धियोगाद्धनञ्जय ।
बुद्धौ शरणमन्विच्छ कृपणाः फलहेतवः ॥ २-४९॥

dūreṇa hy avaram karma buddhiyogād dhanañjaya
buddhau śaraṇam anviccha kṛpaṇāḥ phalahetavaḥ 2.49

बुद्धियुक्तो जहातीह उभे सुकृतदुष्कृते ।
तस्माद्योगाय युज्यस्व योगः कर्मसु कौशलम् ॥ २-५०॥

buddhiyukto jahātīha ubhe sukṛtaduṣkṛte
tasmād yogāya yujyasva yogaḥ karmasu kauśalam 2.50

In the fruits of every action, their senses are held sway
Allured their fickle minds meekly wander away
Such people whose intelligence is thus unfocussed
Never attain contentment and are always depressed.|44|

O *Arjuna*, It is in the *Vedas* that the truth is contained-
The "threefold qualities" within man are explained,
The true state wherein every desire is conquered,
And the net non-dual consciousness that is acquired.|45|

Just as all the usefulness of water in a well
Is all encompassed in a reservoir replete
So too is all the Vedic knowledge as well
Known to him, who has "Self"-realization complete |46|

Vested you are with the authority to perform
But not seek your actions' fruits in any form
When by the fruits of actions you aren't motivated
From discharging your duties, you never get deviated |47|

Perform your every action in this *Yogic* way
All attachments *Arjuna*, you must throw away
From accomplishments and loss find your release
Then shall you attain the *Yogic* poise and peace |48|

O *Arjuna*, The pursuit of fruit is only base and ignoble
This is *Yoga*'s essence as per the knowledgable
Seek refuge in its principles practicable
Because seekers of fruits of actions are despicable |49|

With this knowledge, in this very world itself
From good and bad actions, one can free oneself.
Knowing this, engage yourself in this *Karma-Yoga*
Detachment yet excellence in works is only *Yoga*. |50|

कर्मजं बुद्धियुक्ता हि फलं त्यक्त्वा मनीषिणः ।
जन्मबन्धविनिर्मुक्ताः पदं गच्छन्त्यनामयम् ॥ २-५१॥

karmajam buddhiyuktā hi phalaṃ tyaktvā manīṣiṇaḥ
janmabandhavinirmuktāḥ padaṃ gacchhanty anāmayam 2.51

यदा ते मोहकलिलं बुद्धिर्व्यतितरिष्यति ।
तदा गन्तासि निर्वेदं श्रोतव्यस्य श्रुतस्य च ॥ २-५२॥

yadā te mohakalilam buddhir vyatitariṣyati
tadā gantāsi nirvedaṃ śrotavyasya śrutasya ca 2.52

श्रुतिविप्रतिपन्ना ते यदा स्थास्यति निश्चला ।
समाधावचला बुद्धिस्तदा योगमवाप्स्यसि ॥ २-५३॥

śrutivipratipannā te yadā sthāsyati niścalā
samādhāv acalā buddhis tadā yogam avāpsyasi 2.53

अर्जुन उवाच ।
स्थितप्रज्ञस्य का भाषा समाधिस्थस्य केशव ।
स्थितधीः किं प्रभाषेत किमासीत व्रजेत किम् ॥ २-५४॥

arjuna uvāca
sthitaprajñasya kā bhāṣā samādhisthasya keśava
sthitadhīḥ kim prabhāṣeta kim āsīta vrajeta kim 2.54

श्रीभगवानुवाच ।
प्रजहाति यदा कामान्सर्वान्पार्थ मनोगतान् ।
आत्मन्येवात्मना तुष्टः स्थितप्रज्ञस्तदोच्यते ॥ २-५५॥

śrībhagavān uvāca
prajahāti yadā kāmān sarvān pārtha manogatān
ātmany evātmanā tu ṣṭaḥ sthitaprajñas tadocyate 2.55

दुःखेष्वनुद्विग्नमनाः सुखेषु विगतस्पृहः ।
वीतरागभयक्रोधः स्थितधीर्मुनिरुच्यते ॥ २-५६॥

duḥkheṣvanudvignamanāḥ sukheṣu vigataspṛhaḥ
vītarāgabhayakrodhaḥ sthitadhīr munir ucyate 2.56

The most enlightened amongst men are thus aware
And for the fruits of efforts they don't care
Liberated from the bondages of birth, they stand
And in the highest conscious states they land.|51|

When the mind thus illumined becomes
And desire's web it overcomes
One becomes free, detached and undisturbed
Towards all that was and all that will be heard.|52|

When from the disturbances of all that is heard
You become steady and unperturbed
An awakened state of "*Samadhi*" is then attained
And the union with the cosmic-Divine is obtained.|53|

Arjuna asked:
"O *Krishna*, What is this state- awakened?
What are the indications and signs observed?
How does such a person in "*Samadhi*" talk?
How does he sit? How does he walk?"|54|

Sri Krishna spoke:
"*Arjuna*, when a person gives up all the desires
That the mind conjures and aspires
And is steady and immersed only in the "Self",
Such a person dwells in the state of the awakened "Self". |55|

When one suffers not in times of distress
And in happiness, exuberance one doesn't express
When you see someone free from anger and fear
It is clearly understood that a sage is near.|56|

यः सर्वत्रानभिस्नेहस्तत्तत्प्राप्य शुभाशुभम् ।
नाभिनन्दति न द्वेष्टि तस्य प्रज्ञा प्रतिष्ठिता ॥ २-५७॥

yaḥ sarvatrānabhisnehas tattatprāpya śubhāśubham
nābhinandati na dveṣṭi tasya prajñā pratiṣṭhitā 2.57

यदा संहरते चायं कूर्मोऽङ्गानीव सर्वशः ।
इन्द्रियाणीन्द्रियार्थेभ्यस्तस्य प्रज्ञा प्रतिष्ठिता ॥ २-५८॥

yadā saṃharate cāyaṃ kūrmoṅgānīva sarvaśaḥ
indriyāṇīndriyārthebhyas tasya prajñā pratiṣṭhitā 2.58

विषया विनिवर्तन्ते निराहारस्य देहिनः ।
रसवर्जं रसोऽप्यस्य परं दृष्ट्वा निवर्तते ॥ २-५९॥

viṣayā vinivartante nirāhārasya dehinaḥ
rasavarjaṃ rasopy asya paraṃ dṛṣṭvā nivartate 2.59

यततो ह्यपि कौन्तेय पुरुषस्य विपश्चितः ।
इन्द्रियाणि प्रमाथीनि हरन्ति प्रसभं मनः ॥ २-६०॥

yatato hyapi kaunteya puruṣasya vipaścitaḥ
indriyāṇi pramāthīni haranti prasabhaṃ manaḥ 2.60

तानि सर्वाणि संयम्य युक्त आसीत मत्परः ।
वशे हि यस्येन्द्रियाणि तस्य प्रज्ञा प्रतिष्ठिता ॥ २-६१॥

tāni sarvāṇi saṃyamya yukta āsīta matparaḥ
vaśe hi yasyendriyāṇi tasya prajñā pratiṣṭhitā 2.61

ध्यायतो विषयान्पुंसः सङ्गस्तेषूपजायते ।
सङ्गात्सञ्जायते कामः कामात्क्रोधोऽभिजायते ॥ २-६२॥

dhyāyato viṣayān puṃsaḥ saṅgas teṣūpajāyate
saṅgāt sañjāyate kāmaḥ kāmāt krodhobhijāyate 2.62

क्रोधाद्भवति सम्मोहः सम्मोहात्स्मृतिविभ्रमः ।
स्मृतिभ्रंशाद् बुद्धिनाशो बुद्धिनाशात्प्रणश्यति ॥ २-६३॥

krodhād bhavati sammohaḥ sammohāt smṛtivibhramaḥ
smṛtibhraṃśād buddhināśo buddhināśāt praṇaśyati 2.63

Such a person who is thus detached
And to neither virtue nor sin is he attached,
When in all moments a poise is maintained,
The awakened mind, he is said to have attained.|57|

Like a tortoise receding into its shell's safety
Over all six senses, when he claims mastery
From everything he can then withdraw himself
And dwell in the awakened state of the 'Self'|58|

From sensual temptations one may strongly desist
And all attractions one may control and resist
But still the yearning may remain and persist
For the awakened one only, even desire's root doesn't exist.|59|

O *Arjuna,* Even amongst men who are wisest
Even those who make the efforts hardest
The senses agitate them to go astray
And these defeated minds lose their way |60|

Capable of controlling the senses is only he-
Who focuses and meditates upon Me!
For when the sensual distractions one overcomes
His intelligence awakened and illumined becomes|61|

Those intellectuals who over subjects contemplate
Attached to those subjects, lost they become
And in their attachment, they are by desire overcome
And by desires within themselves anger they generate|62|

And in anger they become hoodwinked by delusion
In delusion, their memory only gets clouded
In this forgetfulness their wisdom is destroyed
And this loss of wisdom furthers their annihilation|63|

रागद्वेषविमुक्तैस्तु विषयानिन्द्रियैश्चरन् ।
वियुक्तैस्तु आत्मवश्यैर्विधेयात्मा प्रसादमधिगच्छति ॥ २-६४॥

rāgadveṣavimuktais tu viṣayān indriyaiś caran
ātmavaśyair vidheyātmā prasādam adhigacchati 2.64

प्रसादे सर्वदुःखानां हानिरस्योपजायते ।
प्रसन्नचेतसो ह्याशु बुद्धिः पर्यवतिष्ठते ॥ २-६५॥

prasāde sarvaduḥkhānāṃ hānir asyopajāyate
prasannacetaso hyāśu buddhiḥ paryavatiṣṭhate 2.65

नास्ति बुद्धिरयुक्तस्य न चायुक्तस्य भावना ।
न चाभावयतः शान्तिरशान्तस्य कुतः सुखम् ॥ २-६६॥

nāsti buddhir ayuktasya na cāyuktasya bhāvanā
na cābhāvayataḥ śāntir aśāntasya kutaḥ sukham 2.66.

इन्द्रियाणां हि चरतां यन्मनोऽनुविधीयते ।
तदस्य हरति प्रज्ञां वायुर्नावमिवाम्भसि ॥ २-६७॥

indriyāṇāṃ hi caratāṃ yan manonuvidhīyate
tad asya harati prajñāṃ vāyur nāvam ivāmbhasi 2.67

तस्माद्यस्य महाबाहो निगृहीतानि सर्वशः ।
इन्द्रियाणीन्द्रियार्थेभ्यस्तस्य प्रज्ञा प्रतिष्ठिता ॥ २-६८॥

tasmād yasya mahābāho nigṛhītāni sarvaśaḥ
indriyāṇīndriyārthebhyas tasya prajñā pratiṣṭhitā 2.68

या निशा सर्वभूतानां तस्यां जागर्ति संयमी ।
यस्यां जाग्रति भूतानि सा निशा पश्यतो मुनेः ॥ २-६९॥

yā niśā sarvabhūtānāṃ tasyāṃ jāgarti saṃyamī
yasyāṃ jāgrati bhūtāni sā niśā paśyato muneḥ 2.69

When one bereft of hatred and desires, lives
And no authority to his senses, he gives
That champion who reins in attraction
Is blessed with the awakened "Self's" satisfaction |64|

Unhappiness in all its forms ends
And all sorrows, away this blessing sends.
Filling the seeker's mind with ethereal joys
He attains the perfect wisdom's poise |65|

He whose wisdom is not focused,
His emotions are also uncontrolled
Uncontrolled emotions only spread disquiet around
And without peace can happiness ever be found? |66|

Wandering to the whims of the senses –
The mind to its own preferred sense attaches
This sense-mind leads the intelligence astray
Just like the wind blowing a rudderless boat away |67|

Therefore, your Self-control you must reaffirm
And in all respects hold your determination firm,
As he who over his senses has mastery obtained
The state of the illumined mind he has verily attained |68|

For what is night for those lost in material dreams
It is day to the dwellers of the spiritual realms
And what is day for the seekers of the material mundane
It is darkness to the illumined man of the spiritual plane|69|

आपूर्यमाणमचलप्रतिष्ठं समुद्रमापः प्रविशन्ति यद्वत् ।
तद्वत्कामा यं प्रविशन्ति सर्वे स शान्तिमाप्नोति न कामकामी ॥ २-७०॥

āpūryamāṇam acalapratiṣṭham samudram āpaḥ praviśanti yadvat
tadvat kāmā yam praviśanti sarve sa śāntim āpnoti
na kāmakāmī 2.70

विहाय कामान्यः सर्वान्पुमांश्चरति निःस्पृहः ।
निर्ममो निरहङ्कारः स शान्तिमधिगच्छति ॥ २-७१॥

vihāya kāmān yaḥ sarvān pumāṃś carati niḥspṛhaḥ
nirmamo nirahaṃkāraḥ sa śāntim adhigacchhati 2.71

एषा ब्राह्मी स्थितिः पार्थ नैनां प्राप्य विमुह्यति ।
स्थित्वास्यामन्तकालेऽपि ब्रह्मनिर्वाणमृच्छति ॥ २-७२॥

eṣā brāhmī sthitiḥ pārtha naināṃ prāpya vimuhyati
sthitvāsyām antakālepi brahmanirvā ṇam ṛcchati 2.72

Just like when the many turbulent rivers converge
And affect not the vast ethereal ocean as they merge
On reaching the awakened stable mind, all attraction dissolves
Not for the one whose mind to senses' whims revolves |70|

He who from all desires abstains,
A complete detachment in life he obtains
From the senses of ownership and ego, he is free
And ergo, purely at peace he can be.|71|

O *Arjuna*! In this conscious state awakened
The veil of illusion is forever lifted
If this state up to the time of death is sustained
A merger with the infinite is then attained |72|"

(Thus ended the Second Canto of the Bhagavad Gita where Sri Krishna began to reveal the hidden knowledge to Arjuna who had been overcome with a terrible depression in the middle of the battle field)

❉ ❉ ❉

अथ तृतीयोऽध्याय: ।
atha tṛtīyodhyāyaḥ

अर्जुन उवाच ।
ज्यायसी चेत्कर्मणस्ते मता बुद्धिर्जनार्दन ।
तत्किं कर्मणि घोरे मां नियोजयसि केशव ॥ ३-१॥

arjuna uvāca
jyāyasī cet karmaṇas te matā buddhir janārdana
tat kiṃ karmaṇi ghore māṃ niyojayasi keśava 3.1

व्यामिश्रेणेव वाक्येन बुद्धिं मोहयसीव मे ।
तदेकं वद निश्चित्य येन श्रेयोऽहमाप्नुयाम् ॥ ३-२॥

vyāmiśreṇeva vākyena buddhiṃ mohayasīva me
tad ekaṃ vada niścitya yena śreyoham āpnuyām 3.2

श्रीभगवानुवाच ।
लोकेऽस्मिन् द्विविधा निष्ठा पुरा प्रोक्ता मयानघ ।
ज्ञानयोगेन साङ्ख्यानां कर्मयोगेन योगिनाम् ॥ ३-३॥

śrībhagavān uvāca
lokesmin dvividhā niṣṭhā purā proktā mayānagha
jñānayogena sāṅkhyānāṃ karmayogena yoginām 3.3

न कर्मणामनारम्भान्नैष्कर्म्यं पुरुषोऽश्नुते ।
न च संन्यसनादेव सिद्धिं समधिगच्छति ॥ ३-४॥

na karmaṇām anārambhān naiṣkarmyaṃ puruṣośnute
na ca saṃnyasanād eva siddhiṃ samadhigacchati 3.4

न हि कश्चित्क्षणमपि जातु तिष्ठत्यकर्मकृत् ।
कार्यते ह्यवशः कर्म सर्वः प्रकृतिजैर्गुणैः ॥ ३-५॥

na hi kaścit kṣaṇamapi jātu tiṣṭhatyakarmakṛt
kāryate hy avaśaḥ karma sarvaḥ prakṛtijair guṇaiḥ 3.5

Canto III: *Unveiling the Spirit in material action*

(Verse 3-9, 19-26, 35: Knowledge of the *Yoga* of Action; 27-29: The Origins of Action; 30-35: Secret of Yoga of Action; 36-40: The Enemies within; 42: Mind and Beyond; 41,43: *Krishna*'s instruction to the seeker of light)

Arjuna asked:
"O *Krishna*, Haven't you just said what is superior,
That spiritual knowledge over material action is better!
Then why is it that you coerce me into action?
This ghastly *"karma"* on me, why do you sanction? |1|

My mind stands confused and disarrayed-
For it fully understands not all that you have said.
Hence, show me which is the correct way?
What will benefit me, I request you to please say! |2|

Sri Krishna said:
Men of two faiths in this world dwell
O Pure one, as I had said before as well,
Those to whom seeking the eternal
knowledge gives satisfaction
And those who believe firmly in the *Yoga* of action.|3|

A state of detached action in works can't be reached
Without man's beginning and performing the action
And great spiritual boundaries can't be breached
By physically renouncing all the works or by inaction|4|

Not a single such moment can pass for man
As without engaging in activity, exist- no one can
This nature's qualities on all beings has been endowed-
A bond of works and actions on man has been bestowed.|5|

कर्मेन्द्रियाणि संयम्य य आस्ते मनसा स्मरन् ।
इन्द्रियार्थान्विमूढात्मा मिथ्याचारः स उच्यते ॥ ३-६॥

karmendriyāṇi saṃyamya ya āste manasā smaran
indriyārthān vimūḍhātmā mithyācāraḥ sa ucyate 3.6

यस्त्विन्द्रियाणि मनसा नियम्यारभतेऽर्जुन ।
कर्मेन्द्रियैः कर्मयोगमसक्तः स विशिष्यते ॥ ३-७॥

yastvindriyāṇi manasā niyamyārabhaterjuna
karmaindriyaiḥ karmayogam asaktaḥ sa viśiṣyate 3.7

नियतं कुरु कर्म त्वं कर्म ज्यायो ह्यकर्मणः ।
शरीरयात्रापि च ते न प्रसिद्ध्येदकर्मणः ॥ ३-८॥

niyataṃ kuru karma tvaṃ karma jyāyo hy akarmaṇaḥ
śarīrayātrāpi ca te na prasidhyedakarmaṇaḥ 3.8
यज्ञार्थात्कर्मणोऽन्यत्र लोकोऽयं कर्मबन्धनः ।

तदर्थं कर्म कौन्तेय मुक्तसङ्गः समाचर ॥ ३-९॥

yajñārthātkarmaṇonyatra lokoyaṃ karmabandhanaḥ
tadarthaṃ karma kaunteya muktasaṅgaḥ samācara 3.9

सहयज्ञाः प्रजाः सृष्ट्वा पुरोवाच प्रजापतिः ।
अनेन प्रसविष्यध्वमेष वोऽस्त्विष्टकामधुक् ॥ ३-१०॥

sahayajñāḥ prajāḥ sṛṣṭvā purovāca prajāpatiḥ
anena prasaviṣyadhvameṣa vostviṣṭakāmadhuk 3.10

देवान्भावयतानेन ते देवा भावयन्तु वः ।
परस्परं भावयन्तः श्रेयः परमवाप्स्यथ ॥ ३-११॥

devān bhāvayatānena te devā bhāvayantu vaḥ
parasparam bhāvayantaḥ śreyaḥ param avāpsyatha 3.11
इष्टान्भोगान्हि वो देवा दास्यन्ते यज्ञभाविताः ।

तैर्दत्तानप्रदायैभ्यो यो भुङ्क्ते स्तेन एव सः ॥ ३-१२॥
iṣṭān bhogān hi vo devā dāsyante yajñabhāvitāḥ
tair dattān apradāyaibhyo yo bhuṅkte stena eva saḥ 3.12

A way to physically control the senses, a man may find-
But if he constantly thinks of the senses in his mind,
He is caught up in self-discipline's wrong notion
Such a being is beguiled by his misplaced devotion.|6|

He who by the mind controls the senses
And is detached, *O Arjuna* from all sensual disturbances,
And performs all his works and actions in this *Yogic* way-
He is considered the most superior person any day.|7|

Without attachment, perform your every action
Because action always supersedes inaction
Even your body's life journey cannot be sustained
Without action no accomplishment can be attained.|8|

Except the actions that are performed in a state of sacrifice,
Chained to *Karma*'s bonds are all actions done otherwise
That is why, *O Arjuna*, Your actions you regulate
With the freedom of detachment as I postulate.|9|

Brahma-The progenitor, through the act of sacrifice,
Bore the first living beings and put forth this edifice
He said- "As from sacrifice, you all originated-
Through sacrifice your life's evolution will be actuated."|10|

Through sacrifice, the Gods you can bolster
And call upon their blessings with your fervor
Thus mutually you can together advance-
With the supreme's blessing, all life you can enhance.|11|

When through sacrifice the gods you impress
All your desired enjoyments they shall bless
These enjoyments to the supreme, whoever doesn't offer
Such a person is naught but a thieving beggar.|12|

यज्ञशिष्टाशिनः सन्तो मुच्यन्ते सर्वकिल्बिषैः ।
भुञ्जते ते त्वघं पापा ये पचन्त्यात्मकारणात् ॥ ३-१३॥

yajñaśiṣṭāśinaḥ santo mucyante sarvakilbiṣaiḥ
bhuñjate te tv agham pāpā ye pacanty ātmakāraṇāt 3.13

अन्नाद्भवन्ति भूतानि पर्जन्यादन्नसम्भवः ।
यज्ञाद्भवति पर्जन्यो यज्ञः कर्मसमुद्भवः ॥ ३-१४॥

annād bhavanti bhūtāni parjanyād annasambhavaḥ
yajñād bhavati parjanyo yajñaḥ karmasamudbhavaḥ 3.14

कर्म ब्रह्मोद्भवं विद्धि ब्रह्माक्षरसमुद्भवम् ।
तस्मात्सर्वगतं ब्रह्म नित्यं यज्ञे प्रतिष्ठितम् ॥ ३-१५॥

karma brahmodbhava m viddhi brahm ākṣarasamudbhavam
tasmāt sarvagatam brahma nityam yajñe pratiṣṭhitam 3.15

एवं प्रवर्तितं चक्रं नानुवर्तयतीह यः ।
अघायुरिन्द्रियारामो मोघं पार्थ स जीवति ॥ ३-१६॥

evam pravartitam cakram nānuvartayatīha yaḥ
aghāyur indriyārāmo mogham pārtha sa jīvati 3.16

यस्त्वात्मरतिरेव स्यादात्मतृप्तश्च मानवः ।
आत्मन्येव च सन्तुष्टस्तस्य कार्यं न विद्यते ॥ ३-१७॥

yas tv ātmaratir eva syād ātmatṛptaś ca mānavaḥ
ātmany eva ca saṃtuṣṭas tasya kāryam na vidyate 3.17

नैव तस्य कृतेनार्थो नाकृतेनेह कश्चन ।
न चास्य सर्वभूतेषु कश्चिदर्थव्यपाश्रयः ॥ ३-१८॥

naiva tasya kṛtenārtho nākṛteneha kaścana
na cāsya sarvabhūteṣu kaścid arthavyapāśrayaḥ 3.18

तस्मादसक्तः सततं कार्यं कर्म समाचर ।
असक्तो ह्याचरन्कर्म परमाप्नोति पूरुषः ॥ ३-१९॥

tasmād asaktaḥ satatam kāryam karma samācara
asakto hy ācarankarma paramāpnoti pūruṣaḥ 3.19

After the sacrifice, whatever is the undistributed left over,
The good who are free of sin, eat the oblation's remainder
The evil offer only to themselves to eat the food
And only consume sin- their actions accumulate no good. |13|

From food-the living beings' existence is found-
And food is formed when rain falls on the ground
And rain comes from the sacrifice or *Yagnya*
And sacrifice originates through works or *Karma*.|14|

Karma is borne of *Brahma* or the progenitor
And *Brahma* of the formless imperishable creator
Thus the all pervading *Brahma* is engaged
And in a state of sacrifice-the universe is arranged|15|

He who follows not this universe's wheel
And succumbs to whatsoever his senses feel
Is base in his pursuit of sensual enjoyment
O *Arjuna,* Such a life is but a wasted predicament.|16|

But He who revels in the delight of the 'Self'
And lives joyously contented within the 'Self'
Such an illumined and awakened person very joyfully exists
As his need for work to be done no longer persists.|17|

Such a great one has nothing to be gained-
Neither in performing actions nor in inaction
Nothing exists thus in all of existence –
That can bind him with dependence.|18|

So perennially perform all of your actions,
Detachedly, fulfill the duties that life sanctions
For when man in detached action engages
With his *Karma* he transcends the highest stages.|19|

कर्मणैव हि संसिद्धिमास्थिता जनकादयः ।
लोकसङ्ग्रहमेवापि सम्पश्यन्कर्तुमर्हसि ॥ ३-२०॥

karmaṇaiva hi saṃsiddhim āsthitā janakādayaḥ
lokasaṃgraham evāpi saṃpaśyan kartum arhasi 3.20

यद्यदाचरति श्रेष्ठस्तत्तदेवेतरो जनः ।
स यत्प्रमाणं कुरुते लोकस्तदनुवर्तते ॥ ३-२१॥

yadyad ācarati śreṣṭhas tattad evetaro janaḥ
sa yat pramāṇaṃ kurute lokas tad anuvartate 3.21

न मे पार्थास्ति कर्तव्यं त्रिषु लोकेषु किञ्चन ।
नानवाप्तमवाप्तव्यं वर्त एव च कर्मणि ॥ ३-२२॥

na me pārthāsti kartavyaṃ triṣu lokeṣu kiṃcana
nānavāptam avāptavyaṃ varta eva ca karmaṇi 3.22

यदि ह्यहं न वर्तेयं जातु कर्मण्यतन्द्रितः ।
मम वर्त्मानुवर्तन्ते मनुष्याः पार्थ सर्वशः ॥ ३-२३॥

yadi hy ahaṃ na varteyaṃ jātu karmaṇy atandritaḥ
mama vartmānuvartante manuṣyāḥ pārtha sarvaśaḥ 3.23

उत्सीदेयुरिमे लोका न कुर्यां कर्म चेदहम् ।
सङ्करस्य च कर्ता स्यामुपहन्यामिमाः प्रजाः ॥ ३-२४॥

utsīdeyur ime lokā na kuryāṃ karma ced aham
saṃkarasya ca kartā syām upahanyām imāḥ prajāḥ 3.24

सक्ताः कर्मण्यविद्वांसो यथा कुर्वन्ति भारत ।
कुर्याद्विद्वांस्तथासक्तश्चिकीर्षुर्लोकसङ्ग्रहम् ॥ ३-२५॥

saktāḥ karmaṇy avidvāṃso yathā kurvanti bhārata
kuryād vidvāṃs tathāsaktaś cikīrṣur lokasaṃgraham 3.25

न बुद्धिभेदं जनयेदज्ञानां कर्मसङ्गिनाम् ।
जोषयेत्सर्वकर्माणि विद्वान्युक्तः समाचरन् ॥ ३-२६॥

na buddhibhedaṃ janayed ajñānāṃ karmasaṃginām
joṣayet sarvakarmāṇi vidvān yuktaḥ samācaran 3.26

King *Janaka* and the rest attained perfection
Only through their works and liberated action
Detached actions for the sake of the world are best
This is said to be the true *Yogic* way by the wisest.|20|

Whatever actions the best amongst men perform
The other men seek to imitate
Whatever standard he sets as the norm
That the world tries to follow and emulate.|21|

O Arjuna, I have no duties to discharge
Towards the peoples of all three worlds at large
There is nothing I haven't gained or seek to gain
And yet I perform my duties-come sun or rain.|22|

If I did not meticulously perform my every action
And lead by example in every aspect
O Arjuna, All men would follow likewise
And ape my path in every respect.|23|

For If I were to not follow this path of action
The peoples shall follow suit and sink to destruction
I would become the perpetuator of pandemonium
And then have to slay them all for the opprobium|24|

O Arjuna, Just as the men of ignorance perform-
Their actions all engrossed in attachment
So too the wise remain motivated as a norm
To better the world, by their works in detachment.|25|

Without creating a divide in the ignorant minds
A middle path, the intelligent mind finds,
He gets the right work done from the attached
Despite his remaining fully detached. |26|

प्रकृतेः क्रियमाणानि गुणैः कर्माणि सर्वशः ।
अहङ्कारविमूढात्मा कर्ताहमिति मन्यते ॥ ३-२७॥

prakṛteḥ kriyamānāni guṇaiḥ karmāṇi sarvaśaḥ
ahaṃkāravimūḍhātmā kartāham iti manyate 3.27

तत्त्वित्तु महाबाहो गुणकर्मविभागयोः ।
गुणा गुणेषु वर्तन्त इति मत्वा न सज्जते ॥ ३-२८॥

tattvavit tu mahābāho guṇakarmavibhāgayoḥ
guṇā guṇeṣu vartanta iti matvā na sajjate 3.28

प्रकृतेर्गुणसम्मूढाः सज्जन्ते गुणकर्मसु ।
तानकृत्स्नविदो मन्दान्कृत्स्नविन्न विचालयेत् ॥ ३-२९॥

prakṛter guṇasammūḍhāḥ sajjante guṇakarmasu
tān akṛtsnavido mandān kṛtsnavin na vicālayet 3.29

मयि सर्वाणि कर्माणि संन्यस्याध्यात्मचेतसा ।
निराशीर्निर्ममो भूत्वा युध्यस्व विगतज्वरः ॥ ३-३०॥

mayi sarvāṇi karmāṇi saṃnyasyādhyātmacetasā
nirāśīr nirmamo bh ūtvā yudhyasva vigatajvara ḥ 3.30

ये मे मतमिदं नित्यमनुतिष्ठन्ति मानवाः ।
श्रद्धावन्तोऽनसूयन्तो मुच्यन्ते तेऽपि कर्मभिः ॥ ३-३१॥

ye me matam idam nityam anutiṣṭhanti mānavāḥ
śraddhāvantonasūyanto mucyante tepi karmabhiḥ 3.31

ये त्वेतदभ्यसूयन्तो नानुतिष्ठन्ति मे मतम् ।
सर्वज्ञानविमूढांस्तान्विद्धि नष्टानचेतसः ॥ ३-३२॥

ye tv etad abhyasūyanto nānutiṣṭhanti me matam
sarvajñānavimūḍhāṃs tān viddhi naṣṭān acetasaḥ 3.32

सदृशं चेष्टते स्वस्याः प्रकृतेर्ज्ञानवानपि ।
प्रकृतिं यान्ति भूतानि निग्रहः किं करिष्यति ॥ ३-३३॥

sadṛśaṃ ceṣṭate svasyāḥ prakṛter jñānavān api
prakṛtim yānti bhūtāni nigrahaḥ kiṃ kariṣyati 3.33

All the types of actions originated
From nature qualities and their interactions
The ignorant one who is by his ego- deluded
Thinks his outer-self performs all actions |27|

O Mighty-armed One, Those who know the foundation
Of how nature's qualities through works function,
Know that the senses attach to the sense objects-
And are unperturbed and detached in all aspects|28|

These qualities of nature bewilder the ignorant,
Who wish not to forgo attachment at any instant -
He who knows should from disturbing them abstain
And from altering their mental state, he should refrain.|29|

Consecrating your actions to Me (the supreme I),
Meditate upon your 'Self' that is a part of Me
Without holding on to desires or prestige
Without grief or remorse, ready your weapons to lay siege|30|

Those amongst men who thus regularly perform
And to My instructions they dutifully conform,
With the purest and blemish-less devotion-
From *Karma's* bondage they attain redemption.|31|

Those who lack the conviction and regard
And my instructions they bluntly disregard
From all knowledge they are by their ignorance deluded -
From a growth in consciousness, they are excluded.|32|

Even the knowledgeable person always, in life acts
And as per one's own nature when he interacts
When all living creatures by their natures are bound
In its suppression, what truth can be found? |33|

इन्द्रियस्येन्द्रियस्यार्थे रागद्वेषौ व्यवस्थितौ ।
तयोर्न वशमागच्छेत्तौ ह्यस्य परिपन्थिनौ ॥ ३-३४॥

indriyasyendriyasy ārthe rāgadveṣau vyavasthitau
tayor na vaśam āgacchhet tau hy asya paripanthinau 3.34

श्रेयान्स्वधर्मो विगुणः परधर्मात्स्वनुष्ठितात् ।
स्वधर्मे निधनं श्रेयः परधर्मो भयावहः ॥ ३-३५॥

śreyān svadharmo viguṇaḥ paradharmāt svanuṣṭhitāt
svadharme nidhanaṃ śreyaḥ paradharmo bhayāvahaḥ 3.35

अर्जुन उवाच ।
अथ केन प्रयुक्तोऽयं पापं चरति पूरुषः ।
अनिच्छन्नपि वार्ष्णेय बलादिव नियोजितः ॥ ३-३६॥

arjuna uvāca
atha kena prayuktoyaṃ pāpaṃ carati pūruṣaḥ
anicchann api vārṣṇeya balād iva niyojitaḥ 3.36

श्रीभगवानुवाच ।
काम एष क्रोध एष रजोगुणसमुद्भवः ।
महाशनो महापाप्मा विद्ध्येनमिह वैरिणम् ॥ ३-३७॥

śrībhagavān uvāca
kāma eṣa krodha eṣa rajoguṇasamudbhavaḥ
mahāśano mahāpāpmā viddhy enam iha vairiṇam 3.37

धूमेनाव्रियते वह्निर्यथादर्शो मलेन च ।
यथोल्बेनावृतो गर्भस्तथा तेनेदमावृतम् ॥ ३-३८॥

dhūmenāvriyate vanhir yathādarśo malena ca
yatholbenāvṛto garbhas tathā tenedam āvṛtam 3.38

आवृतं ज्ञानमेतेन ज्ञानिनो नित्यवैरिणा ।
कामरूपेण कौन्तेय दुष्पूरेणानलेन च ॥ ३-३९॥

āvṛtaṃ jñānam etena jñānino nityavairiṇā
kāmarupeṇa kaunteya duṣpūreṇānalena ca 3.39

Likes and dislikes arise out of the senses
And their emergence one cannot avoid
But one must not fall prey to their pretenses
Else progress on the spirit's path is destroyed. |34|

Working for one's 'Self' even though faultily is much better
Than to serve perfectly under someone else's fetter
Even if death comes while performing one's natural duty
It is better as serving others is a perilous vulnerability.|35|"

Arjuna asked:
"So, What is it that provokes man to sin?
And act against his will –thus against his own kin?
Where from does the force arise to rebel?
O Descendent of *Vrishni*, Please tell! |36|"

Krishna answered:
"It is desire and its furious sibling- anger
Borne from the quality *'Rajas'*- they are related to one another
All ensnaring and all polluting, they cause life to go in vain
These are the two greatest enemies that ought to be slain.|37|

Just as fire is masked by smoke and dust
Or like the embryo is sheathed within the amniotic crust
In this manner similar and precise-
Knowledge is hidden by an outer disguise.|38|

Knowledge is covered by this perennial enemy-
Even in the cases of the knowledgeable many
O *Arjuna*, such is desire's lustful form-
Which rages like a quenchless firestorm.|39|

इन्द्रियाणि मनो बुद्धिरस्याधिष्ठानमुच्यते ।
एतैर्विमोहयत्येष ज्ञानमावृत्य देहिनम् ॥ ३-४०॥

indriyāṇi mano buddhir asyādhiṣṭhānam ucyate
etair vimohayaty eṣa jñānam āvṛtya dehinam 3.40

तस्मात्त्वमिन्द्रियाण्यादौ नियम्य भरतर्षभ ।
पाप्मानं प्रजहि ह्येनं ज्ञानविज्ञाननाशनम् ॥ ३-४१॥

tasmāt tvam indriyāṇy ādau niyamya bharatarṣabha
pāpmānaṃ prajahi hy enaṃ jñānavijñānanāśanam 3.41

इन्द्रियाणि पराण्याहुरिन्द्रियेभ्यः परं मनः ।
मनसस्तु परा बुद्धिर्यो बुद्धेः परतस्तु सः ॥ ३-४२॥

indriyāṇi parāṇy āhur indriyebhyaḥ paraṃ manaḥ
manasas tu parā buddhir yo buddheḥ paratas tu saḥ 3.42

एवं बुद्धेः परं बुद्ध्वा संस्तभ्यात्मानमात्मना ।
जहि शत्रुं महाबाहो कामरूपं दुरासदम् ॥ ३-४३॥

evaṃ buddheḥ paraṃ buddhvā saṃstabhyātmānam
ātmanā jahi śatruṃ mahābāho kāmarūpaṃ durāsadam 3.43

It is said, If senses occupy the governing seat
The mind and the intellect- desires can cheat
Knowledge is bewildered by the sensual stimulants
And hoodwinked become the two instruments |40|

Therefore, know this O mighty seeker of light
Taming the senses is your first fight
Slay the forces that proliferate the sin –
These destroyers of knowledge, conquer and win.|41|

Beyond the senses that are supreme is the mind
Beyond the mind –the awakened intelligence you find
But beyond the awakened intelligence it is thus said-
It is He- the eternal "Self"- the supreme Godhead.|42|

With this knowledge of the Supreme "Self"
Assailing your mind and intellect, gather yourself
O Mighty armed one- this formidable enemy you must slay-
Destroy Desire-For truth's light to make way.|43|"

(Thus ended the third Canto of the Bhagavad Gita where Sri Krishna described the governing spiritual forces that are at play behind the veil of the material objects and actions)

✻ ✻ ✻

अथ चतुर्थोऽध्यायः ।
atha caturthodhyāyaḥ

श्रीभगवानुवाच ।
इमं विवस्वते योगं प्रोक्तवानहमव्ययम् ।
विवस्वान्मनवे प्राह मनुरिक्ष्वाकवेऽब्रवीत् ॥ ४-१॥

śrībhagavān uvāca
imaṃ vivasvate yogaṃ proktavān aham avyayam
vivasvān manave prāha manur ikṣvākavebravīt 4.1

एवं परम्पराप्राप्तमिमं राजर्षयो विदुः ।
स कालेनेह महता योगो नष्टः परन्तप ॥ ४-२॥

evaṃ paramparāprāptam imaṃ rājarṣayo viduḥ
sa kāleneha mahatā yogo naṣṭaḥ paraṃtapa 4.2

स एवायं मया तेऽद्य योगः प्रोक्तः पुरातनः ।
भक्तोऽसि मे सखा चेति रहस्यं ह्येतदुत्तमम् ॥ ४-३॥

sa evāyaṃ mayā tedya yogaḥ proktaḥ purātanaḥ
bhaktosi me sakhā ceti rahasyaṃ hy etad uttamam 4.3

अर्जुन उवाच ।
अपरं भवतो जन्म परं जन्म विवस्वतः ।
कथमेतद्विजानीयां त्वमादौ प्रोक्तवानिति ॥ ४-४॥

arjuna uvāca
aparaṃ bhavato janma paraṃ janma vivasvataḥ
katham etad vijānīyāṃ tvam ādau proktavān iti 4.4

श्रीभगवानुवाच ।

बहूनि मे व्यतीतानि जन्मानि तव चार्जुन ।
तान्यहं वेद सर्वाणि न त्वं वेत्थ परन्तप ॥ ४-५॥

śrībhagavānuvāca
bahūni me vyatītāni janmāni tava cārjuna
tāny ahaṃ veda sarvāṇi na tvaṃ vettha paraṃtapa 4.5

Canto IV: *<u>Krishna opens the gates of knowledge</u>*

(Verse 1-5: The Descent of Knowledge 6-15: Avatarhood; 16, 17: Action and Inaction; 18-23: Way of the Illumined Man; 24-33: The sacrifice to Brahma; 34: The key to Knowledge; 35: Realization of the Godhead; 36-41: The Strength of Faith; 42- The light to dispel darkness)

And His Lordship *Sri Krishna* spoke:
"This Way of Yoga I first taught the sun,
Who then revealed to *Manu*- who was the first mortal one
And this knowledge to the first king *Ikshvaku, Manu* transferred-
Thus in this way knowledge passed on from the first word |1|

This tradition was upheld then by the regal-sages
And from sage to sage, it was conveyed in succession
O Arjuna, this knowledge that was passed on by the sages
With the passage of time got lost in transmission.|2|

The same knowledge that I had first taught
I shared with you to enlighten your thought
This king of secrets to you too, I shall lend,
For you are My devotee, my dear friend. |3|"

Arjuna questioned:
"The Sun- God was the first amongst the living-
Even before your birth was the Sun's beginning
How is it that I can comprehend what you say?-
That you instructed the Sun on the first day! |4|"

Sri Krishna answered:
"Many many births before, *O Arjuna*, I have seen
And many times born, you too have been
The only difference is that of all of them I know
But you are unaware of them and hence don't know |5|

अजोऽपि सन्नव्ययात्मा भूतानामीश्वरोऽपि सन् ।
प्रकृतिं स्वामधिष्ठाय सम्भवाम्यात्ममायया ॥ ४-६॥

ajopi sann avyayātmā bhūtānām īśvaropi san
prakṛtiṃ svām adhiṣṭhāya sambhavāmy ātmamāyayā 4.6

यदा यदा हि धर्मस्य ग्लानिर्भवति भारत ।
अभ्युत्थानमधर्मस्य तदात्मानं सृजाम्यहम् ॥ ४-७॥

yadā yadā hi dharmasya glānir bhavati bhārata
abhyutthānam adharmasya tadātmānaṃ sṛjāmy aham 4.7

परित्राणाय साधूनां विनाशाय च दुष्कृताम् ।
धर्मसंस्थापनार्थाय सम्भवामि युगे युगे ॥ ४-८॥

paritrāṇāya sādhūnāṃ vināśāya ca duṣkṛtām
dharmasaṃsthāpanārthāya sambhavāmi yuge yuge 4.8

जन्म कर्म च मे दिव्यमेवं यो वेत्ति तत्त्वतः ।
त्यक्त्वा देहं पुनर्जन्म नैति मामेति सोऽर्जुन ॥ ४-९॥

janma karma ca me divyam evaṃ yo vetti tattvataḥ
tyaktvā dehaṃ punarjanma naiti mām eti sorjuna 4.9

वीतरागभयक्रोधा मन्मया मामुपाश्रिताः ।
बहवो ज्ञानतपसा पूता मद्भावमागताः ॥ ४-१०॥

vītarāgabhayakrodhā manmayā mām upāśritāḥ
bahavo jñānatapasā pūtā madbhāvam āgatāḥ 4.10

ये यथा मां प्रपद्यन्ते तांस्तथैव भजाम्यहम् ।
मम वर्त्मानुवर्तन्ते मनुष्याः पार्थ सर्वशः ॥ ४-११॥

ye yathā māṃ prapadyante tāṃs tathaiva bhajāmy aham
mama vartmānuvartante manuṣyāḥ pārtha sarvaśaḥ 4.11

काङ्क्षन्तः कर्मणां सिद्धिं यजन्त इह देवताः ।
क्षिप्रं हि मानुषे लोके सिद्धिर्भवति कर्मजा ॥ ४-१२॥

kāṃkṣantaḥ karmaṇām siddhiṃ yajanta iha devatāḥ
kṣipraṃ hi mānuṣe loke siddhir bhavati karmajā 4.12

Though I am imperishable and birth-less,
The Lord of all beings, eternal and timeless
I descend into my *Maya's* existence
And in nature I bring forth My presence |6|

At all times when righteousness is at its wane
O Child of Light, whenever there is a reign of darkness and pain
When injustice and entropy blares on the human side-
My *Avatar* descends into the mortal realm to turn the tide.|7|

For the deliverance of the good- who are oppressed
To obliterate all the world's evil that has coalesced
To once more coronate the kingdom of right
Epoch after epoch I manifest My light|8|

He who understands My birth-Divine
And knows the way of My Divine works
After death his consciousness merges into Mine
And he relapses not into the cycle of endless births.|9|

Thus exempted from attachment, fear and anger
With their minds seeking refuge in My shelter
Such men of knowledge who have performed penance-
In divinizing life, they have been able to advance.|10|

Whichever form of mine, My devotees expect
Their ardent prayers towards Me I accept
Seekers of my path walk in so many ways
O Arjuna, In search of Me all men tread –always!|11|

The mortals to fulfill their works of desire
Sacrifice to the various demigods whom they admire
Because these actions bear fruition quickly
In the human realm the results manifest easily.|12|

चातुर्वर्ण्यं मया सृष्टं गुणकर्मविभागशः ।
तस्य कर्तारमपि मां विद्ध्यकर्तारमव्ययम् ॥ ४-१३॥

cāturvarṇyaṃ mayā sṛṣṭaṃ guṇakarmavibhāgaśaḥ
tasya kartāram api māṃ viddhy akartāram avyayam 4.13

न मां कर्माणि लिम्पन्ति न मे कर्मफले स्पृहा ।
इति मां योऽभिजानाति कर्मभिर्न स बध्यते ॥ ४-१४॥

na māṃ karmāṇi limpanti na me karmaphale spṛhā
iti māṃ yobhijānāti karmabhir na sa badhyate 4.14

एवं ज्ञात्वा कृतं कर्म पूर्वैरपि मुमुक्षुभिः ।
कुरु कर्मैव तस्मात्त्वं पूर्वैः पूर्वतरं कृतम् ॥ ४-१५॥

evaṃ jñātvā kṛtaṃ karma pūrvair api mumukṣubhiḥ
kuru karmaiva tasmāt tvaṃ pūrvaiḥ pūrvataraṃ kṛtam 4.15

किं कर्म किमकर्मेति कवयोऽप्यत्र मोहिताः ।
तत्ते कर्म प्रवक्ष्यामि यज्ज्ञात्वा मोक्ष्यसेऽशुभात् ॥ ४-१६॥

kiṃ karma kimakarmeti kavayopy atra mohitāḥ
tat te karma pravakṣyāmi yaj jñātvā mokṣyaseśubhāt 4.16

कर्मणो ह्यपि बोद्धव्यं बोद्धव्यं च विकर्मणः ।
अकर्मणश्च बोद्धव्यं गहना कर्मणो गतिः ॥ ४-१७॥

karmaṇo hy api boddhavyaṃ boddhavyaṃ ca vikarmaṇaḥ
akarmaṇaś ca boddhavyaṃ gahanā karmaṇo gatiḥ 4.17

कर्मण्यकर्म यः पश्येदकर्मणि च कर्म यः ।
स बुद्धिमान्मनुष्येषु स युक्तः कृत्स्नकर्मकृत् ॥ ४-१८॥

karmaṇy akarma yaḥ paśyed akarmaṇi ca karma yaḥ
sa buddhimān manuṣyeṣu sa yuktaḥ kṛtsnakarmakṛt 4.18

यस्य सर्वे समारम्भाः कामसङ्कल्पवर्जिताः ।
ज्ञानाग्निदग्धकर्माणं तमाहुः पण्डितं बुधाः ॥ ४-१९॥

yasya sarve samārambhāḥ kāmasaṃkalpavarjitāḥ
jñānāgnidagdhakarmāṇaṃ tam āhuḥ paṇḍitaṃ budhāḥ 4.19

I created the four-fold system of order-
On the basis of qualities, activities and ardor
It is I who gave the four fold law sanction-
Imperishable I am, yet I detachedly perform My action.|13|

I cannot be chained or bound by actions
Nor by any fruitive aspirations
He who knows this and understands
In the entanglement of works he never lands|14|

The ancient wise ones who were liberated
Imbibing this knowledge they operated
Therefore you too, all your works perform
Adopting the ancients' practice as your norm|15|

What is action and what is inaction?
Even the wisest seers are thus perplexed
I shall hand you that riddle's explanation-
That knowledge by which all bondages are shed|16|

Understand one must- what is right action
And what is the action that is considered wrong
Also one must know what is considered to be inaction-
And the deep nature to which the way of works belong|17|

He who while performing action, sees inaction
And even in inactivity, he who perceives a latent action
Know him to be the man of the illumined mind
And his actions transcendentally benefit all of mankind.|18|

He who seeks not any gratification
He whose every activity is without desire
He whose very works are consumed by knowledge's fire
He is declared to be the wisest sage in action.|19|

त्यक्त्वा कर्मफलासङ्गं नित्यतृप्तो निराश्रयः ।
कर्मण्यभिप्रवृत्तोऽपि नैव किञ्चित्करोति सः ॥ ४-२०॥

tyaktvā karmaphalāsaṅgaṃ nityatṛpto nirāśrayaḥ
karmaṇy abhipravṛttopi naiva kiṃcit karoti saḥ 4.20

निराशीर्यतचित्तात्मा त्यक्तसर्वपरिग्रहः ।
शारीरं केवलं कर्म कुर्वन्नाप्नोति किल्बिषम् ॥ ४-२१॥

nirāśīr yatacittātmā tyaktasarvaparigrahaḥ
śārīraṃ kevalaṃ karma kurvan nāpnoti kilbiṣam 4.21

यदृच्छालाभसन्तुष्टो द्वन्द्वातीतो विमत्सरः ।
समः सिद्धावसिद्धौ च कृत्वापि न निबध्यते ॥ ४-२२॥

yadṛcchālābhasaṃtuṣṭo dvandvātīto vimatsaraḥ
samaḥ siddhāv asiddhau ca kṛtvāpi na nibadhyate 4.22

गतसङ्गस्य मुक्तस्य ज्ञानावस्थितचेतसः ।
यज्ञायाचरतः कर्म समग्रं प्रविलीयते ॥ ४-२३॥

gatasaṅgasya muktasya jñānāvasthitacetasaḥ
yajñāyācarataḥ karma samagraṃ pravilīyate 4.23

ब्रह्मार्पणं ब्रह्म हविर्ब्रह्माग्नौ ब्रह्मणा हुतम् ।
ब्रह्मैव तेन गन्तव्यं ब्रह्मकर्मसमाधिना ॥ ४-२४॥

brahmārpaṇaṃ brahma havir brahmāgnau brahmaṇā hutam
brahmaiva tena gantavyaṃ brahmakarmasamādhinā 4.24

दैवमेवापरे यज्ञं योगिनः पर्युपासते ।
ब्रह्माग्नावपरे यज्ञं यज्ञेनैवोपजुह्वति ॥ ४-२५॥

daivam evāpare yajñaṃ yoginaḥ paryupāsate
brahmāgnāv apare yajñaṃ yajñenaivopajuvhati 4.25

श्रोत्रादीनीन्द्रियाण्यन्ये संयमाग्निषु जुह्वति ।
शब्दादीन्विषयानन्य इन्द्रियाग्निषु जुह्वति ॥ ४-२६॥

śrotrādīnīndriyāṇy anye saṃyamāgniṣu juvhati
śabdādīn viṣayān anya indriyāgniṣu juvhati 4.26

When he has given up attachment,
Desire-less and unperturbed, he is the blissful one.
In the midst of activity, he is in a state of detachment
He is not the doer of works, but his work is done|20|

He desires naught for his heart or mind
All desires renounced, his senses in his grip you find
In this poise, all bodily actions he does verily perform
But his actions can cause no sin to take form.|21|

With whatever good that naturally comes his way
He is contented, thus never envious on any day
Both success and failure, he greets with poise
Works don't bind him for he has transcended choice.|22|

Devoid of attachment, he is truly free and liberated
In a state of sacrifice, his every action is consecrated
In the 'Self'-his heart and mind are immersed and involved
And all reactions arising from works are dissolved.|23|

It is to *Brahma*-the supreme truth, that all offerings are made
So that into the state of *Brahma,* one can wade
The *Brahmin* –truth seeker, into *Brahma*'s fire, pours oblations
And his works reach the ultimate state of *Brahman* actions.|24|

Some seekers of a Divine union make
Sacrifices only to the Gods whom they prefer
But there are others who in the sacrifice partake
Into *Brahma*'s fire, they offer solely for the sacrifice's sake|25|

Others consecrate their hearing and other senses as a whole
Into the sacrificial fire of complete self-control
Some place the music of sound or the best objects they desire
Thus offering their senses into the sacred sacrificial fire.|26|

सर्वाणीन्द्रियकर्माणि प्राणकर्माणि चापरे ।
आत्मसंयमयोगाग्नौ जुह्वति ज्ञानदीपिते ॥ ४-२७॥

sarvāṇīndriyakarmāṇi prāṇakarmāṇi cāpare
ātmasaṃyamayogāgnau juvhati jñānadīpite 4.27

द्रव्ययज्ञास्तपोयज्ञा योगयज्ञास्तथापरे ।
स्वाध्यायज्ञानयज्ञाश्च यतयः संशितव्रताः ॥ ४-२८॥

dravyayajñās tapoyajñā yogayajñās tathāpare
svādhyāyajñānayajñāś ca yatayaḥ saṃśitavratāḥ 4.28

अपाने जुह्वति प्राणं प्राणेऽपानं तथापरे ।
प्राणापानगती रुद्ध्वा प्राणायामपरायणाः ॥ ४-२९॥

apāne juvhati prāṇaṃ prāṇepānaṃ tathāpare
prāṇāpānagatī ruddhvā prāṇāyāmaparāyaṇāḥ 4.29

अपरे नियताहाराः प्राणान्प्राणेषु जुह्वति ।
सर्वेऽप्येते यज्ञविदो यज्ञक्षपितकल्मषाः ॥ ४-३०॥

apare niyatāhārāḥ prāṇān prāṇeṣu juvhati
sarvepy ete yajñavido yajñak ṣapitakalma ṣāḥ 4.30

यज्ञशिष्टामृतभुजो यान्ति ब्रह्म सनातनम् ।
नायं लोकोऽस्त्ययज्ञस्य कुतोऽन्यः कुरुसत्तम ॥ ४-३१॥

yajñaśiṣṭāmṛtabhujo yānti brahma san ātanam
nāyaṃ lokosty ayajñasya kutonya ḥ kurusattama 4.31

एवं बहुविधा यज्ञा वितता ब्रह्मणो मुखे ।
कर्मजान्विद्धि तान्सर्वानेवं ज्ञात्वा विमोक्ष्यसे ॥ ४-३२॥

evaṃ bahuvidhā yajñā vitatā brahmaṇo mukhe
karmajān viddhi tān sarvān evaṃ jñātvā vimokṣyase 4.32

श्रेयान्द्रव्यमयाद्यज्ञाज्ज्ञानयज्ञः परन्तप ।
सर्वं कर्माखिलं पार्थ ज्ञाने परिसमाप्यते ॥ ४-३३॥

śreyān dravyamayād yajñāj jñānayajñaḥ paraṃtapa
sarvaṃ karmākhilam pārtha jñāne parisamāpyate 4.33

All sense-bound actions are offered by some-
Along with their bodily actions, breath and life force
With Self control all these offerings only oblations become-
Into Knowledge's fire -light's kindling source.|27|

Some make material offerings for their benefaction,
While other *Yogis* practice a rigorous austerity in action
Others into the fire of knowledge as oblations show
Their intellectual prowess, reading and all that they know.|28|

While others practice the sacrifice by breathing
The life force that they are inhaling and exhaling
Thus, they exercise restraint on their very life force
And a regulation over their breaths they enforce.|29|

There are yet others who regulate their food,
Their life-forces, they pour into the sacrifice of life-force
Sacrifice's meaning all these beings have truly understood
And in its fire they obliterate their sins in life's course.|30|

Post-sacrifice, they who enjoy the ambrosial nectar leftover,
In the eternal *Brahma's* consciousness they hover
When even this world isn't for those who sacrifice not
And if not here, O *Arjuna*-elsewhere can anything be got? |31|

Into the fiery mouth of *Brahma,* these sacrifices enter
Through many different ways, whichever one may offer
Know these as the ways of sacrificial works that must be
For this is the knowledge that shall free and set free.|32|

Over any material sacrifice that is performed physically
Superior is the sacrifice of knowledge that is done intellectually
O Arjuna, all actions always ultimately reach
Culminating in knowledge, the supreme truth they teach.|33|

तद्विद्धि प्रणिपातेन परिप्रश्नेन सेवया ।
उपदेक्ष्यन्ति ते ज्ञानं ज्ञानिनस्तत्त्वदर्शिनः ॥ ४-३४॥

tad viddhi praṇipātena paripraśnena sevayā
upadekṣyanti te jñānam jñāninas tattvadarśinah 4.34

यज्ज्ञात्वा न पुनर्मोहमेवं यास्यसि पाण्डव ।
येन भूतान्यशेषेण द्रक्ष्यस्यात्मन्यथो मयि ॥ ४-३५॥

yaj jñātvā na punar moham evam yāsyasi pāṇḍava
yena bhūtāny aśeṣeṇa drakṣyasy ātmany atho mayi 4.35

अशेषाणि अपि चेदसि पापेभ्यः सर्वेभ्यः पापकृत्तमः ।
सर्वं ज्ञानप्लवेनैव वृजिनं सन्तरिष्यसि ॥ ४-३६॥

api ced asi pāpebhyaḥ sarvebhyaḥ pāpakṛttamah
sarvam jñānaplavenaiva vṛjinam samtariṣyasi 4.36

यथैधांसि समिद्धोऽग्निर्भस्मसात्कुरुतेऽर्जुन ।
ज्ञानाग्निः सर्वकर्माणि भस्मसात्कुरुते तथा ॥ ४-३७॥

yathaidhāmsi samiddhognir bhasmasāt kuruterjuna
jñānāgniḥ sarvakarmāṇi bhasmasāt kurute tathā 4.37

न हि ज्ञानेन सदृशं पवित्रमिह विद्यते ।
तत्स्वयं योगसंसिद्धः कालेनात्मनि विन्दति ॥ ४-३८॥

na hi jñānena sadṛśam pavitram iha vidyate
tat svayam yogasamsiddhaḥ kālenātmani vindati 4.38

श्रद्धावाँल्लभते ज्ञानं तत्परः संयतेन्द्रियः ।
ज्ञानं लब्ध्वा परां शान्तिमचिरेणाधिगच्छति ॥ ४-३९॥

śraddhāvāml labhate jñānam tatparaḥ samyatendriyah
jñānam labdhvā parām śāntim acireṇādhigacchati 4.39

अज्ञश्चाश्रद्दधानश्च संशयात्मा विनश्यति ।
नायं लोकोऽस्ति न परो न सुखं संशयात्मनः ॥ ४-४०॥

ajñaś cāśraddadhānaś ca samśayātmā vinaśyati
nāyam lokosti na paro na sukham samśayātmanah 4.40

By humbly bowing to a true master and by worshiping
And by questioning and by dutifully serving
These preceptors who possess the divinity and foresight
Shall bless and part you their knowledge's light.|34|

With this knowledge, *O Arjuna*, you shall know the true way
And your mind's ignorance shall never lead you astray
See you shall first in all living entities the Self's presence
And then witness you shall in Myself every being's exis-
tence.|35|

Even a sinner who has the greatest sin performed
By this knowledge, the sinner can be reformed
Surpassing the sea of wickedness, he shall pass through
Boarding the ship of knowledge, he'll cross a horizon new.|36|

O Arjuna, just like when an inferno blazes
Everything its fire consumes, burns and razes
The fire of ethereal knowledge, everything burns
Every actions and works into ashes it thus turns.|37|

More immaculate than this, there is nothing
Than the radiance of knowledge's unadulterated light
He who has integrated the *Yogic* principles in everything
Attains in himself the true Self's insight.|38|

He whose faith is strongly ordained
And a control over senses, he who has attained
Is by the supreme knowledge enlightened
And his ascent to absolute peace is ascertained|39|

The One who is faithless and ignorant
For whom neither this world nor the other is existent
By infinite doubts, his mind is plagued,
And by his own skepticism he is destroyed.|40|

योगसंन्यस्तकर्माणं ज्ञानसञ्छिन्नसंशयम् ।
आत्मवन्तं न कर्माणि निबध्नन्ति धनञ्जय ॥ ४-४१॥

yogasaṃnyastakarmāṇam jñānasaṃchinnasaṃśayam
ātmavantaṃ na karmāṇi nibadhnanti dhanaṃjaya 4.41

तस्मादज्ञानसम्भूतं हृत्स्थं ज्ञानासिनात्मनः ।
छित्त्वैनं संशयं योगमातिष्ठोत्तिष्ठ भारत ॥ ४-४२॥

tasmād ajñānasañbhūtam hṛtstham jñānāsinātmanaḥ
chittvainam saṃśayam yogam ātiṣṭhottiṣṭha bhārata 4.42

O *Arjuna,* He who has above doubts risen
And sacrificed all, desiring nothing for himself
Is no more bound in *Karma*'s prison
For he has attained a true knowledge of the Self|41|

Therefore this ignorance that your heart has borne
Let its veil be shred and torn
With the saber of knowledge, besiege its disguise
O Son of *Bhaarath*! Attain the union-awaken and arise.|42|

(Thus ended the fourth Canto of the Bhagavad Gita where Sri Krishna described to Arjuna the ways of attaining a conscious liberation from the laws of Karma through the Yoga of Knowledge)

✳ ✳ ✳

अथ पञ्चमोऽध्यायः ।
atha pañcamodhyāyaḥ

अर्जुन उवाच ।
संन्यासं कर्मणां कृष्ण पुनर्योगं च शंससि ।
यच्छ्रेय एतयोरेकं तन्मे ब्रूहि सुनिश्चितम् ॥ ५-१॥
arjuna uvāca
saṃnyāsaṃ karmaṇāṃ kṛṣṇa punar yogaṃ ca śaṃsasi
yac chreya etayor ekaṃ tan me brūhi suniścitam 5.1

श्रीभगवानुवाच ।
संन्यासः कर्मयोगश्च निःश्रेयसकरावुभौ ।
तयोस्तु कर्मसंन्यासात्कर्मयोगो विशिष्यते ॥ ५-२॥
śrībhagavān uvāca
saṃnyāsaḥ karmayogaś ca niḥśreyasakarāv ubhau
tayos tu karmasaṃnyāsāt karmayogo viśiṣyate 5.2

ज्ञेयः स नित्यसंन्यासी यो न द्वेष्टि न काङ्क्षति ।
निर्द्वन्द्वो हि महाबाहो सुखं बन्धात्प्रमुच्यते ॥ ५-३॥
jñeyaḥ sa nityasaṃnyāsī yo na dveṣṭi na kāṅkṣati
nirdvandvo hi mahābāho sukhaṃ bandhāt pramucyate 5.3

साङ्ख्ययोगौ पृथग्बालाः प्रवदन्ति न पण्डिताः ।
एकमप्यास्थितः सम्यगुभयोर्विन्दते फलम् ॥ ५-४॥
sāṃkhyayogau pṛthag bālāḥ pravadanti na paṇḍitāḥ
ekam apy āsthitaḥ samyag ubhayor vindate phalam 5.4

यत्साङ्ख्यैः प्राप्यते स्थानं तद्योगैरपि गम्यते ।
एकं साङ्ख्यं च योगं च यः पश्यति स पश्यति ॥ ५-५॥
yat sāṃkhyaiḥ prāpyate sthānaṃ tad yogair api gamyate
ekaṃ sāṃkhyaṃ ca yogaṃ ca yaḥ paśyati sa paśyati 5.5

Canto V: *Absolute Renunciation*

(Verse 1-5: Liberated action and renunciation; 6-28: The peaceful Bliss of renunciation; 29: The enjoyer of sacrifices)

Arjuna said:
"O *Krishna*, The virtues of renunciation of actions you praise
And yet a union with the Divine in all actions you raise!
Of these two which is the best, please do tell-
Which is the way that will augur me well?" |1|

Lord *Krishna* replied:
"The path of Divine action and the way of renunciation
Both these two lead to the ultimate liberation
.But amongst all paths if one were to choose the best
The way of Divine union in activities is superior to the rest.|2|

A *Sannyasin* can be thus defined, O mighty armed one-
As he who holds attachments none-
For he experiences neither desire nor dislike,
Detachedly, he considers both to be alike|3|

It is the children naïve who thus consider and think,
That renunciation and liberated action are contrasting
For the wise can successfully operate with both in sync.
And the results of such actions are everlasting.|4|

The same status which from renunciation may be won,
By a Divine union in works, can be reached with ease.
For both renunciation and liberated actions are one-
He who can thus see, he truly sees.|5|

संन्यासस्तु महाबाहो दुःखमाप्तुमयोगतः ।
योगयुक्तो मुनिर्ब्रह्म नचिरेणाधिगच्छति ॥ ५-६॥

saṃnyāsas tu mahābāho duḥkham āptum ayogataḥ
yogayukto munir brahma nacireṇādhigacchati 5.6

योगयुक्तो विशुद्धात्मा विजितात्मा जितेन्द्रियः ।
सर्वभूतात्मभूतात्मा कुर्वन्नपि न लिप्यते ॥ ५-७॥

yogayukto viśuddhātmā vijitātmā jitendriyaḥ
sarvabhūtātmabhūtātmā kurvann api na lipyate 5.7

नैव किञ्चित्करोमीति युक्तो मन्येत तत्त्ववित् ।
पश्यञ्शृण्वन्स्पृशञ्जिघ्रन्नश्रनगच्छन्स्वपञ्श्वसन् ॥ ५-८॥

naiva kiṃcit karomīti yukto manyeta tattvavit
paśyañ śṛṇvan spṛśañ jighrann aśnan gacchan svapañ śvasan 5.8

प्रलपन्विसृजनगृह्लन्नुन्मिषन्निमिषन्नपि ।
इन्द्रियाणीन्द्रियार्थेषु वर्तन्त इति धारयन् ॥ ५-९॥

pralapan visṛjan gṛhṇann unmiṣan nimiṣann api
indriyāṇīndriyārtheṣu vartanta iti dhārayan 5.9

ब्रह्मण्याधाय कर्माणि सङ्गं त्यक्त्वा करोति यः ।
लिप्यते न स पापेन पद्मपत्रमिवाम्भसा ॥ ५-१०॥

brahmaṇy ādhāya karmāṇi saṅgaṃ tyaktvā karoti yaḥ
lipyate na sa pāpena padmapatram ivāmbhasā 5.10

कायेन मनसा बुद्ध्या केवलैरिन्द्रियैरपि ।
योगिनः कर्म कुर्वन्ति सङ्गं त्यक्त्वात्मशुद्धये ॥ ५-११॥

kāyena manasā buddhyā kevalair indriyair api
yoginaḥ karma kurvanti saṅgaṃ tyaktvātmaśuddhaye 5.11

युक्तः कर्मफलं त्यक्त्वा शान्तिमाप्नोति नैष्ठिकीम् ।
अयुक्तः कामकारेण फले सक्तो निबध्यते ॥ ५-१२॥

yuktaḥ karmaphalaṃ tyaktvā śāntim āpnoti naiṣṭhikīm
ayuktaḥ kāmakāreṇa phale sakto nibadhyate 5.12

It is difficult to achieve the state of renunciation
Without uniting with the Divine in every action
For the wise sage who has attained this togetherness
The knowledge of *Brahma* he can soon unearth and harness.|6|

That purest soul who in *Yoga* engages
Having gained victory over his six senses
In whose Self, the realization of every being is found
His actions are liberated, for by work he is not bound.|7|

The knower of the true principles of all existence
Knows that he is not the cause of his subsistence
Nor is he performing the acts of seeing, hearing,
touching or smelling
Nor the actions of eating, moving,
sleeping or even breathing.|8|

Neither in the physical acts of speaking or egesting
Nor in the involuntary acts of the eyes –opening or closing.
For he knows that in these actions, it isn't he who is acting
And understands that his senses are but merely reacting.|9|

One who consecrates to the *Brahman* his every action,
And performs them in a state of renunciation,
No sin can ever pollute his immaculate belief -
Just as the droplets of water cling not to a lotus's leaf.|10|

By their bodies, minds, intellect or senses they function
And consider not any of them as their own
For to them a perfect detachment is known
And so they engage in the process of self-purification |11|

By giving up all desires for the outcomes of actions
The zenith of peace, a soul can attain certainly
But those bound by desires of actions live uncertainly-
Obsessed with phantom fruits and their material attractions.|12|

सर्वकर्माणि मनसा संन्यस्यास्ते सुखं वशी ।
नवद्वारे पुरे देही नैव कुर्वन्न कारयन् ॥ ५-१३॥

sarvakarmāṇi manasā saṃnyasyāste sukham vaśī
navadvāre pure dehī naiva kurvan na kārayan 5.13

न कर्तृत्वं न कर्माणि लोकस्य सृजति प्रभुः ।
न कर्मफलसंयोगं स्वभावस्तु प्रवर्तते ॥ ५-१४॥

na kartṛtvam na karmāṇi lokasya sṛjati prabhuḥ
na karmaphalasamyogam svabhāvas tu pravartate 5.14

नादत्ते कस्यचित्पापं न चैव सुकृतं विभुः ।
अज्ञानेनावृतं ज्ञानं तेन मुह्यन्ति जन्तवः ॥ ५-१५॥

nādatte kasyacit pāpam na caiva sukṛtam vibhuḥ
ajñānenāvṛtam jñānam tena muhyanti jantavaḥ 5.15

ज्ञानेन तु तदज्ञानं येषां नाशितमात्मनः ।
तेषामादित्यवज्ज्ञानं प्रकाशयति तत्परम् ॥ ५-१६॥

jñānena tu tad ajñānam yeṣām nāśitam ātmanaḥ
teṣām ādityavaj jñānam prakāśayati tat param 5.16

तद्बुद्धयस्तदात्मानस्तन्निष्ठास्तत्परायणाः ।
गच्छन्त्यपुनरावृत्तिं ज्ञाननिर्धूतकल्मषाः ॥ ५-१७॥

tadbuddhayas tadātmānas tannisṭhās tatparāyaṇāḥ
gacchanty apunarāvṛttim jñānanirdhūtakalmaṣāḥ 5.17

विद्याविनयसम्पन्ने ब्राह्मणे गवि हस्तिनि ।
शुनि चैव श्वपाके च पण्डिताः समदर्शिनः ॥ ५-१८॥

vidyāvinayasampanne brāhmaṇe gavi hastini
śuni caiva śvapāke ca paṇḍitāḥ samadarśinaḥ 5.18

इहैव तैर्जितः सर्गो येषां साम्ये स्थितं मनः ।
निर्दोषं हि समं ब्रह्म तस्माद् ब्रह्मणि ते स्थिताः ॥ ५-१९॥

ihaiva tair jitaḥ sargo yeṣām sāmye sthitam manaḥ
nirdoṣam hi samam brahma tasmād brahmaṇi te sthitāḥ 5.19

Possessing self-control with perfection
With poise, he dwells in nature with satisfaction
Within the nine gates of the physical body, he resides
Neither in being the doer nor in the cause, he prides.|13|

The lord of all living beings –the creator supreme,
Created not works nor their ownership in the mortal realm.
The feelings of doing works and the fruit seeking desire,
It was only nature who thus did conspire.|14|

The omniscient One-God of all subjects
Man's sins or virtues- He neither accepts nor rejects
Over Knowledge, a cloak of ignorance is spread-
And that is why living creatures are thus misled.|15|

For those who, by the Self's knowledge are liberated
Ignorance's darkness within them is verily annihilated
The light of knowledge in these beings glows
Like the immortal sun dispelling night's shadows.|16|

On that Self they meditate, channeling their intellect
Taking refuge, On the Self -they consciously reflect
Cleansed off their sins by the purifying waters of light
Towards the destination of no return their souls take flight.|17|

Those whose eyes are illumined with that knowledge's insight
All living ones appear equivalent and identical to their sight-
From the learned spiritual seeker to the elephant or the cow
From the dog to the consumers of lower animals like the sow.|18|

They are the champions here- in this world itself
For with a poised mind, they have united with their Self
Their faultless mind experiences the *Brahma's* oneness
And they breathe and dwell in the *Brahma's* consciousness.|19|

न प्रहृष्येत्प्रियं प्राप्य नोद्विजेत्प्राप्य चाप्रियम् ।
स्थिरबुद्धिरसम्मूढो ब्रह्मविद् ब्रह्मणि स्थितः ॥ ५-२०॥

na prahṛṣyet priyaṃ prāpya nodvijet pr āpya cāpriyam
sthirabuddhir asa ṃmūḍho brahmavid brahma ṇi sthitaḥ 5.20

बाह्यस्पर्शेष्वसक्तात्मा विन्दत्यात्मनि यत्सुखम् ।
स ब्रह्मयोगयुक्तात्मा सुखमक्षयमश्नुते ॥ ५-२१॥

bāhyasparśeṣv asaktātmā vindaty ātmani yat sukham
sa brahmayogayuktātmā sukham akṣayam aśnute 5.21

ये हि संस्पर्शजा भोगा दुःखयोनय एव ते ।
आद्यन्तवन्तः कौन्तेय न तेषु रमते बुधः ॥ ५-२२॥

ye hi saṃsparśajā bhogā duḥkhayonaya eva te
ādyantavantaḥ kaunteya na teṣu ramate budhaḥ 5.22

शक्नोतीहैव यः सोढुं प्राक्शरीरविमोक्षणात् ।
कामक्रोधोद्भवं वेगं स युक्तः स सुखी नरः ॥ ५-२३॥

śaknotīhaiva yaḥ soḍhuṃ prāk śarīravimokṣaṇāt
kāmakrodhodbhavaṃ vegaṃ sa yuktaḥ sa sukhī naraḥ 5.23

योऽन्तःसुखोऽन्तरारामस्तथान्तज्र्योतिरेव यः ।
स योगी ब्रह्मनिर्वाणं ब्रह्मभूतोऽधिगच्छति ॥ ५-२४॥

yontaḥsukhontarārāmas tathāntarjyotir eva yaḥ
sa yogī brahmanirvāṇaṃ brahmabhūtodhigacchati 5.24

लभन्ते ब्रह्मनिर्वाणमृषयः क्षीणकल्मषाः ।
छिन्नद्वैधा यतात्मानः सर्वभूतहिते रताः ॥ ५-२५॥

labhante brahmanirvāṇam ṛṣayaḥ kṣīṇakalmaṣāḥ
chinnadvaidhā yatātmanaḥ sarvabhūtahite ratāḥ 5.25

कामक्रोधवियुक्तानां यतीनां यतचेतसाम् ।
अभितो ब्रह्मनिर्वाणं वर्तते विदितात्मनाम् ॥ ५-२६॥

kāmakrodhaviyuktānāṃ yatīnāṃ yatacetasām
abhito brahmanirvāṇam vartate viditātmanām 5.26

He rejoices not when his needs are fulfilled
Nor grieves over the wants that are unfulfilled
With the clarity of a mind free from every distress
The awakened one resides in the eternal *Brahma's* oneness |20|

He who is touched not by the sensations external
Enjoys the blissful realization of the supreme Self-eternal
He who has united with the supreme Self- *Brahma*
He enjoys the boundless bliss of union with his soul-his *Atma.*|21|

From the sensual means, all the enjoyments that come,
Portend towards gloom and only sorrow they become
For they are fleeting with a finite beginning and end,
O *Arjuna,* They attract not the wise who clearly comprehend.|22|

He who is able to bear and sustain,
The rush of anger and the gush of desire
In this very birth itself he shall obtain-
The highest realization of bliss that man can acquire.|23|

One who experiences the bliss of realizing the inner Self
And also sees the light kindled within oneself,
That *Yogi* who realizes a state of Divine extinction
Merges into *Brahma* gaining absolute dissolution. |24|

When this extinction into *Brahma* is attained
For those sages-a redemption is gained
These illumined masters with minds free of uncertainty,
Their every work done for the good of all becomes charity.|25|

The sages of the awakened Self are liberated and free-
For in their minds, no desire or wrath can unconquered be
For within themselves the *Nirvana of Brahma* they withhold
And around them-this realization in all directions they unfold.|26|

स्पर्शान्कृत्वा बहिर्बाह्यांश्चक्षुश्चैवान्तरे भ्रुवोः ।
प्राणापानौ समौ कृत्वा नासाभ्यन्तरचारिणौ ॥ ५-२७॥

sparśān kṛtvā bahir bāhyāṃś cakṣuś caivāntare bhruvoḥ
prāṇāpānau samau kṛtvā nāsābhyantaracāriṇau 5.27

यतेन्द्रियमनोबुद्धिर्मुनिर्मोक्षपरायणः ।
विगतेच्छाभयक्रोधो यः सदा मुक्त एव सः ॥ ५-२८॥

yatendriyamanobuddhirmunir mokṣaparāyaṇaḥ
vigatecchābhayakrodho yaḥ sadā mukta eva saḥ 5.28

भोक्तारं यज्ञतपसां सर्वलोकमहेश्वरम् ।
सुहृदं सर्वभूतानां ज्ञात्वा मां शान्तिमृच्छति ॥ ५-२९॥

bhoktāraṃ yajñatapasāṃ sarvalokamaheśvaram
suhṛdaṃ sarvabhūtānāṃ jñātvā māṃ śāntim ṛcchati 5.29

Shunning all external touches they concentrate
Focusing at the centre between eyebrows, they meditate
Controlling the life force entering and leaving the nostril
Their inhalation and exhalation they equalize by their will.|27|

The sages who are the seekers of liberation
Assert a control over their mind and intellect
All senses, anger or wrath can cause them no interruption
For they have attained complete freedom in every respect.|28|

When to man, this singular truth is known –
That all sacrifices I receive with joy for they are My own
And he shall perceive Me as his dearest loving friend.
He shall then experience My perfect peace that has no end.|29|"

(Thus ended the fifth Canto of the Bhagavad Gita where Sri Krishna taught Arjuna the way to achieve the Nirvana of Brahma by performing every mental and physical activity with an absolute renunciation)

❋ ❋ ❋

अथ षष्ठोऽध्यायः ।
atha ṣaṣṭhodhyāyaḥ

श्रीभगवानुवाच ।
अनाश्रितः कर्मफलं कार्यं कर्म करोति यः ।
स संन्यासी च योगी च न निरग्निर्न चाक्रियः ॥ ६-१॥
śrībhagavān uvāca
anāśritaḥ karmaphalaṃ kāryaṃ karma karoti yaḥ
sa saṃnyāsī ca yogī ca na niragnir na cākriyaḥ 6.1

यं संन्यासमिति प्राहुर्योगं तं विद्धि पाण्डव ।
न ह्यसंन्यस्तसङ्कल्पो योगी भवति कश्चन ॥ ६-२॥
yaṃ saṃnyāsam iti prāhur yogaṃ taṃ viddhi pāṇḍava
na hy asaṃnyastasaṃkalpo yogī bhavati kaścana 6.2

आरुरुक्षोर्मुनेर्योगं कर्म कारणमुच्यते ।
योगारूढस्य तस्यैव शमः कारणमुच्यते ॥ ६-३॥
ārurukṣor muner yogaṃ karma kāraṇam ucyate
yogārūḍhasya tasyaiva śamaḥ kāraṇam ucyate 6.3

यदा हि नेन्द्रियार्थेषु न कर्मस्वनुषज्जते ।
सर्वसङ्कल्पसंन्यासी योगारूढस्तदोच्यते ॥ ६-४॥
yadā hi nendriyārtheṣu na karmasv anuṣajjate
sarvasaṃkalpasaṃnyāsī yogārūḍhas tadocyate 6.4

उद्धरेदात्मनात्मानं नात्मानमवसादयेत् ।
आत्मैव ह्यात्मनो बन्धुरात्मैव रिपुरात्मनः ॥ ६-५॥
uddhared ātmanātmānaṃ nātmānam avasādayet
ātmaiva hy ātmano bandhur ātmaiva ripur ātmanaḥ 6.5

बन्धुरात्मात्मनस्तस्य येनात्मैवात्मना जितः ।
अनात्मनस्तु शत्रुत्वे वर्तेतात्मैव शत्रुवत् ॥ ६-६॥
bandhur ātmātmanas tasya yenātmaivātmanā jitaḥ
anātmanas tu śatrutve vartetātmaiva śatruvat 6.6

Canto VI: *The Merger with the Supernal Divine:*

(Verse1-32: *Krishna* describes the way to Divinize life; 33-34: *Arjuna* confesses his inability to imbibe *Krishna*'s postulates; 35-36: *Krishna* emphasizes the need to tame the mind; 37-39: *Arjuna* points out his personal misgivings of the path of spiritual union; 40-47: *Krishna* assures *Arjuna* of the aegis of the Divine that shields the seekers of Yoga)

Sri Krishna said:
"He who dutifully works without desire
Him- the expectations of fruits cannot cage
And he is said to be the *Sannyasin*- the *Yogi* –the real sage.
Not he who renounces actions and kindles not the sacrificial fire. |1|

This O *Arjuna*- is what they call renunciation
The true state of *Yoga*-the integral union
He is not a *Yogi* who has renounced not desire
Not the one whose mind yearns for objects to acquire.|2|

And for the ascending *Yogi*-it is thus affirmed
That action causes his ascent to be confirmed
And for he who has already ascended
Self-Mastery is the cause by which he has transcended.|3|

In his mind too all attachments he has denounced
When all the wills within are renounced
If he is bereft of desires towards all objects of sense
The zenith of *Yoga* he has reached thence|4|

The Self alone can set the Self free
If you allow it to unsuppressed be
For the Self is the Self's closest friend-
And also the worst nemesis that the Self can portend |5|

The Self as a friend can be thus considered
When the lower Self's pull has been conquered
But when the higher Self one does not know
Then the Self is the Self's greatest foe.|6|

जितात्मनः प्रशान्तस्य परमात्मा समाहितः ।
शीतोष्णसुखदुःखेषु तथा मानापमानयोः ॥ ६-७॥

jitātmanaḥ praśāntasya paramātmā samāhitaḥ
śītoṣṇasukhaduḥkheṣu tathā mānāpamānayoḥ 6.7

ज्ञानविज्ञानतृप्तात्मा कूटस्थो विजितेन्द्रियः ।
युक्त इत्युच्यते योगी समलोष्टाश्मकाञ्चनः ॥ ६-८॥

jñānavijñānatṛptātmā kūṭastho vijitendriyaḥ
yukta ity ucyate yogī samaloṣṭāśmakāñcanaḥ 6.8

सुहृन्मित्रार्युदासीनमध्यस्थद्वेष्यबन्धुषु ।
साधुष्वपि च पापेषु समबुद्धिर्विशिष्यते ॥ ६-९॥

suhṛnmitrāryudāsīnamadhyasthadveṣyabandhuṣu
sādhuṣv api ca pāpeṣu samabuddhir viśiṣyate 6.9

योगी युञ्जीत सततमात्मानं रहसि स्थितः ।
एकाकी यतचित्तात्मा निराशीरपरिग्रहः ॥ ६-१०॥

yogī yuñjīta satatam ātmānaṃ rahasi sthitaḥ
ekākī yatacittātmā nirāśīr aparigrahaḥ 6.10

शुचौ देशे प्रतिष्ठाप्य स्थिरमासनमात्मनः ।
नात्युच्छ्रितं नातिनीचं चैलाजिनकुशोत्तरम् ॥ ६-११॥

śucau deśe pratiṣṭhāpya sthiram āsanam ātmanaḥ
nātyucchritaṃ nātinīcaṃ cailājinakuśottaram 6.11

तत्रैकाग्रं मनः कृत्वा यतचित्तेन्द्रियक्रियः ।
उपविश्यासने युञ्ज्याद्योगमात्मविशुद्धये ॥ ६-१२॥

tatraikāgraṃ manaḥ kṛtvā yatacittendriyakriyaḥ
upaviśyāsane yuñjyād yogam ātmaviśuddhaye 6.12

समं कायशिरोग्रीवं धारयन्नचलं स्थिरः ।
सम्प्रेक्ष्य नासिकाग्रं स्वं दिशश्चानवलोकयन् ॥ ६-१३॥

samaṃ kāyaśirogrīvaṃ dhārayann acalam sthiraḥ
saṃprekṣya nāsikāgraṃ svaṃ diśaś cānavalokayan 6.13

The victor of the Self experiences the perfect peace
And in that greatest oneness all fluctuations cease
Neither in heat or cold nor in loss or gain
And in honor or dishonor finds not he glory or pain|7|

With the Self's gnosis, poised he remains
Unaffected by senses and tranquil in all planes
And regards alike clay, gold or stone,
Towards all objects an equanimity is shown |8|

The enemies or the friends who are dearest
Sowers of discord or the callous or indifferent nearest
The holy saint or the wretched sinner
He who as one perceives is the ultimate progressor.|9|

The *Yogi* should seclude and devote himself
On immersing and becoming one with the supreme Self
In his solitude with mind and body in his control
Free of desire he should meditate on the soul|10|

For this a pure and clean place should be assigned
A position neither too high nor too low he may find
Meditating steadfast on the Self, he must assume his seat
Made of deer skin, *Kusha* grass or a natural cloth sheet|11|

There with a single-minded devotion that is firm
With his mind, a control over senses he must affirm
On his *Asana*- the seat deeply absorbed in meditation
He must engage in his whole being's integral purification|12|

Keeping the body-neck-head erect and immobile,
A stable position he must take in this style
Without his mind or eyes glancing in any other direction-
On the nose's tip, he must focus his attention|13|

प्रशान्तात्मा विगतभीर्ब्रह्मचारिव्रते स्थितः ।
मनः संयम्य मच्चित्तो युक्त आसीत मत्परः ॥ ६-१४॥

praśāntātmā vigatabhīr brahmacārivrate sthitaḥ
manaḥ saṃyamya maccitto yukta āsīta matparaḥ 6.14

युञ्जन्नेवं सदात्मानं योगी नियतमानसः ।
शान्तिं निर्वाणपरमां मत्संस्थामधिगच्छति ॥ ६-१५॥

yuñjann evaṃ sadātmānaṃ yogī niyatamānasaḥ
śāntiṃ nirvāṇaparamāṃ matsaṃsthām adhigacchati 6.15

नात्यश्नतस्तु योगोऽस्ति न चैकान्तमनश्नतः ।
न चातिस्वप्नशीलस्य जाग्रतो नैव चार्जुन ॥ ६-१६॥

nātyaśnatas tu yogosti na caikāntam anaśnataḥ
na cātisvapnaśīlasya jāgrato naiva cārjuna 6.16

युक्ताहारविहारस्य   युक्तचेष्टस्य कर्मसु ।
युक्तस्वप्नावबोधस्य योगो भवति दुःखहा ॥ ६-१७॥

yuktāhāravihārasya yuktaceṣṭasya karmasu
yuktasvapnāvabodhasya yogo bhavati duḥkhahā 6.17

यदा विनियतं चित्तमात्मन्येवावतिष्ठते ।
निःस्पृहः सर्वकामेभ्यो युक्त इत्युच्यते तदा ॥ ६-१८॥

yadā viniyataṃ cittam ātmany evāvatiṣṭhate
niḥspṛhaḥ sarvakāmebhyo yukta ity ucyate tadā 6.18

यथा दीपो निवातस्थो नेङ्गते सोपमा स्मृता ।
योगिनो यतचित्तस्य युञ्जतो योगमात्मनः ॥ ६-१९॥

yathā dīpo nivātastho neṅgate sopamā smṛtā
yogino yatacittasya yuñjato yogam ātmanaḥ 6.19

यत्रोपरमते चित्तं निरुद्धं योगसेवया ।
यत्र चैवात्मनात्मानं पश्यन्नात्मनि तुष्यति ॥ ६-२०॥

yatroparamate cittaṃ niruddhaṃ yogasevayā
yatra caivātmanātmānaṃ paśyann ātmani tuṣyati 6.20

With a peaceful mind that is without fear
The vow of celibacy he must bear
He must seek with his mind firmly in his control
A merger into My consciousness as a whole|14|

Towards the Self -directing and channeling the mind
Always in *Yoga* that being when you find
The supreme peace attains he
With the *Nirvana of Brahma* that is founded in Me |15|

O *Arjuna*, Understand this *Yoga*'s way
And to whom this path is barred I verily say
It is certainly not for him who in sleep and food indulges
And also not for he who rigidly renounces both urges.|16|

All sorrows begin to cease and disappear
When the state of *Yoga* approaches near
Wherein the sleep, awakening and food is in regulation
And works too when the mind engages
in regulated action.|17|

When the mind and the intellect have perfectly converged
In state of the Self they have truly merged
When from all forms of desires, he is liberated-
The state of Union or *Yoga* he is said to have attained|18|

Like the light of the lamp that burns with a steady face
Motionless and still in a windless place
So too is the mind of the *Yogi* of the awakened Self
Who has consciously attained mastery over himself|19|

Where the mind is tamed by a disciplined will
By the awakened knowledge it is purified and still
And the awakened being perceives the Self by the Self's gnosis
Thus dwelling in the contented state of the supreme's bliss|20|

सुखमात्यन्तिकं यत्तद् बुद्धिग्राह्यमतीन्द्रियम्।
वेत्ति यत्र न चैवायं स्थितश्चलति तत्त्वतः ॥ ६-२१॥

sukham ātyantikaṃ yat tad buddhigrāhyam atīndriyam
vetti yatra na caivāyaṃ sthitaś calati tattvataḥ 6.21

यं लब्ध्वा चापरं लाभं मन्यते नाधिकं ततः।
यस्मिन्स्थितो न दुःखेन गुरुणापि विचाल्यते ॥ ६-२२॥

yaṃ labdhvā cāparaṃ lābhaṃ manyate nādhikaṃ tataḥ
yasmin sthito na duḥkhena guruṇāpi vicālyate 6.22

तं विद्याद् दुःखसंयोगवियोगं योगसंज्ञितम्।
स निश्चयेन योक्तव्यो योगोऽनिर्विण्णचेतसा ॥ ६-२३॥

taṃ vidyād.h duḥkhasaṃyogaviyogaṃ yogasaṃjñitam
sa niścayena yoktavyo yogonirviṇṇacetasā 6.23

सङ्कल्पप्रभवान्कामांस्त्यक्त्वा सर्वानशेषतः।
मनसैवेन्द्रियग्रामं विनियम्य समन्ततः ॥ ६-२४॥

saṅkalpaprabhavān kāmāṃs tyaktvā sarvān aśeṣataḥ
manasaivendriyagrāmaṃ viniyamya samantataḥ 6.24

शनैः शनैरुपरमेद् बुद्ध्या धृतिगृहीतया।
आत्मसंस्थं मनः कृत्वा न किञ्चिदपि चिन्तयेत् ॥ ६-२५॥

śanaiḥ śanair uparamed buddhyā dhṛtigṛhītayā
ātmasaṃsthaṃ manaḥ kṛtvā na kiṃcid api cintayet 6.25

यतो यतो निश्चरति मनश्चञ्चलमस्थिरम्।
ततस्ततो नियम्यैतदात्मन्येव वशं नयेत् ॥ ६-२६॥

yato yato niścarati manaś cañcalam asthiram
tatas tato niyamyaitad ātmany eva vaśaṃ nayet 6.26

प्रशान्तमनसं ह्येनं योगिनं सुखमुत्तमम्।
उपैति शान्तरजसं ब्रह्मभूतमकल्मषम् ॥ ६-२७॥

praśāntamanasaṃ hy enaṃ yoginaṃ sukham uttamam
upaiti śāntarajasaṃ brahmabhūtam akalmaṣam 6.27

When the infinitely blissful Self's truth is thus known-
Perceived beyond the domains that the senses can own,
The *Yogi* is established firmly in the awakened state
From the origins Divine, such a being does not deviate|21|

This is the gain of gains –the greatest treasure
Nothing is greater or even comparable in measure
When that unperturbed state is thoroughly gained
Even by the worst grief one can't be disturbed or pained|22|

It is from the sufferings that the mind has to be freed
A union with the Divine is *Yoga*'s true aim and need
An inseparable union is to be courageously sought
Cheerfully bracing the hurdles by which
the path is wrought|23|

Originating from the thoughts, the desires of every kind
Must be dispelled and banished from the mind
The senses that scatter the thoughts must be in control held
From dispersing to their whims the mind must be withheld |24|

Step by step one must gradually turn inwards
And think of nothing else that is outwards
With the intelligence focused in concentration
One must engage in the Self's meditation|25|

And every single time when the mind goes astray
Becoming unsteady and when it begins to sway
The mind must be reined in and secured
And the consciousness of the Self must be reassured|26|

A pure quietude devoid of any strong emotion
Is the gain of the seeker of the Divine union
Attains he a gnosis of the *Brahma*- the supreme realization
Experiencing the infinite bliss of the soul's emancipation|27|

युञ्जन्नेवं सदात्मानं योगी विगतकल्मषः ।
सुखेन ब्रह्मसंस्पर्शमत्यन्तं सुखमश्नुते ॥ ६-२८॥

yuñjann evaṃ sadātmānaṃ yogī vigatakalmaṣaḥ
sukhena brahmasaṃsparśam atyantaṃ sukham aśnute 6.28

सर्वभूतस्थमात्मानं सर्वभूतानि चात्मनि ।
ईक्षते योगयुक्तात्मा सर्वत्र समदर्शनः ॥ ६-२९॥

sarvabhūtastham ātmānaṃ sarvabhūtāni cātmani
īkṣate yogayuktātmā sarvatra samadarśanaḥ 6.29

यो मां पश्यति सर्वत्र सर्वं च मयि पश्यति ।
तस्याहं न प्रणश्यामि स च मे न प्रणश्यति ॥ ६-३०॥

yo māṃ paśyati sarvatra sarvaṃ ca mayi paśyati
tasyāhaṃ na praṇaśyāmi sa ca me na praṇaśyati 6.30

सर्वभूतस्थितं यो मां भजत्येकत्वमास्थितः ।
सर्वथा वर्तमानोऽपि स योगी मयि वर्तते ॥ ६-३१॥

sarvabhūtasthitaṃ yo māṃ bhajaty ekatvam āsthitaḥ
sarvathā vartamānopi sa yogī mayi vartate 6.31

आत्मौपम्येन सर्वत्र समं पश्यति योऽर्जुन ।
सुखं वा यदि वा दुःखं स योगी परमो मतः ॥ ६-३२॥

ātmaupamyena sarvatra samaṃ paśyati yorjuna
sukhaṃ vā yadi vā duḥkhaṃ sa yogī paramo mataḥ 6.32

अर्जुन उवाच ।

योऽयं योगस्त्वया प्रोक्तः साम्येन मधुसूदन ।
एतस्याहं न पश्यामि चञ्चलत्वात्स्थितिं स्थिराम् ॥ ६-३३॥

arjuna uvāca
yoyaṃ yogas tvayā proktaḥ sāmyena madhusūdana
etasyāhaṃ na paśyāmi cañcalatvāt sthitiṃ sthirām 6.33

When he is thus unblemished, passionless and free
Constantly in the state of union he can be
Such a *Yogi* is always in the state of highest joy
As the understanding of the creator, he can enjoy|28|

Such a man who has attained the union universal
Acquires he a perspective equal and global-
For he sees the Self in all and all in the Self
And he discriminates not others from himself|29|

He who everywhere sees only Me
And in everyone, Me only he can see
To him I can never lost be
And he is never lost to Me.|30|

He who in every beings'oneness believes firmly
And loves Me in every living being truly
His action and living, whatsoever may be his way
He lives and acts in My consciousness every day|31|

As the Self's image, when everything he perceives
O *Arjuna*, In an equanimity and oneness he believes
In both joy and grief a steadfast poise he retains
Becoming closest to Me, the highest
position he attains|32|"

Arjuna said:

"O *Krishna*, This *Yoga* of Oneness expounded by Ye
Finds not any understanding or resonance with me
For its nuances I still cannot grasp or find
I am still feeling quite restless within my mind|33|

चञ्चलं हि मनः कृष्ण प्रमाथि बलवद् दृढम् ।
तस्याहं निग्रहं मन्ये वायोरिव सुदुष्करम् ॥ ६-३४॥

cañcalam hi manah krsna pramāthi balavad drdham
tasyāham nigraham manye vāyor iva suduskaram 6.34

श्रीभगवानुवाच ।

असंशयं महाबाहो मनो दुर्निग्रहं चलम् ।
अभ्यासेन तु कौन्तेय वैराग्येण च गृह्यते ॥ ६-३५॥

śrībhagavān uvāca
asañśayam mahābāho mano durnigraham calam
abhyāsena tu kaunteya vairāgyeṇa ca gṛhyate 6.35

असंयतात्मना योगो दुष्प्राप इति मे मतिः ।
वश्यात्मना तु यतता शक्योऽवाप्तुमुपायतः ॥ ६-३६॥

asamyatātmanā yogo dusprāpa iti me matih
vaśyātmanā tu yatatā śakyovāptum upāyatah 6.36

अर्जुन उवाच ।

अयतिः श्रद्धयोपेतो योगाच्चलितमानसः ।
अप्राप्य योगसंसिद्धिं कां गतिं कृष्ण गच्छति ॥ ६-३७॥

arjuna uvāca
ayatih śraddhayopeto yogāc calitamānasah
aprāpya yogasamsiddhim kām gatim krsna gacchati 6.37

कच्चिन्नोभयविभ्रष्टश्छिन्नाभ्रमिव नश्यति ।
अप्रतिष्ठो महाबाहो विमूढो ब्रह्मणः पथि ॥ ६-३८॥

kacchin nobhayavibhrastaś chinnābhram iva naśyati
apratistho mahābāho vimūḍho brahmaṇah pathi 6.38

एतन्मे संशयं कृष्ण छेत्तुमर्हस्यशेषतः ।
त्वदन्यः संशयस्यास्य छेत्ता न ह्युपपद्यते ॥ ६-३९॥

etan me samśayam krsna chettum arhasy aśesatah
tvadanyah samśayasyāsya chettā na hy upapadyate 6.39

Despite your words, my mind seems so restless
Its nature seems so stubborn and relentless
O *Krishna*, To tame it I can't find a way
It seems as hard as controlling a wind blowing away |34|"

Lord *Krishna* spoke:
"O mighty-armed one, taming the mind is difficult indeed
For its restless nature tries to always mislead
With regular practice, the mind can be trained
And with detachment a control over it can be attained|35|

When a control over Self, one cannot maintain
They fail in *Yoga* and a union they cannot attain
Through disciplined efforts- a mastery
over Self they can retain
With regulated practice a control,
they can surely ascertain|36|"

Arjuna said:
"O *Krishna*, What happens to the one who goes astray?
After embarking on the path of *Yoga*, I wish to earnestly know,
When despite his faith, a seeker's mind wanders away,
If he fails to attain perfection, in the end, where does he go?|37|

O Warrior mighty, does he not lose out on both lives here,
When the human desires he fails to completely give up,
And the Union with *Brahma* when he fails to keep up?
And perish like a cloud that will always only disappear!|38|

This great uncertainty, O *Krishna* you must dispel
And the smallest of my queries you must expel
For this seems to be the only way out
And You alone can destroy this grave doubt|39|

श्रीभगवानुवाच ।
पार्थ नैवेह नामुत्र विनाशस्तस्य विद्यते ।
न हि कल्याणकृत्कश्चिद् दुर्गतिं तात गच्छति ॥ ६-४०॥

śrībhagavān uvāca
pārtha naiveha n āmutra vināśas tasya vidyate
na hi kalyāṇakṛt kaścid durgatiṃ tāta gacchati 6.40

प्राप्य पुण्यकृतां लोकानुषित्वा शाश्वतीः समाः ।
शुचीनां श्रीमतां गेहे योगभ्रष्टोऽभिजायते ॥ ६-४१॥

prāpya puṇyakṛtāṃ lokān uṣitvā śāśvatīḥ samāḥ
śucīnāṃ śrīmatāṃ gehe yogabhra ṣṭobhijāyate 6.41

अथवा योगिनामेव कुले भवति धीमताम् ।
एतद्धि दुर्लभतरं लोके जन्म यदीदृशम् ॥ ६-४२॥

athavā yoginām eva kule bhavati dh īmatām
etad dhi durlabhatara ṃ loke janma yad īdṛśam 6.42

तत्र तं बुद्धिसंयोगं लभते पौर्वदेहिकम् ।
यतते च ततो भूयः संसिद्धौ कुरुनन्दन ॥ ६-४३॥

tatra taṃ buddhisaṃyogaṃ labhate paurvadehikam
yatate ca tato bhūyaḥ saṃsiddhau kurunandana 6.43

पूर्वाभ्यासेन तेनैव ह्रियते ह्यवशोऽपि सः ।
जिज्ञासुरपि योगस्य शब्दब्रह्मातिवर्त्तते ॥ ६-४४॥

pūrvābhyāsena tenaiva hriyate hy avaśopi saḥ
jijñāsur api yogasya śabdabrahmātivartate 6.44

प्रयत्नाद्यतमानस्तु योगी संशुद्धकिल्बिषः ।
अनेकजन्मसंसिद्धस्ततो याति परां गतिम् ॥ ६-४५॥

prayatnād yatamānas tu yogī saṃśuddhakilbiṣaḥ
anekajanmasaṃsiddhas tato yāti parāṃ gatim 6.45

Sri *Krishna* spoke:
"O *Arjuna*, Know this- there is no destruction
Neither in this life or the next for there is no regression
For him who selflessly works for the greater good
No ultimate harm can befall him.
May this be understood! |40|

The one who on the path of *Yoga* falters
Attains the realm of the pious sentient beings
And after dwelling there for many years
Is once more born in the household of pure beings|41|

Or he may be born in a *Yogi*'s house
And to the family of the pious and wise
For it is a privilege so very rare
To be born in a household with a spiritual air.|42|

And there, he slowly assumes his previous birth's status
And resumes his *Yoga* after an outer-worldly hiatus
And his works gradually evolve towards perfection
O *Arjuna*, In *Yoga* there is only ascension.|43|

By virtue of previous birth, His *Yoga* is carried forward,
And the soul is towards the science of union allured
And beyond the ritualistic practices the seeker then ascends
And the principles of Vedas & Upanishads,
he verily transcends.|44|

But by concerted efforts and a sincerity in action
The seeker of union gravitates slowly towards perfection
Over a period of many births, he becomes sinless and purified
And with the knowledge highest, his endeavors are justified.|45|

तपस्विभ्योऽधिको योगी ज्ञानिभ्योऽपि मतोऽधिकः ।
कर्मिभ्यश्चाधिको योगी तस्माद्योगी भवार्जुन ॥ ६-४६॥

tapasvibhyodhiko yogī jñānibhyopi matodhikaḥ
karmibhyaś cādhiko yogī tasmād yogī bhavārjuna 6.46

योगिनामपि सर्वेषां मद्गतेनान्तरात्मना ।
श्रद्धावान्भजते यो मां स मे युक्ततमो मतः ॥ ६-४७॥

yogīnām api sarveṣāṃ madgatenāntarātmanā
śraddhāvān bhajate yo māṃ sa me yuktatamo mataḥ 6.47

In comparison to the firm ascetic, He is greater
Amongst men of knowledge and works too he is better
He who practices *Yoga* integrally is most superior for me
And so a *Yogi* is what, O *Arjuna*, I ask you to be|46|

He whose inner Self to Me has been consecrated
For Me an infinite faith and love he has accommodated
Amongst all the *Yogis* who hold the Divine dear
He is in union with Me and to Me- he is most near|47|"

(Thus ended the sixth canto of the Bhagavad Gita where Sri Krishna taught Arjuna the way to divinize all life on earth)

अथ सप्तमोऽध्यायः ।

atha saptamodhyāyaḥ

श्रीभगवानुवाच ।

मय्यासक्तमनाः पार्थ योगं युञ्जन्मदाश्रयः ।

असंशयं समग्रं मां यथा ज्ञास्यसि तच्छृणु ॥ ७-१॥

śrībhagavān uvāca
mayy āsaktamanāḥ pārtha yogaṃ yuñjan madāśrayaḥ
asaṃśayaṃ samagraṃ māṃ yathā jñāsyasi tac chṛṇu 7.1

ज्ञानं तेऽहं सविज्ञानमिदं वक्ष्याम्यशेषतः ।

यज्ज्ञात्वा नेह भूयोऽन्यज्ज्ञातव्यमवशिष्यते ॥ ७-२॥

jñānaṃ teham savijñānam idaṃ vakṣyāmy aśeṣataḥ
yaj jñātvā neha bhūyo.anyaj jñātavyam avaśiṣyate 7.2

मनुष्याणां सहस्रेषु कश्चिद्यतति सिद्धये ।

यततामपि सिद्धानां कश्चिन्मां वेत्ति तत्त्वतः ॥ ७-३॥

manuṣyāṇāṃ sahasreṣu kaścid yatati siddhaye
yatatām api siddhānāṃ kaścin māṃ vetti tattvataḥ 7.3

भूमिरापोऽनलो वायुः खं मनो बुद्धिरेव च ।

अहङ्कार इतीयं मे भिन्ना प्रकृतिरष्टधा ॥ ७-४॥

bhūmir āponalo vāyuḥ khaṃ mano buddhir eva ca
ahaṃkāra itīyam me bhinnā prakṛtir aṣṭadhā 7.4

अपरेयमितस्त्वन्यां प्रकृतिं विद्धि मे पराम् ।

जीवभूतां महाबाहो ययेदं धार्यते जगत् ॥ ७-५॥

apareyam itas tvanyāṃ prakṛtiṃ viddhi me parām
jīvabhūtāṃ mahābāho yayedaṃ dhāryate jagat 7.5

एतद्योनीनि भूतानि सर्वाणीत्युपधारय ।

अहं कृत्स्नस्य जगतः प्रभवः प्रलयस्तथा ॥ ७-६॥

etadyonīni bhūtāni sarvāṇīty upadhāraya
ahaṃ kṛtsnasya jagataḥ prabhavaḥ pralayas tathā 7.6

Canto VII: <u>The Union through Knowledge</u>

(Verse 1-11: *Krishna* parts the high knowledge that is the foundation of the supreme Union; 12-15: The web of Maya; 16: The Four types of Seekers; 17: *Krishna*'s beloved seeker; 18-30: The Integral Knowledge)

Sri *Krishna* said-
"O *Arjuna*, With the consciousness fully absorbed
When In Me a firm foundation is resolved-
Your every doubt will be answered and cleared
And the undiluted knowledge from Me, you'll hear|1|

That science of union to you I shall explain
That which by engaging in *Yoga*, one can attain
That undiluted knowledge after which doubts won't persist
That knowledge beyond which nothing does exist|2|

Among the thousands of men who seek perfection
And the many thousands who strive in this aspiration
The Self's realization by hardly one is won
And My entire truth is known to only that rarest one |3|

The elements: earth, fire, water, ether and air
And senses: mind, reason and ego are there
Functioning as the eight fold divisions of Mine
On all beings, their impositions -nature tries to assign|4|

But these divisions eight-fold are still inferior
For My energies that become life force are superior
O mighty-armed warrior, know you must and behold-
Only a fraction of My forces all material beings hold!|5|

Know these two types of energies to be Mine
Manifested in all living things of My creation Divine
For I am the creator of this creation
And It is also I who am its destruction|6|

मत्तः परतरं नान्यत्किञ्चिदस्ति धनञ्जय ।
मयि सर्वमिदं प्रोतं सूत्रे मणिगणा इव ॥ ७-७॥

mattah parataram nānyat kimcid asti dhanamjaya
mayi sarvam idam protam sūtre maṇigaṇā iva 7.7

रसोऽहमप्सु कौन्तेय प्रभास्मि शशिसूर्ययोः ।
प्रणवः सर्ववेदेषु शब्दः खे पौरुषं नृषु ॥ ७-८॥

raso.aham apsu kaunteya prabhāsmi śaśisūryayoḥ
praṇavaḥ sarvavedeṣu śabdaḥ khe pauruṣam nṛṣu 7.8

पुण्यो गन्धः पृथिव्यां च तेजश्चास्मि विभावसौ ।
जीवनं सर्वभूतेषु तपश्चास्मि तपस्विषु ॥ ७-९॥

puṇyo gandhaḥ pṛthivyām ca tejaś cāsmi vibhāvasau
jīvanam sarvabhūteṣu tapaś cāsmi tapasviṣu 7.9

बीजं मां सर्वभूतानां विद्धि पार्थ सनातनम् ।
बुद्धिर्बुद्धिमतामस्मि तेजस्तेजस्विनामहम् ॥ ७-१०॥

bījam mām sarvabhūtānām viddhi pārtha sanātanam
buddhir buddhimatām asmi tejas tejasvinām aham 7.10

बलं बलवतां चाहं कामरागविवर्जितम् ।
धर्माविरुद्धो भूतेषु कामोऽस्मि भरतर्षभ ॥ ७-११॥

balam balavatām cāham kāmarāgavivarjitam
dharmāviruddho bhūteṣu kāmo.asmi bharatarṣabha 7.11

ये चैव सात्त्विका भावा राजसास्तामसाश्च ये ।
मत्त एवेति तान्विद्धि न त्वहं तेषु ते मयि ॥ ७-१२॥

ye caiva sātvikā bhāvā rājasās tāmasāś ca ye
matta eveti tān viddhi na tv aham teṣu te mayi 7.12

त्रिभिर्गुणमयैर्भावैरेभिः सर्वमिदं जगत् ।
मोहितं नाभिजानाति मामेभ्यः परमव्ययम् ॥ ७-१३॥

tribhir guṇamayair bhāvair ebhiḥ sarvam idam jagat
mohitam nābhijānāti mām ebhyaḥ param avyayam 7.13

O *Arjuna*, there is naught that exists beyond Me
For nothing can more supreme be
For all existence I am the connecting seed
Like the thread linking the pearl necklace's every bead|7|

In the flavor and taste of the waters, it is I
O *Arjuna*, I am the light of the sun and moon in the sky
The primordial word of genesis – I am Om- the Vedic sound
The manhood in man and in ether's subsonic element,
I am found|8|

On the earth, I am the purest original fragrance
And for the fire that burns, I am its heat and radiance
I am the vitality that nourishes all beings living
I strengthen the ascetic who is askesis performing|9|

Know Me to be the seed of all lives, eternal
O *Arjuna*, My truth is for you to conceive
I am the wisdom in the awakened intellectual
And it is My radiance that the illumined receive|10|

I am the strength of the mighty and strong
Devoid of attachment and passion
O *Arjuna*, I am the energy of procreation
I am the *Dharma's* desire that is not wrong |11|

All modes of ignorance, passion or goodness
It is from me that they have manifested from.
Even though they all exist within My oneness
I exist not in their outer form|12|

By these three modes, man bewildered goes
And the truth of My divinity he never knows
For when one is hoodwinked by the three
My supreme, imperishable existence he can never see|13|

दैवी ह्येषा गुणमयी मम माया दुरत्यया ।
मामेव ये प्रपद्यन्ते मायामेतां तरन्ति ते ॥ ७-१४॥

daivī hy eṣā guṇamayī mama māyā duratyayā
mām eva ye prapadyante māyām etāṃ taranti te 7.14

न मां दुष्कृतिनो मूढाः प्रपद्यन्ते नराधमाः ।
माययापहृतज्ञाना आसुरं भावमाश्रिताः ॥ ७-१५॥

na māṃ duṣkṛtino mūḍhāḥ prapadyante narādhamāḥ
māyayāpahṛtajñānā āsuraṃ bhāvam āśritāḥ 7.15

चतुर्विधा भजन्ते मां जनाः सुकृतिनोऽर्जुन ।
आर्तो जिज्ञासुरर्थार्थी ज्ञानी च भरतर्षभ ॥ ७-१६॥

caturvidhā bhajante māṃ janāḥ sukṛtinorjuna
ārto jijñāsur arthārthī jñānī ca bharatarṣabha 7.16

तेषां ज्ञानी नित्ययुक्त एकभक्तिर्विशिष्यते ।
प्रियो हि ज्ञानिनोऽत्यर्थमहं स च मम प्रियः ॥ ७-१७॥

teṣāṃ jñānī nityayukta ekabhaktir viśiṣyate
priyo hi jñāninotyartham ahaṃ sa ca mama priyaḥ 7.17

उदाराः सर्व एवैते ज्ञानी त्वात्मैव मे मतम् ।
आस्थितः स हि युक्तात्मा मामेवानुत्तमां गतिम् ॥ ७-१८॥

udārāḥ sarva evaite jñānī tv ātmaiva me matam
āsthitaḥ sa hi yuktātmā mām evānuttamāṃ gatim 7.18

बहूनां जन्मनामन्ते ज्ञानवान्मां प्रपद्यते ।
वासुदेवः सर्वमिति स महात्मा सुदुर्लभः ॥ ७-१९॥

bahūnāṃ janmanām ante jñānavān māṃ prapadyate
vāsudevaḥ sarvam iti sa mahātmā sudurlabhaḥ 7.19

कामैस्तैस्तैर्हृतज्ञानाः प्रपद्यन्तेऽन्यदेवताः ।
तं तं नियममास्थाय प्रकृत्या नियताः स्वया ॥ ७-२०॥

kāmais tais tair hṛtajñānāḥ prapadyantenyadevatāḥ
taṃ taṃ niyamam āsthāya prakṛtyā niyatāḥ svayā 7.20

This is *Maya*- the illusion Divine-
That engulfs every creation of Mine.
Crossing over beyond the veil can very hard be
But only by surpassing it can one approach Me!|14|

The foolish and evil do not attain Me
For in their bewilderment the truth they do not see
Disillusioned by *Maya* they resort to base means
Governed by the lower nature of the demonic realms|15|

Amongst the pure ones who their devotion offer
Four fold are the ones, who to Me surrender
The suffering, the seekers of the greater good
The knowledge seekers and devotees by whom I am under-
stood|16|

Amongst them is the knower who is in Divine union
With a single minded devotion he engages in My communion
And to that wise knower, I am most dear
To Me too, he is most beloved and near|17|

All these beings are most definitely worthy
But amongst them, I consider him most noteworthy
Who seeks My union as his life's ultimate ambition
For he dwells in the awakened Self's condition|18|

After many successive births can this fortune arise
When the Divine is perceived through the mortal's eyes
Very rare and blessed indeed is that seeking soul
Who experiences the Divine's omniscience as a whole |19|

By various outer desires, many seekers are mislead
Who to fulfill their desires seek a personal godhead
And the demigods by conditions and rules they bind
Arbitrarily based upon the nature of their mind.|20|

यो यो यां यां तनुं भक्तः श्रद्धयार्चितुमिच्छति ।
तस्य तस्याचलां श्रद्धां तामेव विदधाम्यहम् ॥ ७-२१॥

yo yo yāṃ yāṃ tanuṃ bhaktaḥ śraddhayārcitum icchati
tasya tasyācalāṃ śraddhāṃ tām eva vidadhāmy aham 7.21

स तया श्रद्धया युक्तस्तस्याराधनमीहते ।
लभते च ततः कामान्मयैव विहितान्हि तान् ॥ ७-२२॥

sa tayā śraddhayā yuktas tasyārādhanam īhate
labhate ca tataḥ kāmān mayaivaḥ vihitān hi tān 7.22

अन्तवत्तु फलं तेषां तद्भवत्यल्पमेधसाम् ।
देवान्देवयजो यान्ति मद्भक्ता यान्ति मामपि ॥ ७-२३॥

antavat tu phalaṃ teṣāṃ tad bhavaty alpamedhasām
devān devayajo yānti madbhaktā yānti mām api 7.23

अव्यक्तं व्यक्तिमापन्नं मन्यन्ते मामबुद्धयः ।
परं भावमजानन्तो ममाव्ययमनुत्तमम् ॥ ७-२४॥

avyaktaṃ vyaktim āpannaṃ manyante mām abuddhayaḥ
paraṃ bhāvam ajānanto mamāvyayam anuttamam 7.24

नाहं प्रकाशः सर्वस्य योगमायासमावृतः ।
मूढोऽयं नाभिजानाति लोको मामजमव्ययम् ॥ ७-२५॥

nāhaṃ prakāśaḥ sarvasya yogamāyāsamāvṛtaḥ
mūḍhoyaṃ nābhijānāti loko mām ajam avyayam 7.25

वेदाहं समतीतानि वर्तमानानि चार्जुन ।
भविष्याणि च भूतानि मां तु वेद न कश्चन ॥ ७-२६॥

vedāhaṃ samatītāni vartamānāni cārjuna
bhaviṣyāṇi ca bhūtāni māṃ tu veda na kaścana 7.26

इच्छाद्वेषसमुत्थेन द्वन्द्वमोहेन भारत ।
सर्वभूतानि सम्मोहं सर्गे यान्ति परन्तप ॥ ७-२७॥

icchādveṣasamutthena dvandvamohena bhārata
sarvabhūtāni sammohaṃ sarge yānti paraṃtapa 7.27

Whatever form of Mine that the devotees choose,
Their devotion towards me I do not refuse
I ensure that their confidence remains firm
And their faith in their desired forms I only affirm|21|

Enthused with this faith his devotion he pursues
And a force in his worship I then infuse
Even though through faith objects he seeks
When fulfilled they are My fruits that he keeps|22|

But these fruits are temporary and do not last long-
For their founding reasons are petty and not strong
Whichever demigod they worship that demigod they obtain
But My devotees come to Me and My oneness they attain.|23|

The minds ignorant and small consider Me the unmanifest
Who am limited and finite and cannot wholly manifest
For they know not the truth of my being immutable-
I am the Supreme- most perfect and imperishable.|24|

To all beings I am not revealed
For behind *Maya*'s veil I am concealed
This world is hoodwinked and bewildered
About My immortal truth, it hasn't pondered|25|

O *Arjuna*, The past, present and the future
Of every existence I know for sure
Though I know equally about every living one
With the knowledge of My existence, there is none |26|

In likes and dislikes, they are lost in desire's illusion
By the dualities of aversion and dislike they are deluded
And from truth's gnosis they are excluded
O *Arjuna*, bewildered is every living creation|27|

येषां त्वन्तगतं पापं जनानां पुण्यकर्मणाम् ।
ते द्वन्द्वमोहनिर्मुक्ता भजन्ते मां दृढव्रताः ॥ ७-२८॥

yeṣāṃ tv antagataṃ pāpaṃ janānāṃ puṇyakarmaṇām
te dvandvamohanirmuktā bhajante māṃ dṛḍhavratāḥ 7.28

जरामरणमोक्षाय मामाश्रित्य यतन्ति ये ।
ते ब्रह्म तद्विदुः कृत्स्नमध्यात्मं कर्म चाखिलम् ॥ ७-२९॥

jarāmaraṇamokṣāya mām āśritya yatanti ye
te brahma tad viduḥ kṛtsnam adhyātmaṃ karma cākhilam 7.29

साधिभूताधिदैवं मां साधियज्ञं च ये विदुः ।
प्रयाणकालेऽपि च मां ते विदुर्युक्तचेतसः ॥ ७-३०॥

sādhibhūtādhidaivaṃ māṃ sādhiyajñaṃ ca ye viduḥ
prayāṇakālepi ca māṃ te vidur yuktacetasaḥ 7.30

But those virtuous men who are from sin freed
Who have given up their every material need
Steadfastly they believe in My overlordship
And engage devotedly in My worship|28|

Seeking My refuge those beings who to Me bow
And from cyclic births and deaths they seek release
They experience *Brahma's* knowledge and peace
And the integral knowledge of Divine *karma* they know|29|

Recognizing Me to be the supreme living one-
The primordial master and receiver of sacrifices of everyone
At the critical moment of death when they are aware of Me
They attain a merger and unite into my ethereal sea!|30|"

(Thus ended the seventh canto of the Bhagavad Gita where Sri Krishna parted the knowledge by which a being can attain a complete union with the Divine)

✳ ✳ ✳

अथ अष्टमोऽध्यायः ।
atha aṣṭamodhyāyaḥ

अर्जुन उवाच ।
किं तद् ब्रह्म किमध्यात्मं किं कर्म पुरुषोत्तम ।
अधिभूतं च किं प्रोक्तमधिदैवं किमुच्यते ॥ ८-१॥
arjuna uvāca
kiṃ tad brahma kim adhyātmaṃ kiṃ karma puruṣottama
adhibhūtaṃ ca kiṃ proktam adhidaivaṃ kim ucyate 8.1

अधियज्ञः कथं कोऽत्र देहेऽस्मिन्मधुसूदन ।
प्रयाणकाले च कथं ज्ञेयोऽसि नियतात्मभिः ॥ ८-२॥
adhiyajñaḥ kathaṃ kotra dehesmin madhusūdana
prayāṇakāle ca kathaṃ jñeyosi niyatātmabhiḥ 8.2

श्रीभगवानुवाच ।
अक्षरं ब्रह्म परमं स्वभावोऽध्यात्ममुच्यते ।
भूतभावोद्भवकरो विसर्गः कर्मसंज्ञितः ॥ ८-३॥
śrībhagavān uvāca
akṣaraṃ brahma paramaṃ svabhāvodhyātmam ucyate
bhūtabhāvodbhavakaro visargaḥ karmasaṃjñitaḥ 8.3

अधिभूतं क्षरो भावः पुरुषश्चाधिदैवतम् ।
अधियज्ञोऽहमेवात्र देहे देहभृतां वर ॥ ८-४॥
adhibhūtaṃ kṣaro bhāvaḥ puruṣaś cādhidaivatam
adhiyajñoham evātra dehe dehabhṛtāṃ vara 8.4

अन्तकाले च मामेव स्मरन्मुक्त्वा कलेवरम् ।
यः प्रयाति स मद्भावं याति नास्त्यत्र संशयः ॥ ८-५॥
antakāle ca mām eva smaran muktvā kalevaram
yaḥ prayāti sa madbhāvaṃ yāti nāsty atra saṃśayaḥ 8.5

Canto VIII: _Brahma and the kinetics of the departing soul_

(Verse 1-2: _Arjuna_'s metaphysical query on Brahma, material nature, the Self's Karma, the Gods and the soul journey post-death; 3-28: _Krishna_'s answer to all his questions)

Arjuna asked:

"What is this perception that is known as _Brahma_?
What can be truly termed as the _Self's Karma_?
What phenomenon dominates the material coexistence?
O _Krishna_, Who was the first God that came into existence? |1|

What was the first sacrifice in the physical?
O _Krishna_ , How was it in the embodied being practical?
At the time of death where does the soul further go?
Your existence's truth, How can one really know?|2|"

Sri _Krishna_ answered:

"The formless infinite is _Brahma_- it is thus perceived
And the immortal Self's existence in nature is conceived
That sacrifice made at the movement of formation
Is the Self's _Karma_ performed for every being's creation|3|

Perishable is the nature of material coexistence
The first God is the omniscient transcendental existence
The first sacrifice is My dwelling in all physical beings' auspices
And I am also the receiving Lord of all their sacrifices|4|

Whoever while leaving the body remembers Me
At the time of death, if he can thus focused be
Of traversing the unknown realms he shall have no fear
And to the supreme- My consciousness will take him near|5|

यं यं वापि स्मरन्भावं त्यजत्यन्ते कलेवरम् ।
तं तमेवैति कौन्तेय सदा तद्भावभावितः ॥ ८-६॥

yaṁ yaṁ vāpi smaran bhāvaṁ tyajaty ante kalevaram
taṁ tam evaiti kaunteya sadā tadbhāvabhāvitaḥ 8.6

तस्मात्सर्वेषु कालेषु मामनुस्मर युध्य च ।
मय्यर्पितमनोबुद्धिर्मामेवैष्यस्यसंशयः ॥ ८-७॥

tasmāt sarveṣu kāleṣu mām anusmara yudhya ca
mayy arpitamanobuddhir mām evaiṣyasy asaṁśayaḥ 8.7

अभ्यासयोगयुक्तेन चेतसा नान्यगामिना ।
परमं पुरुषं दिव्यं याति पार्थानुचिन्तयन् ॥ ८-८॥

abhyāsayogayuktena cetasā nānyagāminā
paramaṁ puruṣaṁ divyaṁ yāti pārthānucintayan 8.8

कविं पुराणमनुशासितारमणोरणीयंसमनुस्मरेद्यः ।
सर्वस्य धातारमचिन्त्यरूपमादित्यवर्णं तमसः परस्तात् ॥ ८-९॥

kaviṁ purāṇam anuśāsitāraṁ aṇor aṇīyāṁsam anusmared yaḥ
sarvasya dhātāram acintyarūpaṁ ādityavarṇaṁtamasaḥ parastāt 8.9

प्रयाणकाले मनसाऽचलेन भक्त्या युक्तो योगबलेन चैव ।
भ्रुवोर्मध्ये प्राणमावेश्य सम्यक् स तं परं
पुरुषमुपैति दिव्यम् ॥ ८-१०॥

prayāṇakāle manasācalena bhaktyā yukto yogabalena caiva
bhruvor madhye prāṇam āveśya samyak sa taṁ paraṁ puruṣam
upaiti divyam 8.10

यदक्षरं वेदविदो वदन्ति विशन्ति यद्यतयो वीतरागाः ।
यदिच्छन्तो ब्रह्मचर्यं चरन्ति तत्ते पदं सङ्ग्रहेण
प्रवक्ष्ये ॥ ८-११॥

yad akṣaraṁ vedavido vadanti viśanti yad yatayo vītarāgāḥ
yad icchanto brahmacaryaṁ caranti tat te padaṁ saṁgraheṇa
pravakṣye 8.11

O *Arjuna*, when the physical body one leaves
At the time of departure, whatever one believes
That idea which is strong in his final contemplation
He takes that form and object of his imagination|6|

In all your battles and actions, let your insight be fixed
Upon Me let your mind and intellect be affixed
At all times when you remember Me constantly
O *Arjuna*, you shall then come to Me certainly |7|

O *Arjuna*, by regulated efforts of consecration
With the devoted mind focussed in concentration
When one practices *Yoga* seeking the union Divine
He merges into the supreme consciousness of Mine|8|

The Self - the supreme seer, the ancient and most subtle one
The inconceivable being whose golden
radiance surpasses the sun
The formless atomic form that holds everything material
Beyond darkness- is the Divine refulgent and ethereal|9|

He who at the time of departure engages in My deliberation
His soul is powered with the force of his firm devotion
At the mystic seat between the brows,
by focussing his concentration
He can verily attain My Divine and supreme realization|10|

What the knowers of the Vedas preach
Of the imperishable infinite Self that one must reach
The gnosis sought through askesis by the sages and celibate
That same knowledge to you -I shall now elucidate|11|

सर्वद्वाराणि संयम्य मनो हृदि निरुध्य च ।
मूर्ध्न्याधायात्मनः प्राणमास्थितो योगधारणाम् ॥ ८-१२॥

sarvadvārāṇi saṃyamya mano hṛdi nirudhya ca
mūrdhny ādhāyātmanaḥ prāṇam āsthito yogadhāraṇām 8.12

ओमित्येकाक्षरं ब्रह्म व्याहरन्मामनुस्मरन् ।
यः प्रयाति त्यजन्देहं स याति परमां गतिम् ॥ ८-१३॥

om ity ekākṣaram brahma vyāharan mām anusmaran
yaḥ prayāti tyajan deham sa yāti paramām gatim 8.13

अनन्यचेताः सततं यो मां स्मरति नित्यशः ।
तस्याहं सुलभः पार्थ नित्ययुक्तस्य योगिनः ॥ ८-१४॥

ananyacetāḥ satatam yo mām smarati nityaśaḥ
tasyāham sulabhaḥ pārtha nityayuktasya yoginaḥ 8.14

मामुपेत्य पुनर्जन्म दुःखालयमशाश्वतम् ।
नाप्नुवन्ति महात्मानः संसिद्धिं परमां गताः ॥ ८-१५॥

mām upetya punarjanma duḥkhālayam aśāśvatam
nāpnuvanti mahātmānaḥ samsiddhim paramām gatāḥ 8.15

आब्रह्मभुवनाल्लोकाः पुनरावर्तिनोऽर्जुन ।
मामुपेत्य तु कौन्तेय पुनर्जन्म न विद्यते ॥ ८-१६॥

ā brahmabhuvanāl lokāḥ punarāvartinorjuna
mām upetya tu kaunteya punarjanma na vidyate 8.16

सहस्रयुगपर्यन्तमहर्यद् ब्रह्मणो विदुः ।
रात्रिं युगसहस्रान्तां तेऽहोरात्रविदो जनाः ॥ ८-१७॥

sahasrayugaparyantam ahar yad brahmaṇo viduḥ
rātrim yugasahasrāntām te.ahorātravido janāḥ 8.17

अव्यक्ताद् व्यक्तयः सर्वाः प्रभवन्त्यहरागमे ।
रात्र्यागमे प्रलीयन्ते तत्रैवाव्यक्तसंज्ञके ॥ ८-१८॥

avyaktād vyaktayaḥ sarvāḥ prabhavanty aharāgame
rātryāgame pralīyante tatraivāvyaktasaṃjñake 8.18

With all the sensory doors of the beings closed,
The mind into the heart - shut and firmly enclosed
Focusing the life force of the body and raising it upto the head
Meditate upon attaining the union with the supreme Godhead|12|

By chanting Om-the singular syllable
The vibration of the primordial truth imperishable
Remembering the overlord when the body, he leaves behind
The highest status of the supreme he does find|13|

He who practices *Yoga* with an un-deviated mind
Striving to merge his consciousness with Me , him you'll find
In whose memory My remembrance never does cease
He, O *Arjuna*, can attain the union in Me with ease|14|

These liberated souls after having come to My door
Descend not into mortal birth once more-
And return not to the mortal world- transient and full of pain.
The highest state of perfection they verily gain|15|

Even the beings of *Brahma*'s most perfect planet
And all other worlds are to rebirths subject
But the souls that seek refuge in Me alone find release
And their cycles of endless births and deaths then cease|16|

He who has the eternal *Brahma*'s insight
Knows the duration of His cosmic day and night
Each single day and night of *Brahma*'s life Span
Equals a Yuga of Man|17|

On the Day of the Supreme creator unmanifest
All creations are verily borne to manifest
And for all the created beings destruction comes
When the Night of the *Brahma*-Supreme becomes.|18|

भूतग्रामः स एवायं भूत्वा भूत्वा प्रलीयते ।
रात्र्यागमेऽवशः पार्थ प्रभवत्यहरागमे ॥ ८-१९॥

bhūtagrāmaḥ sa evāyaṃ bhūtvā bhūtvā pralīyate
rātryāgamevaśaḥ pārtha prabhavaty aharāgame 8.19

परस्तस्मात्तु भावोऽन्योऽव्यक्तोऽव्यक्तात्सनातनः ।
यः स सर्वेषु भूतेषु नश्यत्सु न विनश्यति ॥ ८-२०॥

paras tasmāt tu bhāvonyovyaktovyaktāt sanātanaḥ
yaḥ sa sarveṣu bhūteṣu naśyatsu na vinaśyati 8.20

अव्यक्तोऽक्षर इत्युक्तस्तमाहुः परमां गतिम् ।
यं प्राप्य न निवर्तन्ते तद्धाम परमं मम ॥ ८-२१॥

avyaktokṣara ity uktas tam āhuḥ paramāṃ gatim
yaṃ prāpya na nivartante tad dhāma paramaṃ mama 8.21

पुरुषः स परः पार्थ भक्त्या लभ्यस्त्वनन्यया ।
यस्यान्तःस्थानि भूतानि येन सर्वमिदं ततम् ॥ ८-२२॥

puruṣaḥ sa paraḥ pārtha bhaktyā labhyas tv ananyayā
yasyāntaḥsthāni bhūtāni yena sarvam idaṃ tatam 8.22

यत्र काले त्वनावृत्तिमावृत्तिं चैव योगिनः ।
प्रयाता यान्ति तं कालं वक्ष्यामि भरतर्षभ ॥ ८-२३॥

yatra kāle tv anāvṛttim āvṛttiṃ caiva yoginaḥ
prayātā yānti taṃ kālaṃ vakṣyāmi bharatarṣabha 8.23

अग्निर्ज्योतिरहः शुक्लः षण्मासा उत्तरायणम् ।
तत्र प्रयाता गच्छन्ति ब्रह्म ब्रह्मविदो जनाः ॥ ८-२४॥

agnir jotir ahaḥ śuklaḥ ṣaṇmāsā uttarāyaṇam
tatra prayātā gacchanti brahma brahmavido janāḥ 8.24

धूमो रात्रिस्तथा कृष्णः षण्मासा दक्षिणायनम् ।
तत्र चान्द्रमसं ज्योतिर्योगी प्राप्य निवर्तते ॥ ८-२५॥

dhūmo rātris tathā kṛṣṇaḥ ṣaṇmāsā dakṣiṇāyanam
tatra cāndramasaṃ jyotir yogī prāpya nivartate 8.25

At the dawn of His day, take birth innumerable lives
All then disappear and die when His night finally arrives
And At the next dawn once more living entities thrive
And the loop never ends every time the night and day arrive|19|

But there still exists in that Supreme a divinity
An immutable and supra-cosmic ethereal entity
Whose existence can never perish,
Even when all living things vanish.|20|

He is the immutable unmanifest, it is exclaimed
Knowing Him is the highest goal that can be gained
Those who attain Him return not to the material realm
For they have reached His abode supreme|21|

O *Arjuna*, the gnosis of the ultimate Supreme one
By the purest unwavering devotion must be won
He dwells in all living beings on the earth's face
And pervades all matter that exists in space|22|

O *Arjuna*, To you I shall now declare
At life's final moment how the awakened beings fare
Under what conditions the *Yogi*s at the time of death
They do and do not attain re-birth|23|

In the six months when the solstice northern starts
By day of fire or light in the phase of
the waxing moon who departs
That *Yogi*- the knower of *Brahma*, aided by the earth's rotation
Reaches the abode of *Brahma* thus attaining salvation|24|

And the six months when the solstice southern starts
By night of smoke or mist, In the waning moon's phase who parts
In lunar light world, the *Yogi* enjoys and his time spends
Exhausting his energies, back to earth he then descends|25|

शुक्लकृष्णे गती ह्येते जगतः शाश्वते मते ।
एकया यात्यनावृत्तिमन्ययावर्तते पुनः ॥ ८-२६॥

śuklakṛṣṇe gatī hy ete jagataḥ śāśvate mate
ekayā yāty anāvṛttim anyayāvartate punaḥ 8.26

नैते सृती पार्थ जानन्योगी मुह्यति कश्चन ।
तस्मात्सर्वेषु कालेषु योगयुक्तो भवार्जुन ॥ ८-२७॥

naite sṛtī pārtha jānan yogī muhyati kaścana
tasmāt sarveṣu kāleṣu yogayukto bhavārjuna 8.27

वेदेषु यज्ञेषु तपःसु चैव दानेषु यत्पुण्यफलं प्रदिष्टम् ।
अत्येति तत्सर्वमिदं विदित्वा योगी परं स्थानमुपैति
चाद्यम् ॥ ८-२८॥

vedeṣu yajñeṣu tapaḥsu caiva dāneṣu yat puṇyaphalaṃ pradiṣṭam
atyeti tat sarvam idaṃ viditvā yogī paraṃ sthānam
upaiti cādyam 8.28

These are the light and dark pathways-
Respectively the Gods and Forefather's stairways
The souls ascending by the former, earthwards do not turn
While those who ascend the latter, back to earth they return.|26|

The *Yogi* who is of both paths aware
Is never misled and always takes care
And makes no error as he dwells in My communion
Therefore O *Arjuna*, engage in this science of union|27|

The deeds of merit that the Vedas have recommended-
All the sacrifices, austerities, offerings and gifts charitable
These duties the *Yogi* has verily transcended
By attaining the knowledge of the Supreme-immutable|28|"

(Thus ended the eighth Canto of the Bhagavad Gita where Sri Krishna described to Arjuna the post-death journey of the soul and the pathway that lead to realization of Brahma)

✳ ✳ ✳

अथ नवमोऽध्यायः ।

atha navamodhyāyaḥ

श्रीभगवानुवाच ।

इदं तु ते गुह्यतमं प्रवक्ष्याम्यनसूयवे ।

ज्ञानं विज्ञानसहितं यज्ज्ञात्वा मोक्ष्यसेऽशुभात् ॥ ९-१॥

śrībhagavān uvāca
idaṃ tu te guhyatamaṃ pravakṣyāmy anasūyave
jñānaṃ vijñānasahitaṃ yaj jñātvā mokṣyaseśubhāt 9.1

राजविद्या राजगुह्यं पवित्रमिदमुत्तमम् ।

प्रत्यक्षावगमं धर्म्यं सुसुखं कर्तुमव्ययम् ॥ ९-२॥

rājavidyā rājaguhya ṃ pavitram idam uttamam
pratyakṣāvagamaṃ dharmyaṃ susukhaṃ kartum avyayam 9.2

अश्रद्दधानाः पुरुषा धर्मस्यास्य परन्तप ।

अप्राप्य मां निवर्तन्ते मृत्युसंसारवर्त्मनि ॥ ९-३॥

aśraddadhānāḥ puruṣā dharmasyāsya para ṃtapa
aprāpya māṃ nivartante m ṛtyusaṃsāravartmani 9.3

मया ततमिदं सर्वं जगदव्यक्तमूर्तिना ।

मत्स्थानि सर्वभूतानि न चाहं तेष्ववस्थितः ॥ ९-४॥

mayā tatam ida ṃ sarvaṃ jagad avyaktamūrtinā
matsthāni sarvabhūtāni na cāhaṃ teṣv avasthitaḥ 9.4

न च मत्स्थानि भूतानि पश्य मे योगमैश्वरम् ।

भूतभृन्न च भूतस्थो ममात्मा भूतभावनः ॥ ९-५॥

na ca matsthāni bhūtāni paśya me yogam aiśvaram
bhūtabhṛn na ca bhūtastho mamātmā bhūtabhāvana ḥ 9.5

यथाकाशस्थितो नित्यं वायुः सर्वत्रगो महान् ।

तथा सर्वाणि भूतानि मत्स्थानीत्युपधारय ॥ ९-६॥

yathākāśasthito nityaṃ vāyuḥ sarvatrago mahān
tathā sarvāṇi bhūtāni matsthānīty upadhāraya 9.6

Canto IX: *The Knowledge Supreme- the Secret of Secrets*

(Verse 1-26: *Krishna* parts the knowledge of the Supreme's existence, 27-30: *Krishna*'s Call for consecration; 31: *Krishna*'s promise to his every lover; 32-34: The fate of His lovers)

Lord *Krishna* spoke:
"Now to you, that knowledge will be revealed
The secret of secrets that was before always concealed
That science - knowing which you shall released be
And from this world of sorrow you shall be set free|1|

This is the king knowledge, the secret highest
That which is resplendent, purest and best,
The right and just knowledge that is verifiable-
Of the laws of living that are spiritual and imperishable.|2|

But those faithless souls who for Me have no belief
They sink and return to the mortal realm of grief
O *Arjuna* on My path of truth, they cannot tread or ascend
Dwelling on the mundane path - they only descend|3|

From I the formless one, came into existence
the universe complete
The universe is My effable mystery replete
Within My consciousness dwell all living beings
But My consciousness surfaces not in all things |4|

But all the living creatures exist not in Me-
This surrealness of My creation, don't you see?
It is I who support every mortal existence
For I am the constitution of every being's essence.|5|

Just as the mighty winds that flow
Pervading all of space, in all directions they blow,
So too you can conceive of My existence as well
Wherever all living beings persist, there I dwell.|6|

सर्वभूतानि कौन्तेय प्रकृतिं यान्ति मामिकाम् ।
कल्पक्षये पुनस्तानि कल्पादौ विसृजाम्यहम् ॥ ९-७॥

sarvabhūtāni kaunteya prakṛtiṃ yānti māmikām
kalpakṣaye punas tāni kalpādau visṛjāmy aham 9.7

प्रकृतिं स्वामवष्टभ्य विसृजामि पुनः पुनः ।
भूतग्राममिमं कृत्स्नमवशं प्रकृतेर्वशात् ॥ ९-८॥

prakṛtiṃ svām avaṣṭabhya visṛjāmi punaḥ punaḥ
bhūtagrāmam imaṃ kṛtsnam avaśaṃ prakṛter vaśāt 9.8

न च मां तानि कर्माणि निबध्नन्ति धनञ्जय ।
उदासीनवदासीनमसक्तं तेषु कर्मसु ॥ ९-९॥

na ca māṃ tāni karmāṇi nibadhnanti dhanaṃjaya
udāsīnavad āsīnam asaktaṃ teṣu karmasu 9.9

मयाध्यक्षेण प्रकृतिः सूयते सचराचरम् ।
हेतुनानेन कौन्तेय जगद्विपरिवर्तते ॥ ९-१०॥

mayādhyakṣeṇa prakṛtiḥ sūyate sacarācaram
hetunānena kaunteya jagad viparivartate 9.10

अवजानन्ति मां मूढा मानुषीं तनुमाश्रितम् ।
परं भावमजानन्तो मम भूतमहेश्वरम् ॥ ९-११॥

avajānanti māṃ mūḍhā mānuṣīṃ tanum āśritam
paraṃ bhāvam ajānanto mama bhūtamaheśvaram 9.11

मोघाशा मोघकर्माणो मोघज्ञाना विचेतसः ।
राक्षसीमासुरीं चैव प्रकृतिं मोहिनीं श्रिताः ॥ ९-१२॥

moghāśā moghakarmāṇo moghajñānā vicetasaḥ
rākṣasīm āsurīṃ caiva prakṛtiṃ mohinīṃ śritāḥ 9.12

महात्मानस्तु मां पार्थ दैवीं प्रकृतिमाश्रिताः ।
भजन्त्यनन्यमनसो ज्ञात्वा भूतादिमव्ययम् ॥ ९-१३॥

mahātmānas tu māṃ pārtha daivīṃ prakṛtim āśritāḥ
bhajanty ananyamanaso jñātvā bhūtādim avyayam 9.13

All things belonging to this creation of Mine
Ultimately return and merge into My nature Divine,
A cyclic relapse of end and beginning, they undergo
From Me they come and I lose them when they go.|7|

Descending into My own created nature,
I configure multitudes of existences of many a stature
But under nature's control is every living object
And governed by its law is every subject.|8|

I am the detached and indifferent overlord
Seated above all, I watch over my every ward
In nature's grip I am not found
For by nature's works I cannot be bound|9|

I am the presiding control over nature's creations
From my creative spirit arise the abundant manifestations
O *Arjuna*-in nature's cycle everyone has to involve
For this what causes the world to rotate and revolve|10|

Caged within the human bodies are minds eluded
About My eternal truth, they are deluded
My supreme nature they do not apprehend
Its existence ethereal- they cannot comprehend.|11|

These ignorant forms are crude and profane
As their hopes, knowledge and actions are all vain
In banal and demoniac natures they thrive and dwell
And their will and intellect are lost under their spell|12|

But the high souls contemplate and mediate
For they are aware of My nature's eternal state
For with love they turn towards only Me
As the imperishable creator of all-only Me they see|13|

सततं कीर्तयन्तो मां यतन्तश्च दृढव्रताः ।
नमस्यन्तश्च मां भक्त्या नित्ययुक्ता उपासते ॥ ९-१४॥

satatam kīrtayanto mām yatantaś ca dṛḍhavratāḥ
namasyantaś ca mām bhaktyā nityayuktā upāsate 9.14

ज्ञानयज्ञेन चाप्यन्ये यजन्तो मामुपासते ।
एकत्वेन पृथक्त्वेन बहुधा विश्वतोमुखम् ॥ ९-१५॥

jñānayajñena cāpy anye yajanto mām upāsate
ekatvena pṛthaktvena bahudhā viśvatomukham 9.15

अहं क्रतुरहं यज्ञः स्वधाहमहमौषधम् ।
मन्त्रोऽहमहमेवाज्यमहमग्निरहं हुतम् ॥ ९-१६॥

aham kratur aham yajñaḥ svadhāham aham auṣadham
mantro.aham aham evājyam aham agnir aham hutam 9.16

पिताहमस्य जगतो माता धाता पितामहः ।
वेद्यं पवित्रमोङ्कार ऋक्साम यजुरेव च ॥ ९-१७॥

pitāham asya jagato mātā dhātā pitāmaha ḥ
vedyam pavitram omkāra ṛk sāma yajur eva ca 9.17

गतिर्भर्ता प्रभुः साक्षी निवासः शरणं सुहृत् ।
प्रभवः प्रलयः स्थानं निधानं बीजमव्ययम् ॥ ९-१८॥

gatir bhartā prabhu ḥ sākṣī nivāsaḥ śaraṇam suhṛt
prabhavaḥ pralayaḥ sthānam nidhānam bījam avyam 9.18

तपाम्यहमहं वर्षं निगृह्णाम्युत्सृजामि च ।
अमृतं चैव मृत्युश्च सदसच्चाहमर्जुन ॥ ९-१९॥

tapāmy aham aham varṣam nigṛṇhāmy utsṛjāmi ca
amṛtam caiva mṛtyuś ca sad asac cāham arjuna 9.19

Adoring Me with the greatest love and spiritual fervor
Consecrated efforts they put in their every endeavor
In My surrender and worship they kneel and bow
And a perfect union with Me they seek to know.|14|

Through the sacrifice of knowledge those who seek
Their knowledge -as offerings in
the gnostic sacrifice, they keep
They worship in all life forms My Divine unity
And also in all, they adore My masked multiplicity |15|

I am the ritual action and the sacrifice that is performed
I am the food-oblation, medicinal-herb
by which the sacrifice is formed
I am clarified butter and the incantation transcendental
For the sacrifice, I am the flame and
also the offering central|16|

For all -I am the true Father and the Mother,
For the world I am the Father supreme and perpetuator
I am Om- the first word and the purifying sound
I am the knowledge-that in the three Vedas can be found.|17|

I am the master, the journey, the goal and the shelter
The witness, the refuge, the residence and the well-wisher
The creation, the preservation and destruction of everything
I am the seed and the eternal destination of every living thing|18|

I am heat's energy. It is I who withhold and send
The waters from the heavens that descend
O *Arjuna* I am both death and immortality
Nescient and Existent, I am the quintessential reality.|19|

त्रैविद्या मां सोमपाः पूतपापा यज्ञैरिष्ट्वा स्वर्गतिं प्रार्थयन्ते ।
ते पुण्यमासाद्य सुरेन्द्रलोकमश्नन्ति दिव्यान्दिवि देवभोगान् ॥ ९-२०॥

traividyā māṃ somapāḥ pūtapāpā yajñair iṣṭvā svargatiṃ prārthayante
te puṇyam āsādya surendralokam aśnanti divyān
divi devabhogān 9.20

ते तं भुक्त्वा स्वर्गलोकं विशालं क्षीणे पुण्ये मर्त्यलोकं विशन्ति ।
एवं त्रयीधर्ममनुप्रपन्ना गतागतं कामकामा लभन्ते ॥ ९-२१॥

te taṃbhuktvā svargalokaṃ viśālaṃkṣīṇe puṇye martyalokaṃ viśanti
evaṃ trayīdharmam anuprapannā gatāgataṃ kāmakāmā labhante 9.21

अनन्याश्चिन्तयन्तो मां ये जनाः पर्युपासते ।
तेषां नित्याभियुक्तानां योगक्षेमं वहाम्यहम् ॥ ९-२२॥

ananyāś cintayanto māṃ ye janāḥ paryupāsate
teṣāṃ nityābhiyuktānāṃ yogak ṣemaṃ vahāmy aham 9.22

येऽप्यन्यदेवता भक्ता यजन्ते श्रद्धयान्विताः ।
तेऽपि मामेव कौन्तेय यजन्त्यविधिपूर्वकम् ॥ ९-२३॥

yepy anyadevatābhaktā yajante śraddhayānvitāḥ
tepi mām eva kaunteya yajanty avidhipūrvakam 9.23

अहं हि सर्वयज्ञानां भोक्ता च प्रभुरेव च ।
न तु मामभिजानन्ति तत्त्वेनातश्च्यवन्ति ते ॥ ९-२४॥

ahaṃ hi sarvayajñānāṃ bhoktā ca prabhur eva ca
na tu mām abhijānanti tattvenātaś cyavanti te 9.24

यान्ति देवव्रता देवान्पितृन्यान्ति पितृव्रताः ।
भूतानि यान्ति भूतेज्या यान्ति मद्याजिनोऽपि माम् ॥ ९-२५॥

yānti devavratā devān pitṛn yānti pitṛvratāḥ
bhūtāni yānti bhūtejyā yānti madyājinopi mām 9.25

Those to whom the knowledge of the triple Vedas is known
They consume *Soma*-the ambrosial nectar for it's their own
Worshipping Me with the sacrifices, for the heavens they aspire
By their righteousness, Divine feasts in paradise
they enjoy and acquire|20|

Having enjoyed the rewards of the heavenly realm
With their good deeds exhausted, they return to
the mortal dream
Seeking satisfaction, to the prescribed Vedic virtues they resort
Ultimately back to cycle of birth and demise they retort|21|

But those seekers by whom I am integrally sought
Focus only on Me in their every thought
To those whose consciousness is one with Mine
To them, I bring the prosperity Divine.|22|

Even those who offer to other Godheads, sacrifice to Me
For by coming to Me only their sacrifices can fulfilled be
As their devotion and faith are pure and without flaw
I receive them, though they offer not as per the true law.|23|

For every sacrifice performed, I am the enjoyer
The overlord of sacrifices, I am the true receiver
But they know not My truth fundamental
And in their growth this is detrimental|24|

To the abode of the deities, go the God worshippers
Worshippers of the Divine ancestors,
to the realm of the ancestors
Performers of the sacrifice to the spirit,
to the elements they enjoin
But My worshippers – To Me they come and directly join|25|

पत्रं पुष्पं फलं तोयं यो मे भक्त्या प्रयच्छति ।
तदहं भक्त्युपहृतमश्नामि प्रयतात्मनः ॥ ९-२६॥

patraṃ puṣpam phalaṃ toyaṃ yo me bhaktyā prayacchati
tad ahaṃ bhaktyupahṛtam aśnāmi prayatātmanaḥ 9.26

यत्करोषि यदश्नासि यज्जुहोषि ददासि यत् ।
यत्तपस्यसि कौन्तेय तत्कुरुष्व मदर्पणम् ॥ ९-२७॥

yat karoṣi yad aśnāsi yaj juhoṣi dadāsi yat
yat tapasyasi kaunteya tat kuruṣva madarpaṇam 9.27

शुभाशुभफलैरेवं मोक्ष्यसे कर्मबन्धनैः ।
संन्यासयोगयुक्तात्मा विमुक्तो मामुपैष्यसि ॥ ९-२८॥

śubhāśubhaphalair evaṃ mokṣyase karmabandhanaiḥ
saṃnyāsayogayuktātmā vimukto mām upai ṣyasi 9.28

समोऽहं सर्वभूतेषु न मे द्वेष्योऽस्ति न प्रियः ।
ये भजन्ति तु मां भक्त्या मयि ते तेषु चाप्यहम् ॥ ९-२९॥

samohaṃ sarvabhūteṣu na me dveṣyosti na priyaḥ
ye bhajanti tu māṃ bhaktyā mayi te teṣu cāpy aham 9.29

अपि चेत्सुदुराचारो भजते मामनन्यभाक् ।
साधुरेव स मन्तव्यः सम्यग्व्यवसितो हि सः ॥ ९-३०॥

api cet sudurācāro bhajate māṃ ananyabhāk
sādhur eva sa mantavyaḥ samyag vyavasito hi saḥ 9.30

क्षिप्रं भवति धर्मात्मा शश्वच्छान्तिं निगच्छति ।
कौन्तेय प्रतिजानीहि न मे भक्तः प्रणश्यति ॥ ९-३१॥

kṣipraṃ bhavati dharmātmā śaśvacchānti ṃ nigacchhati
kaunteya pratijānīhi na me bhaktaḥ praṇaśyati 9.31

मां हि पार्थ व्यपाश्रित्य येऽपि स्युः पापयोनयः ।
स्त्रियो वैश्यास्तथा शूद्रास्तेऽपि यान्ति परां गतिम् ॥ ९-३२॥

māṃ hi pārtha vyapāśritya yepi syu ḥ pāpayonayaḥ
striyo vaiśyās tathā śūdrās tepi yānti parā ṃ gatim 9.32

He who offers with devotion a leaf or a flower
A fruit or even a singular cup of water
When the offering is with love replete
It is to Me acceptable and complete|26|

Your sacrifice, your enjoyment and your every action
All your austerities, offerings and your every donation
Channel your soul's effort and its inner will
Let all your offerings be as per my Divine will.|27|

From good and evil, you shall attain liberation
And from the bonds of *Karma*, you shall attain dissolution
With your soul engaged purely in My consecration
You shall be free and experience My realization|28|

To all beings I am disposed with equanimity
For towards all I am impartial, bereft of acerbity
But those who see with devotion -a holy commuion
I reside in them and they dwell in My union.|29|

Even the most evil amongst men can transformed be
When with love and soul they turn towards Me
For when his adverse nature and will, he has conquered.
That changed being even as a saint may be considered|30|

His soul then gets purified with a Divine haste
And in My ethereal peace he shall then awake
O *Arjuna*, This promise to all My lovers I make
Your love for Me shall not go waste.|31|

O *Arjuna*, All those who seek refuge in Me
Even if in a womb of sin, born they may be
The wretchedly ostracized downtrodden men or women
They all attain to Me; To their sincere calls I hearken.|32|

किं पुनर्ब्राह्मणाः पुण्या भक्ता राजर्षयस्तथा ।
अनित्यमसुखं लोकमिमं प्राप्य भजस्व माम् ॥ ९-३३॥

kiṃ punar brāhmaṇāḥ puṇyā bhaktā rājarṣayas tathā
anityam asukham lokam imaṃ prāpya bhajasva mām 9.33

मन्मना भव मद्भक्तो मद्याजी मां नमस्कुरु ।
मामेवैष्यसि युक्त्वैवमात्मानं मत्परायणः ॥ ९-३४॥

manmanā bhava madbhakto madyājī māṃ namaskuru
mām evaiṣyasi yuktvaivam ātmānaṃ matparāyaṇaḥ 9.34

What then to speak of the *Brahma's* seeker
And the most devoted sages regal and fine!
This transient and sorrowful world's every dweller
Can channel their love to seek the Divine|33|

Sacrifice unto Me and unite with Me through your mind
My Self-Supreme you shall know, experience and find
Bowing to Me and with love, when Me alone you adore
Then for the Divine union you shall open the door.|34|

(Thus ended the ninth Canto of the Bhagavad Gita where Sri Krishna parted the knowledge of the Supreme's existence and called upon Arjuna to engage in complete devotion to live in communion with the Divine)

❈ ❈ ❈

अथ दशमोऽध्यायः ।

atha daśamodhyāyaḥ

श्रीभगवानुवाच ।

भूय एव महाबाहो शृणु मे परमं वचः ।

यत्तेऽहं प्रीयमाणाय वक्ष्यामि हितकाम्यया ॥ १०-१॥

śrībhagavānuvāca
bhūya eva mahābāho śṛṇu me paramaṃ vacaḥ
yat teham prīyamāṇāya vakṣyāmi hitakāmyayā 10.1

न मे विदुः सुरगणाः प्रभवं न महर्षयः ।

अहमादिर्हि देवानां महर्षीणां च सर्वशः ॥ १०-२॥

na me viduḥ suragaṇāḥ prabhavam na maharṣayaḥ
aham ādir hi devānāṃ maharṣīṇām ca sarvaśaḥ 10.2

यो मामजमनादिं च वेत्ति लोकमहेश्वरम् ।

असम्मूढः स मर्त्येषु सर्वपापैः प्रमुच्यते ॥ १०-३॥

yo mām ajam anādiṃ ca vetti lokamaheśvaram
asammūḍhah sa martyeṣu sarvapāpaiḥ pramucyate 10.3

बुद्धिर्ज्ञानमसम्मोहः क्षमा सत्यं दमः शमः ।

सुखं दुःखं भवोऽभावो भयं चाभयमेव च ॥ १०-४॥

buddhir jñānam asaṃmohaḥ kṣamā satyaṃ damaḥ śamaḥ
sukhaṃ duḥkhaṃ bhavobhāvo bhayaṃ cābhayam eva ca 10.4

अहिंसा समता तुष्टिस्तपो दानं यशोऽयशः ।

भवन्ति भावा भूतानां मत्त एव पृथग्विधाः ॥ १०-५॥

ahiṃsā samatā tuṣṭis tapo dānam yaśoyaśaḥ
bhavanti bhāvā bhūtānām matta eva pṛthagvidhāḥ 10.5

Canto X: *<u>The Cosmic Divine, World-Gods,</u>*
<u>and their representations</u>

(Verse 1-11: The Cosmic Divine's Existence; 12-18: *Arjuna* requests *Krishna* to elaborate on His worldly manifestations; 19-42: The Gods and the representatives of the Divine)

Sri *Krishna* spoke:
"Listen, to the words supreme that I shall now say
For I will to part the Divine wisdom to you in this way.
They shall certainly lead to your soul's betterment
As your heart is receiving my words with merriment.|1|

Neither the mighty sages nor the Gods know
My transcendental origins- many aeons ago
For I am Myself the cause and origin
Of every God, sage and his kin.|2|

He who knows that I am beginning-less,
The overlord of all worlds and peoples, I am birth-less,
Free of delusion-the mortal world he inhabits
And falls not prey to evil's sinful gambits|3|

Knowledge, intelligence and a clarity berefet of pretenses
Forgiveness, truth and a control over mind and senses
Joy and sorrow, creation and destruction
The state of being fearless and also fear's sensation|4|

Also equanimity, contentment and charity
Non-violence, fame, infamy and austerity
They are but manifestations arising from Me alone
All objective qualities of My own.|5|

महर्षयः सप्त पूर्वे चत्वारो मनवस्तथा ।
मद्भावा मानसा जाता येषां लोक इमाः प्रजाः ॥ १०-६॥

maharṣayaḥ sapta pūrve catvāro manavas tathā
madbhāvā mānasā jātā yeṣāṃ loka imāḥ prajāḥ 10.6

एतां विभूतिं योगं च मम यो वेत्ति तत्त्वतः ।
सोऽविकम्पेन योगेन युज्यते नात्र संशयः ॥ १०-७॥

etāṃ vibhūtiṃ yogaṃ ca mama yo vetti tattvataḥ
sovikampena yogena yujyate nātra saṃśayaḥ 10.7

अहं सर्वस्य प्रभवो मत्तः सर्वं प्रवर्तते ।
इति मत्वा भजन्ते मां बुधा भावसमन्विताः ॥ १०-८॥

ahaṃ sarvasya prabhavo mattaḥ sarvaṃ pravartate
iti matvā bhajante māṃ budhā bhāvasamanvitāḥ 10.8

मच्चित्ता मद्गतप्राणा बोधयन्तः परस्परम् ।
कथयन्तश्च मां नित्यं तुष्यन्ति च रमन्ति च ॥ १०-९॥

maccittā madgataprāṇā bodhayantaḥ parasparam
kathayantaś ca māṃ nityaṃ tuṣyanti ca ramanti ca 10.9

तेषां सततयुक्तानां भजतां प्रीतिपूर्वकम् ।
ददामि बुद्धियोगं तं येन मामुपयान्ति ते ॥ १०-१०॥

teṣāṃ satatayuktānāṃ bhajatāṃ prītipūrvakam
dadāmi buddhiyogaṃ taṃ yena mām upayānti te 10.10

तेषामेवानुकम्पार्थमहमज्ञानजं तमः ।
नाशयाम्यात्मभावस्थो ज्ञानदीपेन भास्वता ॥ १०-११॥

teṣām evānukampārtham aham ajñānajaṃ tamaḥ
nāśayāmy ātmabhāvastho jñānadīpena bhāsvatā 10.11

अर्जुन उवाच ।
परं ब्रह्म परं धाम पवित्रं परमं भवान् ।
पुरुषं शाश्वतं दिव्यमादिदेवमजं विभुम् ॥ १०-१२॥

arjuna uvāca
paraṃ brahma paraṃ dhāma pavitraṃ paramaṃ bhavān
puruṣaṃ śāśvataṃ divyam ādidevam ajaṃ vibhum 10.12

The heavenly *Saptarishis*- the seven sages
As well as the four *Manus* of the ancient ages
They are but creations of my impulses mental
And from them arose all living beings in the physical.|6|

He who understands my principles Divine
And knows this all pervading truth that is Mine
United in *Yoga*, with Me he becomes one
About this there are doubts none.|7|

I am the birth of all living things that can exist to be
And their growth only proceeds from Me
For I set their development into motion
Knowing this, the wise love Me with the highest emotion.|8|

With their consciousness flooded with that of Mine
With their lives surrendered completely to the Divine
With Me only in their dialogues they go around
Contentment and joy only in their lives can be found|9|

To those yearning for a constant state of union,
With the purest intensity, seeking My communion
To them I give *Yoga*'s understanding that sets them apart
And unites them with Me and they never again part.|10|

For them My compassion begins to stem
From within the Self that resides within them
The lamp of knowledge within them I ignite
And the ignorance of darkness disappears by My Light|11|"

Arjuna said:
"Thou art the immaculate *Brahman*-supreme
Thou art the permanent one of the highest esteem
Thou art the Divine *Purusha* – The Supernal God
Unborn, Thou art the all-pervading Lord|12|

आहुस्त्वामृषयः सर्वे देवर्षिर्नारदस्तथा ।
असितो देवलो व्यासः स्वयं चैव ब्रवीषि मे ॥ १०-१३॥

āhus tvām ṛṣayaḥ sarve devarṣir nāradas tathā
asito devalo vyāsaḥ svayaṃ caiva bravīṣi me 10.13

सर्वमेतदृतं मन्ये यन्मां वदसि केशव ।
न हि ते भगवन्व्यक्तिं विदुर्देवा न दानवाः ॥ १०-१४॥

sarvam etad ṛtaṃ manye yan māṃ vadasi keśava
na hi te bhagavan vyaktiṃ vidur devā na dānavāḥ 10.14

स्वयमेवात्मनात्मानं वेत्थ त्वं पुरुषोत्तम ।
भूतभावन भूतेश देवदेव जगत्पते ॥ १०-१५॥

svayam evātmanātmānaṃ vettha tvaṃ puruṣottama
bhūtabhāvana bhūteśa devadeva jagatpate 10.15

वक्तुमर्हस्यशेषेण दिव्या ह्यात्मविभूतयः ।
याभिर्विभूतिभिर्लोकानिमांस्त्वं व्याप्य तिष्ठसि ॥ १०-१६॥

vaktum arhasy aśeṣeṇa divyā hy ātmavibhūtayaḥ
yābhir vibhūtibhir lokān imāṃs tvaṃ vyāpya tiṣṭhasi 10.16

कथं विद्यामहं योगिंस्त्वां सदा परिचिन्तयन् ।
केषु केषु च भावेषु चिन्त्योऽसि भगवन्मया ॥ १०-१७॥

kathaṃ vidyām ahaṃ yogiṃs tvāṃ sadā paricintayan
keṣu keṣu ca bhāveṣu cintyosi bhagavan mayā 10.17

विस्तरेणात्मनो योगं विभूतिं च जनार्दन ।
भूयः कथय तृप्तिर्हि शृण्वतो नास्ति मेऽमृतम् ॥ १०-१८॥

vistareṇātmano yogaṃ vibhūtiṃ ca janārdana
bhūyaḥ kathaya tṛptir hi śṛṇvato nāsti memṛtam 10.18

श्रीभगवानुवाच ।
हन्त ते कथयिष्यामि दिव्या ह्यात्मविभूतयः ।
प्राधान्यतः कुरुश्रेष्ठ नास्त्यन्तो विस्तरस्य मे ॥ १०-१९॥

śrībhagavān uvāca
hanta te kathayiṣyāmi divyā hy ātmavibhūtayaḥ
prādhānyataḥ kuruśreṣṭha nāsty anto vistarasya me 10.19

This the wisest of the sages have thus said
When Thy words they have sought to spread
Narada, Asita, Devala and *Vyasa*- the seers have portrayed
And O Lord, Thou hast to me explained.|13|

Whatever it is that is spoken by Thee
For my mind – that is the only truth that can be
But O Lord gracious – neither God nor Titan,
About Thy manifestations can they enlighten.|14|

O Greatest Supreme one, It is only thee
Who knows Thyself completely.
For all creations and beings, Thou art the Lord
Overlord of the world, Even for the Gods, thou art the God.|15|

I solicit Ye to completely tell
Of all Thy manifestations that in this world dwell-
Thy richest of forms that the mortal realm has received
Without exception do reveal all that can be perceived.|16|

How is it that I can know and unite with Thee,
By always meditating in all places only upon Ye?
What are the embodiments that I should aspire to see?
Which forms should be contemplated upon by me? |17|

O Father of all peoples, lucidly please explain
Of your *Yoga* and Thy many forms that in this world reign
Eager I am to hear of your manifestations, more the better
To my insatiable thirst, This is an immortal nectar|18|"

Sri *Krishna* spoke:-
Yes. I shall speak to you of my representatives Divine
But only some forms that are most prominent and fine
For my manifestations, O *Arjuna*, There is no end
All across the universe, It is only I who extend.|19|

अहमात्मा गुडाकेश सर्वभूताशयस्थितः ।
अहमादिश्च मध्यं च भूतानामन्त एव च ॥ १०-२०॥

aham ātmā guḍākeśa sarvabhūtāśayasthitaḥ
aham ādiś ca madhyaṃ ca bhūtānām anta eva ca 10.20

आदित्यानामहं विष्णुर्ज्योतिषां रविरंशुमान् ।
मरीचिर्मरुतामस्मि नक्षत्राणामहं शशी ॥ १०-२१॥

ādityānām ahaṃ viṣṇur jyotiṣāṃ ravir aṃśumān
marīcir marutām asmi nakṣatrāṇām ahaṃ śaśī 10.21

वेदानां सामवेदोऽस्मि देवानामस्मि वासवः ।
इन्द्रियाणां मनश्चास्मि भूतानामस्मि चेतना ॥ १०-२२॥

vedānāṃ sāmavedosmi devānām asmi vāsavaḥ
indriyāṇāṃ manaś cāsmi bhūtānām asmi cetanā 10.22

रुद्राणां शङ्करश्चास्मि वित्तेशो यक्षरक्षसाम् ।
वसूनां पावकश्चास्मि मेरुः शिखरिणामहम् ॥ १०-२३॥

rudrāṇāṃ śaṃkaraś cāsmi vitteśo yakṣarakṣasām
vasūnāṃ pāvakaś cāsmi meruḥ śikhariṇām aham 10.23

पुरोधसां च मुख्यं मां विद्धि पार्थ बृहस्पतिम् ।
सेनानीनामहं स्कन्दः सरसामस्मि सागरः ॥ १०-२४॥

purodhasāṃ ca mukhyaṃ māṃ viddhi pārtha
bṛhaspatim senānīnām ahaṃ skandaḥ sarasām
asmi sāgaraḥ 10.24

महर्षीणां भृगुरहं गिरामस्म्येकमक्षरम् ।
यज्ञानां जपयज्ञोऽस्मि स्थावराणां हिमालयः ॥ १०-२५॥

maharṣīṇāṃ bhṛgur ahaṃ girām asmy ekam akṣaram
yajñānāṃ japayajñosmi sthāvarāṇāṃ himālayaḥ 10.25

O *Arjuna*, It is My Self that abides
And within all being My divinity resides
For every living being big and small,
It is I who am the beginning, middle and end of all.|20|

Amongst *Adityas* the seven suns, I am *Vishnu* the most radiant
Amongst splendorous lights, I am the brilliant sun
Amongst *Maruts* the storm deities- I am *Marichi* the mightiest one
I am the Moon, amongst constellations most prominent|21|

I am Sama-Veda, amongst the *Vedas*
I am *Indra*, leader amongst the Gods-the *Devas*
Amongst the senses, I am the mind
In all living beings it is My consciousness that you find|22|

Amongst the *Rudras* eleven, I am *Shankara*-the lord
I am *Kubera*-prosperity and wealth's overlord-
Amongst demons and nature spirits benevolent.
I am- the God of Fire amongst *Vasus, Meru*- of the peaks mag-
nificent.|23|

O *Arjuna*, Know and understand Me to be
Amongst reservoirs of water, I am the oceanic sea.
Brihaspati- the chief amongst the demigods.
I am *Skanda*, the commanding battle lord of lords|24|

I am *Bhrigu* amongst the greatest of sages
I am *Himalaya*, the greatest of mountain ranges.
I am amongst words, *Om* the sacred syllable of creation
Amongst ways of worship,
I am *Japa*-the silent chants' repetition|25|

अश्वत्थः सर्ववृक्षाणां देवर्षीणां च नारदः ।
गन्धर्वाणां चित्ररथः सिद्धानां कपिलो मुनिः ॥ १०-२६॥

aśvatthaḥ sarvavṛkṣāṇām devarṣīṇām ca nāradaḥ
gandharvāṇām citrarathaḥ siddhānām kapilo muniḥ 10.26

उच्चैःश्रवसमश्वानां विद्धि माममृतोद्भवम् ।
ऐरावतं गजेन्द्राणां नराणां च नराधिपम् ॥ १०-२७॥

uccaiḥśravasam aśvānām viddhi mām amṛtodbhavam
airāvatam gajendrāṇām narāṇām ca narādhipam 10.27

आयुधानामहं वज्रं धेनूनामस्मि कामधुक् ।
प्रजनश्चास्मि कन्दर्पः सर्पाणामस्मि वासुकिः ॥ १०-२८॥

āyudhānām aham vajram dhenūnām asmi kāmadhuk
prajanaś cāsmi kandarpaḥ sarpāṇām asmi vāsukiḥ 10.28

अनन्तश्चास्मि नागानां वरुणो यादसामहम् ।
पितॄणामर्यमा चास्मि यमः संयमतामहम् ॥ १०-२९॥

anantaś cāsmi nāgānām varuṇo yādasām aham
pitṛṇām aryamā cāsmi yamaḥ samyamatām aham 10.29

प्रह्लादश्चास्मि दैत्यानां कालः कलयतामहम् ।
मृगाणां च मृगेन्द्रोऽहं वैनतेयश्च पक्षिणाम् ॥ १०-३०॥

pralhādaś cāsmi daityānām kālaḥ kalayatām aham
mṛgāṇām ca mṛgendroham vainateyaś ca pakṣiṇām 10.30

पवनः पवतामस्मि रामः शस्त्रभृतामहम् ।
झषाणां मकरश्चास्मि स्रोतसामस्मि जाह्नवी ॥ १०-३१॥

pavanaḥ pavatām asmi rāmaḥ śastrabhṛtām aham
jhaṣāṇām makaraś cāsmi strotasām asmi jāhnavī 10.31

सर्गाणामादिरन्तश्च मध्यं चैवाहमर्जुन ।
अध्यात्मविद्या विद्यानां वादः प्रवदतामहम् ॥ १०-३२॥

sargāṇām ādir antaś ca madhyam caivāham arjuna
adhyātmavidyā vidyānām vādaḥ pravadatām aham 10.32

Amongst the most sacred trees- I am the *Peepal* tree
I am *Chitraratha* amongst the heavenly beings free
Amongst the Divine sages, I am *Narada Muni*
And amongst the perfected saints, I am *Kapila-Muni*.|26|

Know me to be *Uchhaisravas*, the best horse that came to be
Born of nectar, that arose from the churning of the milk-sea
I am *Airavata*- the lord of elephants white and regal
I am the one king and all mankind are my subjects loyal.|27|

I am *Vajra*- the Divine thunderbolt amongst weapons in battle
I am *Kamadhenu*- the wish yielding Divine cow amongst cattle
I am *Kandarpa*-the cupid that motivates the procreation
Amongst single headed serpents,*Vasuki* is my manifestation.|28|

The best amongst the *Naga* races- I am *Ananta*
Amongst the peoples of all the oceans- I am *Varuna*
I am *Aryaman*- the father of the deified ancestor
I am the death god *Yama*, who is justice's upholder|29|

I am *Prahlada* amongst the titans of might
Amongst measurements, I am time that never stops day or night
Amongst forest beasts, I am the lion king of kings
I am *Garuda*-the king eagle amongst the birds of wings|30|

I am the wind- purifying and swift moving
Amongst master warriors, I am *Rama*-the valiant and daring
I am the alligator amongst the aquatic creatures
I am the *Ganges* amongst the pristine rivers|31|

I am the beginning, middle and end of all creation
Arjuna, I am the logic of those involved in debate and discussion.
I am the knowledge of the spiritual-sciences
That is higher than all philosophies, art and sciences.|32|

अक्षराणामकारोऽस्मि द्वन्द्वः सामासिकस्य च ।
अहमेवाक्षयः कालो धाताहं विश्वतोमुखः ॥ १०-३३॥

akṣarāṇām akārosmi dvandvaḥ sāmāsikasya ca
aham evākṣayaḥ kālo dhātāham viśvatomukhaḥ 10.33

मृत्युः सर्वहरश्चाहमुद्भवश्च भविष्यताम् ।
कीर्तिः श्रीर्वाक्च नारीणां स्मृतिर्मेधा धृतिः क्षमा ॥ १०-३४॥

mṛtyuḥ sarvaharaś cāham udbhavaś ca bhaviṣyatām
kīrtiḥ śrīr vāk ca nārīṇāṃ smṛtir medhā dhṛtiḥ kṣamā 10.34

बृहत्साम तथा साम्नां गायत्री छन्दसामहम् ।
मासानां मार्गशीर्षोऽहमृतूनां कुसुमाकरः ॥ १०-३५॥

bṛhatsāma tathā sāmnāṃ gāyatrī chandasām aham
māsānāṃ mārgaśīrṣoham ṛtūnāṃ kusumākaraḥ 10.35

द्यूतं छलयतामस्मि तेजस्तेजस्विनामहम् ।
जयोऽस्मि व्यवसायोऽस्मिसत्त्वं सत्त्ववतामहम्॥ १०-३६॥

dyutaṃ chalayatām asmi tejas tejasvinām aham
jayosmi vyavasāyosmi sattvaṃ sattvavatām aham 10.36

वृष्णीनां वासुदेवोऽस्मि पाण्डवानां धनञ्जयः ।
मुनीनामप्यहं व्यासः कवीनामुशना कविः ॥ १०-३७॥

vṛṣṇīnāṃ vāsudevosmi pāṇḍavānāṃ dhanaṃjayaḥ
munīnāṃ apy aham vyāsaḥ kavīnām uśanā kaviḥ 10.37

दण्डो दमयतामस्मि नीतिरस्मि जिगीषताम् ।
मौनं चैवास्मि गुह्यानां ज्ञानं ज्ञानवतामहम् ॥ १०-३८॥

daṇḍo damayatām asmi nītir asmi jigīṣatām
maunaṃ caivāsmi guhyānāṃ jñānam jñānavatām aham 10.38

यच्चापि सर्वभूतानां बीजं तदहमर्जुन ।
न तदस्ति विना यत्स्यान्मया भूतं चराचरम् ॥ १०-३९॥

yac cāpi sarvabhūtānām bījaṃ tad aham arjuna
na tad asti vinā yat syān mayā bhūtam carācaram 10.39

Amongst letters, in the all-encompassing letter 'A' I am found
Amongst words, I am the dual compound
I am the imperishable time that ceases not to persist
The master of all existences, in all their faces I exist.|33|

I am for the living, the all-ensnaring death
And for the beings to come, I am also birth.
Glory, speech, intellect, and memory- the qualities Divine
And forgiveness are all my best virtues feminine |34|

I am the *Brihat Sama* of the *Sama Veda's* mantra chimes
I am *Gayatri* amongst the established metrical rhymes
Amongst the months I am *Mrigashirsha* – the month first
Amongst the seasons, I am spring's delicate burst |35|

I am the cunning in the gambler's deception
And in the good-natured, I am purity's inception.
I am the glory of the glorious and victory of the victors
I am the enterprise of the entrepreneurs|36|

I am *Krishna* amongst the *Vrishnis*
And I am *Arjuna* amongst the *Pandavas*
I am *Vyasa* amongst the great sages
And amongst the poetic seers, I am *Ushanas*|37|

I am the mastery of the ruler and the power of the tamer
I am the winning strategy of the invincible conqueror
I am the secret of silent things that are unknown
I am the knowledge of the knower
who then becomes known|38|

O *Arjuna*, whatever be the existence and life form-
I am the seed from which they all sprouted from
Nothing motile or immotile, animate or inanimate can be
As their existence is impossible without Me.|39|

नान्तोऽस्ति मम दिव्यानां विभूतीनां परन्तप ।
एष तूद्देशतः प्रोक्तो विभूतेर्विस्तरो मया ॥ १०-४०॥

nāntosti mama divyānāṃ vibhūtīnāṃ paraṃtapa
eṣa tūddeśataḥ prokto vibhūter vistaro mayā 10.40

यद्यद्विभूतिमत्सत्त्वं श्रीमदूर्जितमेव वा ।
तत्तदेवावगच्छ त्वं मम तेजोंऽशसम्भवम् ॥ १०-४१॥

yad yad vibhūtimat sattvaṃ śrīmad ūrjitam eva vā
tat tad evāvagaccha tvaṃ mama tejoṃśasambhavam 10.41

अथवा बहुनैतेन किं ज्ञातेन तवार्जुन ।
विष्टभ्याहमिदं कृत्स्नमेकांशेन स्थितो जगत् ॥ १०-४२॥

athavā bahunaitena kiṃ jñātena tavārjuna
viṣṭabhyāham idaṃ kṛtsnam ekāṃśena sthito jagat 10.42

My manifestations are transcendental and innumerable
O *Arjuna*! My Divine representations are immeasurable
For what I have spoken is nothing but a brief summary
A glimpse of what truth's light is indicatory.|40|

All creatures that are beautiful and splendorous
And all things that are brilliant, powerful and glorious
I am the source from which their energies come to be
Know them to be an infinitesimal fraction of Me|41|

But O *Arjuna*, what is the need for you to understand
In detail all My Divine forms that manifest on the mortal land,
Take it from Me that I am both here and everywhere
And the entire universe within a fraction of My-Self, I bear.|42|"

(Thus ended the tenth Canto of the Bhagavad Gita where Sri Krishna parted the knowledge of the Cosmic Divine and His multifarious manifestations)

अथैकादशोऽध्यायः ।
athaikādaśodhyāyaḥ

अर्जुन उवाच ।
मदनुग्रहाय परमं गुह्यमध्यात्मसंज्ञितम् ।
यत्त्वयोक्तं वचस्तेन मोहोऽयं विगतो मम ॥ ११-१॥
arjuna uvāca
madanugrahāya paramaṃ guhyam adhyātmasaṃjñitam
yat tvayoktaṃ vacas tena mohoyaṃ vigato mama 11.1

भवाप्ययौ हि भूतानां श्रुतौ विस्तरशो मया ।
त्वत्तः कमलपत्राक्ष माहात्म्यमपि चाव्ययम् ॥ ११-२॥
bhavāpyayau hi bhūtānāṃ śrutau vistaraśo mayā
tvattaḥ kamalapatrākṣa māhātmyam api cāvyayam 11.2

एवमेतद्यथात्थ त्वमात्मानं परमेश्वर ।
द्रष्टुमिच्छामि ते रूपमैश्वरं पुरुषोत्तम ॥ ११-३॥
evam etad yathāttha tvam ātmānaṃ parameśvara
draṣṭum icchāmi te rūpam aiśvaram puruṣottama 11.3

मन्यसे यदि तच्छक्यं मया द्रष्टुमिति प्रभो ।
योगेश्वर ततो मे त्वं दर्शयात्मानमव्ययम् ॥ ११-४॥
manyase yadi tac chakyaṃ mayā draṣṭum iti prabho
yogeśvara tato me tvaṃ darśayātmānam avyayam 11.4

Canto XI: The *full vision of the Universal-Divine being*

(Verses: 1-4 *Arjuna* solicits the vision of the universal Godhead; 5-8: *Krishna* grants the Divine sight; 9-14: Sanjaya 's description of the vision; 15-22: *Arjuna*'s vision; 23-31: *Arjuna*'s horror and plea; 32-34: The thunderous call of the universal Divine; 35: Sanjaya describes *Arjuna*'s reaction , 36-46: *Arjuna*'s prostration and request; 47-50: *Krishna* assumes His four armed form; 51: *Arjuna*'s relief; 52-54: *Krishna* speaks of the power of devotion ;55: *Krishna*'s invitation to *Arjuna*)

Arjuna said:
"The secret of spiritual secrets Thou hast unveiled
The occult and highest knowledge has been revealed
By the compassion that Thou hast upon me showered
My delusion is lifted and I am by Thy grace, empowered|1|

I have heard about all the existences from their birth
And also in detail of their progression to and after death
O lotus-eyed One, I have listened of the soul
And its imperishable all pervading greatness as a whole|2|

O Lord, as Thou hast said about Thy divinity
So art Thou, I do understand with clarity,
But O Greatest Supreme, I desire to see
Thy physical Self and form, please display to me.|3|

If it is Thy will, O supreme God,
I shall be able to see Thee, my Lord
For it is only by Thy Divine grace
That your Almighty form I can witness or face |4|"

श्रीभगवानुवाच ।
पश्य मे पार्थ रूपाणि शतशोऽथ सहस्रशः ।
नानाविधानि दिव्यानि नानावर्णाकृतीनि च ॥ ११-५॥

śrībhagavān uvāca
paśya me pārtha rūpāṇi śataśotha sahastraśa ḥ
nānāvidhāni divyāni nānāvar ṇākṛtīni ca 11.5

पश्यादित्यान्वसून्रुद्रानश्विनौ मरुतस्तथा ।
बहून्यदृष्टपूर्वाणि पश्याश्चर्याणि भारत ॥ ११-६॥

paśyādityān vasūn rudrān aśvinau marutas tathā
bahūny adṛṣṭapūrvāṇi paśyāścaryāṇi bhārata 11.6

इहैकस्थं जगत्कृत्स्नं पश्याद्य सचराचरम् ।
मम देहे गुडाकेश यच्चान्यद् द्रष्टुमिच्छसि ॥ ११-७॥

ihaikasthaṃ jagat kṛtsnaṃ paśyādya sacarācaram
mama dehe gu ḍākeśa yac cānyad dra ṣṭum icchasi 11.7

न तु मां शक्यसे द्रष्टुमनेनैव स्वचक्षुषा ।
दिव्यं ददामि ते चक्षुः पश्य मे योगमैश्वरम् ॥ ११-८॥

na tu māṃ śakyase draṣṭum anenaiva svacakṣuṣā
divyaṃ dadāmi te cakṣuḥ paśya me yogam aiśvaram 11.8

सञ्जय उवाच ।
एवमुक्त्वा ततो राजन्महायोगेश्वरो हरिः ।
दर्शयामास पार्थाय परमं रूपमैश्वरम् ॥ ११-९॥

sañjaya uvāca
evam uktvā tato rājan mahāyogeśvaro hariḥ
darśayām āsa pārthāya paramaṃ rūpam aiśvaram 11.9

अनेकवक्त्रनयनमनेकाद्भुतदर्शनम् ।
अनेकदिव्याभरणं दिव्यानेकोद्यतायुधम् ॥ ११-१०॥

anekavaktranayanam anekādbhutadarśanam
anekadivyābharaṇam divyānekodyatāyudham 11.10

Sri *Krishna* then spoke:-
"O *Arjuna*, Behold for I will display to you
My hundred thousand forms shall stand in your view
All Divine in their multitudinous shapes, hues and kind
In all their dimensions that are otherwise beyond the mind|5|

Observe, O *Arjuna*, the many forms of the *Adityas*
The *Vasus*, the *Ashwini* twins, the *Maruts* and the *Rudras*
None before on earth have ever thus witnessed
These supra-mortal wonders none has experienced.|6|

Witness today, O *Arjuna*- the universe complete
With all the mobile and immobile forms replete
Observe them to be united but yet a part of Me
And also glimpse everything else that you wish to see|7|

By the mortal eye, you cannot just see
And bear the vision that will soon be
There is an inner eye which I shall now awaken within you
So that a vision of my Divine *Yoga* you can behold and view.|8|"

Sanjaya spoke:
"With these words, O King, the Lord of *Yoga-Krishna*
Blessed *Arjuna* with His supreme form's revelation- the *darshana*
The destroyer of all sins, the godhead Divine
Displayed to him all his infinite forms resplendent and fine.|9|

The Godhead with the infinite eyes and faces
Armed with weapons and warheads Divine at different places
Displayed His innumerable forms wondrous and dazzling
With countless Divine jewels and ornaments gleaming|10|

दिव्यमाल्याम्बरधरं दिव्यगन्धानुलेपनम् ।
सर्वाश्चर्यमयं देवमनन्तं विश्वतोमुखम् ॥ ११-११॥

divyamālyāmbaradharam divyagandhānulepanam
sarvāścaryamayam devam anantam viśvatomukham 11.11

दिवि सूर्यसहस्रस्य भवेद्युगपदुत्थिता ।
यदि भाः सदृशी सा स्याद्भासस्तस्य महात्मनः ॥ ११-१२॥

divi sūryasahastrasya bhaved yugapad utthitā
yadi bhāḥ sadṛśī sā syād bhāsas tasya mahātmanaḥ 11.12

तत्रैकस्थं जगत्कृत्स्नं प्रविभक्तमनेकधा ।
अपश्यद्देवदेवस्य शरीरे पाण्डवस्तदा ॥ ११-१३॥

tatraikastham jagat kṛtsnam pravibhaktam anekadhā
apaśyad devadevasya śarīre pāṇḍavas tadā 11.13

ततः स विस्मयाविष्टो हृष्टरोमा धनञ्जयः ।
प्रणम्य शिरसा देवं कृताञ्जलिरभाषत ॥ ११-१४॥

tataḥ sa vismayāviṣṭo hṛṣṭaromā dhanaṃjayaḥ
praṇamya śirasā devam kṛtāñjalir abhāṣata 11.14

अर्जुन उवाच ।
पश्यामि देवांस्तव देव देहे सर्वांस्तथा भूतविशेषसङ्घान् ।
ब्रह्माणमीशं कमलासनस्थ- मृषींश्च सर्वानुरगांश्च
दिव्यान् ॥ ११-१५॥

arjuna uvāca
paśyāmi devāṃs tava deva dehe sarvāṃs tathā bhūtaviśeṣasaṃghān
brahmāṇam īśam kamalāsathnasam ṛṣīṃś ca sarvān uragāṃś ca divyān 11.15

अनेकबाहूदरवक्त्रनेत्रं पश्यामि त्वां सर्वतोऽनन्तरूपम् ।
नान्तं न मध्यं न पुनस्तवादिं पश्यामि विश्वेश्वर
विश्वरूप ॥ ११-१६॥

anekabāhūdaravaktranetra ṃ paśyāmi tvāṃ sarvatonantarūpam
nāntam na madhyam na punas tavādi ṃ paśyāmi viśveśvara viśvarūpa
11.16

Garlanded with heavenly adornments
And celestial scents and fragrant anointments
A surreal being stood before him with infinite mouths replete
And a splendorous brilliance embellished the God complete |11|

As if a thousand suns had together emerged
And their brilliance had coalesced and merged
So was the Divine's glorious refulgence,
So overwhelming was the heavenly magnificence|12|

And *Arjuna* was struck with awe
As in the very mortal envelope of *Krishna* he saw
The vision of the God of Gods supreme
The mighty creator of existence's every realm.|13|

Seeing the *Vishwaroopam*-most magnificent and beautiful
And also inconceivably terrible and powerful
Trembling at the hair rising and surreal vision
Arjuna prostrated offering his
full bodily submission|14|

Arjuna then spoke:
"All the Gods and Divine beings I now see
Emanating and expanding from within Thee
Seated in the cosmic lotus, *Brahma* is
the epitome of grace
I also see the mystic sages and those
of the Divine serpent race|15|

Countless arms, stomachs, heads and eyes
I can see all- Your infinite form vaster than the skies
Neither a beginning nor an end to it can I conform
O, I behold once more the Lord
of the universe's universal form|16|

किरीटिनं गदिनं चक्रिणं च तेजोराशिं सर्वतो दीप्तिमन्तम् ।
पश्यामि त्वां दुर्निरीक्ष्यं समन्ताद् दीप्तानलार्कद्युतिमप्रमेयम् ॥ ११-१७॥

kirīṭinaṃ gadinaṃ cakriṇaṃ ca tejorāśiṃ sarvato dīptimantam
paśyāmi tvāṃ durnirīkṣyaṃ samantād dīptānalārkadyutim aprameyam
11.17

त्वमक्षरं परमं वेदितव्यं त्वमस्य विश्वस्य परं निधानम् ।
त्वमव्यय: शाश्वतधर्मगोप्ता सनातनस्त्वं पुरुषो
मतो मे ॥ ११-१८॥

tvam akṣaraṃ paramaṃ veditavyaṃ tvam asya viśvasya paraṃ
nidhānam
tvam avyayaḥ śāśvatadharmagoptā sanātanas tvaṃ puruṣo
mato me 11.18

अनादिमध्यान्तमनन्तवीर्यमनन्तबाहुं शशिसूर्यनेत्रम् ।
पश्यामि त्वां दीप्तहुताशवक्त्रं स्वतेजसा विश्वमिदं तपन्तम् ॥ ११-१९॥

anādimadhyāntam anantavīryam anantabāhu ṃ śaśisūryanetram
paśyāmi tvāṃ dīptahutāśavaktra ṃ svatejasā viśvam idaṃ
tapantam 11.19

द्यावापृथिव्योरिदमन्तरं हि व्याप्तं त्वयैकेन दिशश्च सर्वा: ।
दृष्ट्वाद्भुतं रूपमुग्रं तवेदं लोकत्रयं प्रव्यथितं महात्मन् ॥ ११-२०॥

dyāvāpṛthivyor idam antaraṃhi vyāptaṃtvayaikena diśaś ca sarvāḥ
dṛṣṭvādbhutaṃ rupam ugraṃ tavedaṃ lokatrayam pravyathitam
mahātman 11.20

अमी हि त्वां सुरसङ्घा विशन्ति केचिद्भीता: प्राञ्जलयो गृणन्ति ।
स्वस्तीत्युक्त्वा महर्षिसिद्धसङ्घा: स्तुवन्ति त्वां स्तुतिभि: पुष्कलाभि: ॥
११-२१॥

amī hi tvāṃ surasaṃghā viśanti kecid bhītāḥ prāñjalayo gṛṇanti
svastīty uktvā maharṣisiddhasaṃghāḥ stuvanti tvāṃ stutibhiḥ
puṣkalābhiḥ 11.21

With Thy crowns, maces and the discs of destruction
I witness Thy opulence that pervades in every direction
Thy overwhelming iridescent luminescence O so bright
Thou art like a brilliant blazing mass of fire and light.|17|

The highest immaculate truth that
by man can be known,
The foundation upon which our universe has grown
The indestructible guardian of righteousness eternal
I believe, Thou art the one -celestial and supernal|18|

Thou hast neither beginning nor middle nor end
The universe burns with the heat that Thy fires send.
Thy arms infinite and Thy eyes are the sun and the moon
And Thy face appears to me like a blazing fiery cocoon|19|

The heavens, the earth and all of space-
Are but extensions of Thy Divine grace
By a vision of Thy fiery form only fear reigns
Amongst the skies, the earth and the nether planes.|20|

The groups of demigods are all entering thee-
Both adoring and afraid, I see
The liberated beings and sages-Thy prayers sing
Hymns for the prosperity of every living thing.|21|

रुद्रादित्या वसवो ये च साध्या विश्वेऽश्विनौ मरुतश्चोष्मपाश्च ।

गन्धर्वयक्षासुरसिद्धसङ्घा वीक्षन्ते त्वां विस्मिताश्चैव सर्वे ॥ ११-२२॥

rudrādityā vasavo ye ca sādhyā viśveśvinau marutaś coṣmapāś ca
gandharvayakṣāsurasiddhasaṃghā vīkṣante tvāṃ vismitāś caiva sarve
11.22

रूपं महत्ते बहुवक्त्रनेत्रं महाबाहो बहुबाहूरुपादम् ।

बहूदरं बहुदंष्ट्राकरालं दृष्ट्वा लोकाः प्रव्यथितास्तथाहम् ॥ ११-२३॥

rūpaṃ mahat te bahuvaktranetraṃ mahābāho bahubāhūrupādam
bahūdaraṃ bahudañṣṭrākarālaṃ dṛṣṭvā lokāḥ pravyathitās
tathāham 11.23

नभःस्पृशं दीप्तमनेकवर्णं व्यात्ताननं दीप्तविशालनेत्रम् ।

दृष्ट्वा हि त्वां प्रव्यथितान्तरात्मा धृतिं न विन्दामि शमं च विष्णो ॥ ११-२४॥

nabhaḥspṛśaṃ dīptam anekavaṇaṃ vyāttānanaṃ dīptaviśālanetram
dṛṣṭvā hi tvāṃ pravyathitāntarātmā dhṛtiṃ na vindāmi śamaṃ ca
viṣṇo 11.24

दंष्ट्राकरालानि च ते मुखानि दृष्ट्वैव कालानलसन्निभानि ।

दिशो न जाने न लभे च शर्म प्रसीद देवेश जगन्निवास ॥ ११-२५॥

daṃṣṭrākarālāni ca te mukhāni dṛṣṭvaiva kālānalasaṃnibhāni
diśo na jāne na labhe ca śarma prasīda deveśa jagannivāsa 11.25

अमी च त्वां धृतराष्ट्रस्य पुत्राःसर्वे सहैवावनिपालसङ्घैः ।

भीष्मो द्रोणः सूतपुत्रस्तथासौ सहास्मदीयैरपि योधमुख्यैः ॥ ११-२६॥

amī ca tvāṃ dhṛtarāṣṭrasya putrāḥ sarve sa-
haivāvanipālasaṃghaiḥ
bhīṣmo droṇaḥ sūtaputras tathāsau sahāsmadīyair api yodhamu-
khyaiḥ 11.26

The *Rudras,* the *Adityas,* the *Vasus* and *Sadhyas*
The *Ashwini Kumars, Vishwas,* the *Maruts* and *Ushmapas*
The *Gandharvas,* the *Yakshas,*
the *Asuras* and the beings perfect
Transfixed on Thy vision – only awe their eyes reflect.|22|

O magnificent Lord with many faces and eyes limitless
With strong arms, bellies and feet –each countless
Myself, all the nations and the world finds Thy form terrible
With infinite teeth, Thou striketh a fear unbearable.|23|

Blazing the heavens, is Thy burning manifestation
Multihued, open-mouthed with eyes in every dimension
Thy vision I am unable to grasp with joy or peace
For the panic within me does not seem to cease.|24|

I witness Thy mouths, with destructive tusks numerous
Thy faces are death and time 'O' so fierce and enormous
O Lord of Lords supreme, a great despair overwhelms me
O shelter of the worlds, May Thy merciful
grace upon me be.|25|

I see all of *Dhritarashtra's* children
And the host of all the kings and the strongest of men
Bheeshma, Drona, and Karna- I see them too-
And the prominent amongst warriors
proceeding in queue! |26|

वक्त्राणि ते त्वरमाणा विशन्ति दंष्ट्राकरालानि भयानकानि ।
केचिद्विलग्ना दशनान्तरेषु सन्दृश्यन्ते चूर्णितैरुत्तमाङ्गैः ॥ ११-२७॥

vaktrāṇi te tvaramāṇā viśanti daṃṣṭrākarālāni bhayānakāni
kecid vilagnā daśanāntareṣu saṃdṛśyante cūrṇitair uttamāṅgaiḥ 11.27

यथा नदीनां बहवोऽम्बुवेगाः समुद्रमेवाभिमुखा द्रवन्ति ।
तथा तवामी नरलोकवीरा विशन्ति वक्त्राण्यभिविज्वलन्ति ॥ ११-२८॥

yathā nadīnāṃ bahavombuvegāḥ samudram evābhimukhā dravanti
tathā tavāmī naralokavīrā viśanti vaktrāṇy abhivijvalanti 11.28

यथा प्रदीप्तं ज्वलनं पतङ्ग विशन्ति नाशाय समृद्धवेगाः ।
तथैव नाशाय विशन्ति लोकास् तवापि वक्त्राणि समृद्धवेगाः ॥ ११-२९॥

yathā pradīpta ṃ jvalanam pataṅgā viśanti nāśāya sam ṛddhavegāḥ
tathaiva nāśāya viśanti lokās tavāpi vaktrā ṇi samṛddhavegāḥ 11.29

लेलिह्यसे ग्रसमानः समन्ताल्लोकान्समग्रान्वदनैर्ज्वलद्भिः ।
तेजोभिरापूर्य जगत्समग्रं भासस्तवोग्राः प्रतपन्ति विष्णो ॥ ११-३०॥

lelihyase grasamānaḥ samantāl lokān samagrān vadanair jvaladbhiḥ
tejobhir āpūrya jagat samagra ṃ bhāsas tavogrāḥ pratapanti viṣṇo 11.30

आख्याहि मे को भवानुग्ररूपो नमोऽस्तु ते देववर प्रसीद ।
विज्ञातुमिच्छामि भवन्तमाद्यं न हि प्रजानामि तव प्रवृत्तिम् ॥ ११-३१॥

ākhyāhi me ko bhavān ugrarūpo namostu te devavara prasīda
vijñātum icchāmi bhavantam ādyaṃ na hi prajānāmi tava pravṛttim
11.31

Into Thy dreaded mouth of fire they are receding
All of them overpowered and helplessly squirming
Between Thy teeth, I see their bleeding heads protruding-
Crushed and ground by Thy razor teeth and tusks horrifying|27|

Just as the many rivers that turbulently gush
And merge into the ocean vast and overwhelming
So too do the heroes of the mortal plane rush
Into Thy mouth-the ethereal inferno blazing.|28|

Like the moths that by nature's instinct
Dive into fires to become extinct
All the men too are rapidly proceeding to destruction
Allured by default into Thy fiery mouth's suction.|29|

Thy many tongues lick all the ten directions
And Thy flaming mouths devour all the world's nations
Thy terrible brilliance scorches Thy infinite creations
O Vishnu, Thy energies feed all manifestations.|30|

O greatest God, show Thy compassion- I salute and appeal
Who art thou behind this terrible form, please reveal
Before the beginning thou wert- I wish to know
To my ignorant mind, the will of Thy workings please show|31|"

श्रीभगवानुवाच ।
कालोऽस्मि लोकक्षयकृत्प्रवृद्धो लोकान्समाहर्तुमिह प्रवृत्तः ।
ऋतेऽपि त्वां न भविष्यन्ति सर्वे येऽवस्थिताः प्रत्यनीकेषु योधाः ॥ ११-३२॥

śrībhagavān uvāca
kālosmi lokakṣayakṛt pravṛddho lokān samāhartum iha pravṛttaḥ
ṛtepi tvāṃ na bhaviṣyanti sarve yevasthitāḥ
pratyanīkeṣu yodhāḥ 11.32

तस्मात्त्वमुत्तिष्ठ यशो लभस्व जित्वा शत्रून् भुङ्क्ष्व राज्यं समृद्धम् ।
मयैवैते निहताः पूर्वमेव निमित्तमात्रं भव सव्यसाचिन् ॥ ११-३३॥

tasmāt tvam uttiṣṭha yaśo labhasva jitvā śatrūn
bhuṅkṣva rājyaṃ samṛddham
mayaivaite nihatāḥ pūrvam eva nimittamātraṃ
bhava savyasācin 11.33

द्रोणं च भीष्मं च जयद्रथं च कर्णं तथान्यानपि योधवीरान् ।
मया हतांस्त्वं जहि मा व्यथिष्ठा युध्यस्व जेतासि रणे सपत्नान् ॥ ११-३४॥

droṇaṃ ca bhīṣmaṃ ca jayadrathaṃ ca karṇaṃ
tathānyān api yodhavīrān
mayā hatāṃs tvaṃ jahi mā vyathiṣṭhā yudhyasva jetāsi
raṇe sapatnān 11.34

सञ्जय उवाच ।
एतच्छुत्वा वचनं केशवस्य कृताञ्जलिर्वेपमानः किरीटी ।
नमस्कृत्वा भूय एवाह कृष्णं सगद्गदं भीतभीतः प्रणम्य ॥ ११-३५॥

sañjaya uvāca
etac chrutvā vacanaṃ keśavasya kṛtāñjalir vepamānaḥ kirīṭī
namaskṛtvā bhūya evāha kṛṣṇaṃ sagadgadaṃ bhītabhītaḥ
praṇamya 11.35

Lord *Krishna* spoke:-
"I am time- harbinger of destruction of everything
I am the colossal destroyer of all that is living
Even without you, these warriors shall not live
To the ranks of the opposing forces, only death I shall give|32|

Arise to the opulence of the conqueror that beckons
And garner the glory that a victor reckons
Know that by Me all are already slain
So become My instrument, let your arrows rain|33|

Defeat all the warriors, *Bheeshma,* and *Drona*
And vanquish the heroes-*Jayadrata* and *Karna*
Fight without being troubled or in pain
Know that by My hands alone they have been slain.|34|"

Sanjaya spoke:
"On listening to the voice of *Krishna,*
With folded hands stood a trembling *Arjuna*
Bowing to the lord in obeisance, he shuddered
And in a faltering voice *Arjuna*
the following words he uttered-|35|

अर्जुन उवाच ।

स्थाने हृषीकेश तव प्रकीर्त्या जगत्प्रहृष्यत्यनुरज्यते च ।

रक्षांसि भीतानि दिशो द्रवन्ति सर्वे नमस्यन्ति च सिद्धसङ्घाः ॥ ११-३६॥

arjuna uvāca

sthāne hṛṣīkeśa tava prakīrtyājagat prahṛṣyaty anurajyate ca

rakṣāmsi bhītāni diśo dravanti sarve namasyanti ca siddhasaṃghāḥ11.36

कस्माच्च ते न नमेरन्महात्मन् गरीयसे ब्रह्मणोऽप्यादिकर्त्रे ।

अनन्त देवेश जगन्निवास त्वमक्षरं सदसत्तत्परं यत् ॥ ११-३७॥

kasmāc ca te na nameran mahātman garīyase brahmaṇopy ādikartre

ananta deveśa jagannivāsa tvam akṣaram sad asat tatparam yat 11.37

त्वमादिदेवः पुरुषः पुराणस्त्वमस्य विश्वस्य परं निधानम् ।

वेत्तासि वेद्यं च परं च धाम त्वया ततं विश्वमनन्तरूप ॥ ११-३८॥

tvam ādidevaḥ puruṣaḥ purāṇas tvam asya viśvasya paramnidhānam

vettāsi vedyam ca param ca dhāma tvayā tatam viśvam

anantarūpa 11.38

वायुर्यमोऽग्निर्वरुणः शशाङ्कःप्रजापतिस्त्वं प्रपितामहश्च ।

नमो नमस्तेऽस्तु सहस्रकृत्वः पुनश्च भूयोऽपि नमो नमस्ते ॥ ११-३९॥

vāyur yamognir varuṇaḥ śaśāṅkaḥ prajāpatis tvam prapitāmahaś ca

namo namas testu sahastrak ṛtvaḥ punaś ca bhūyopi namo

namas te 11.39

नमः पुरस्तादथ पृष्ठतस्ते नमोऽस्तु ते सर्वत एव सर्व ।

अनन्तवीर्यामितविक्रमस्त्वं सर्वं समाप्नोषि ततोऽसि सर्वः ॥ ११-४०॥

namaḥ purastād atha pṛṣṭhatas te namostu te sarvata eva sarva

anantavīryāmitavikramas tvam sarvam samāpnoṣi tatosi sarvaḥ 11.40

Arjuna declared:
"Of your name, O *Krishna*, It is thus rightly perceived
That by uttering it, a joyous bliss across the world is achieved
While the forces of evil in all directions flutter and flee,
All the awakened beings and sages adore thee with glee.|36|

O How can they not worship Ye or offer their respects?
Thou hast created the creator and all His mortal subjects!
O Infinite -lord of gods, in whom the universe resides
Over all that is and is not –Thy insuperable lordship presides.|37|

Thou art the *Purusha* of the *Puranas*- the primeval Lord,
The highest knowledge to the knower-only Thou dost accord
The final abode for this world, the end of destinations.
The universe is pervaded by Thy infinite manifestations|38|

Death, Moon, the ethereal waters, the wind and the fire deities
Thou art the creator or creators, the father of all living entities
Again and again bowing in a thousand repetitions
Once more I bow, offering yet again my salutations.|39|

From the front and from the back, I offer my salutations
To Ye in all the quadrants and all the directions
Thou art in all and in every living thing
Almighty and all pervading, thou art everything.|40|

सखेति मत्वा प्रसभं यदुक्तं हे कृष्ण हे यादव हे सखेति ।
अजानता महिमानं तवेदं मया प्रमादात्प्रणयेन वापि ॥ ११-४१॥

sakheti matvā prasabham yad uktam he kṛṣṇa he yādava he sakheti
ajānatā mahimānam tavedam mayā pramādāt praṇayena vāpi 11.41

यच्चावहासार्थमसत्कृतोऽसि विहारशय्यासनभोजनेषु ।
एकोऽथवाप्यच्युत तत्समक्षं तत्क्षामये त्वामहमप्रमेयम् ॥ ११-४२॥

yac cāvahāsārtham asatkṛtosi vihāraśayyāsanabhojaneṣu
ekothavāpy acyuta tatsamakṣam tat kṣāmaye tvām aham
aprameyam 11.42

पितासि लोकस्य चराचरस्य त्वमस्य पूज्यश्च गुरुर्गरीयान् ।
न त्वत्समोऽस्त्यभ्यधिकः कुतोऽन्यो लोकत्रयेऽप्यप्रतिमप्रभाव ॥ ११-४३॥

pitāsi lokasya carācarasya tvam asya pūjyaś ca gurur garīyān
na tvatsamosty abhyadhikaḥ kutonyo lokatrayepy apratimaprab-
hāva 11.43

तस्मात्प्रणम्य प्रणिधाय कायं प्रसादये त्वामहमीशमीड्यम् ।
पितेव पुत्रस्य सखेव सख्युः प्रियः प्रियायार्हसि देव सोढुम् ॥ ११-४४॥

tasmāt praṇamya praṇidhāya kāyam prasādaye tvām aham īśam īḍyam
piteva putrasya sakheva sakhyuḥ priyaḥ priyāyārhasi deva
soḍhum 11.44

अदृष्टपूर्वं हृषितोऽस्मि दृष्ट्वा भयेन च प्रव्यथितं मनो मे ।
तदेव मे दर्शय देव रूपं प्रसीद देवेश जगन्निवास ॥ ११-४५॥

adṛṣṭapūrvam hṛṣitosmi dṛṣṭvā bhayena ca pravyathitam mano me
tad eva me darśaya deva rūpam prasīda deveśa jagannivāsa
11.45

किरीटिनं गदिनं चक्रहस्तं इच्छामि त्वां द्रष्टुमहं तथैव ।
तेनैव रूपेण चतुर्भुजेन सहस्रबाहो भव विश्वमूर्ते ॥ ११-४६॥

kirīṭinam gadinam cakrahastam icchāmi tvām draṣṭum aham tathaiva
tenaiva rūpeṇa caturbhujena sahastrabāho bhava viśvamūrte 11.46

Assuming Thee to be my mortal friend
I spoke rudely, even though I did not intend
Of Thy greatness, O *Krishna*, O *Yadava*, O beloved
Out of love or ignorance I was thoroughly deluded|41|

Whatever disrespect to Thee I may have shown
Out of jest or play, either amongst companions or alone
Else while resting or eating- O Lord I did not know-
O Faultless one, Thy forgiveness upon me please show.|42|

O Divine teacher, the Father of every single being
Thou art the highest worship capable to the living
If in the three worlds – equal to Ye there is none
Superior to Ye, how can there exist anyone? |43|

Hence to Ye, I perform a full body prostration
And to thee I offer my surrender and submission
Thou art the father to the son, the companion of a friend
The beloved to the lover,
O Lord, Thy mercy upon me extend.|44|

What was never seen before I now saw,
But my mind trembles with both fear and awe
O Refuge of The Universe,
shower Thy compassionate grace
Thy earlier peaceful form let my vision embrace.|45|

I crave to see the form my mind understands
With Thy crown, mace and discus in hands
O thousand armed universal form, do unveil
The Divine four-armed figure of thine,
please reveal|46|"

श्रीभगवानुवाच ।
मया प्रसन्नेन तवार्जुनेदं रूपं परं दर्शितमात्मयोगात् ।
तेजोमयं विश्वमनन्तमाद्यं यन्मे त्वदन्येन न दृष्टपूर्वम् ॥ ११-४७॥

śrībhagavān uvāca
mayā prasannena tavārjunedaṃ rūpaṃ paraṃ darśitam ātmayogāt
tejomayaṃ viśvam anantam ādyaṃ yan me tvadanyena na
dṛṣṭapūrvam 11.47

न वेदयज्ञाध्ययनैर्न दानैर्न च क्रियाभिर्न तपोभिरुग्रैः ।
एवंरूपः शक्य अहं नृलोके द्रष्टुं त्वदन्येन कुरुप्रवीर ॥ ११-४८॥

na veda yajñādhyayanair na dānaiḥ na ca kriyābhir
na tapobhir ugraiḥ
evaṃrūpaḥ śakya ahaṃ nṛloke draṣṭuṃ tvadanyena
kurupravīra 11.48

मा ते व्यथा मा च विमूढभावो दृष्ट्वा रूपं घोरमीदृङ्ममेदम् ।
व्यपेतभीः प्रीतमनाः पुनस्त्वं तदेव मे रूपमिदं प्रपश्य ॥ ११-४९॥

mā te vyathā mā ca vimūḍhabhāvo dṛṣṭvā rūpaṃ ghoram īdṛṅ
mamedam
vyapetabhīḥ prītamanāḥ punas tvaṃ tad eva me rūpam idaṃ
prapaśya 11.49

सञ्जय उवाच ।
इत्यर्जुनं वासुदेवस्तथोक्त्वा स्वकं रूपं दर्शयामास भूयः ।
आश्वासयामास च भीतमेनं भूत्वा पुनः सौम्यवपुर्महात्मा ॥ ११-५०॥

sañjaya uvāca
ity arjunaṃ vāsudevas tathoktvā svakaṃ rūpaṃ darśayām āsa bhūyaḥ
āśvāsayām āsa ca bhītam enaṃ bhūtvā puna ḥ saumyavapur
mahātmā 11.50

Lord *Krishna* spoke:
"O *Arjuna*, By My favor alone this form can you see
My luminous form from which the world came to be
My original Self that mortal eyes before have never gazed
This infinite universal form that
you have witnessed and praised|47|

Not by researching the *Vedas* or by pouring sacrificial oblations
Neither by charity nor by performing right actions
Not even by the strictest of penances, is it possible for man
To see My perfect form, apart fromt you- no one has or can.|48|

Seeing this tremendous form of Mine you should not fret
This ignorant state of panic you must starkly reject
Cast away your fear as I show you the milder form of Mine
Behold and rejoice- witnessing
My other embodiment Divine.|49|"

Sanjaya said:
"After saying these words to *Arjuna*,
The four-armed manifestation was assumed by *Krishna*
Then resuming His peaceful form full of love and grace
The Lord returned to console the fear-struck face."|50|

अर्जुन उवाच ।
दृष्ट्वेदं मानुषं रूपं तव सौम्यं जनार्दन ।
इदानीमस्मि संवृत्तः सचेताः प्रकृतिं गतः ॥ ११-५१॥

arjuna uvāca
dṛṣṭvedam mānuṣam rūpam tava saumyam janārdana
idānīm asmi samvṛttaḥ sacetāḥ prakṛtim gataḥ 11.51

श्रीभगवानुवाच ।
सुदुर्दर्शमिदं रूपं दृष्टवानसि यन्मम ।
देवा अप्यस्य रूपस्य नित्यं दर्शनकाङ्क्षिणः ॥ ११-५२॥

śrībhagavān uvāca
sudurdarśam idam rūpam dṛṣṭvān asi yan mama
devā apy asya rūpasya nityam darśanakāṅkṣiṇaḥ 11.52

नाहं वेदैर्न तपसा न दानेन न चेज्यया ।
शक्य एवंविधो द्रष्टुं दृष्टवानसि मां यथा ॥ ११-५३॥

nāham vedair na tapasā na dānena na cejyayā
śakya evamvidho draṣṭum dṛṣṭavān asi mām yathā 11.53

भक्त्या त्वनन्यया शक्य अहमेवंविधोऽर्जुन ।
ज्ञातुं द्रष्टुं च तत्त्वेन प्रवेष्टुं च परन्तप ॥ ११-५४॥

bhaktyā tv ananyayā śakya aham evamvidhorjuna
jñātum draṣṭum ca tattvena praveṣṭum ca paramtapa 11.54

मत्कर्मकृन्मत्परमो मद्भक्तः सङ्गवर्जितः ।
निर्वैरः सर्वभूतेषु यः स मामेति पाण्डव ॥ ११-५५॥

matkarmakṛn matparamo madbhaktaḥ saṅgavarjitaḥ
nirvairaḥ sarvabhūteṣu yaḥ sa mām eti pāṇḍava 11.55

Arjuna spoke:
"Seeing your four-armed form coming to the fore
An ecstatic delight overwhelms me once more
O So soothing this peaceful form of yours I find,
A silent sea of bliss now fills my mind.|51|"

Lord *Krishna* :
"My four-armed form that has been seen by you
Has been witnessed by only the rarest few
For even the demigods wonder and desire
To see this *Avatar,* forever they aspire|52|

The form that you saw cannot be seen
Neither by *Vedas* nor by the penances strictest
Nor by sacrifices nor by charities to the poorest
To see this form by all it has not possible been |53|

Arjuna, Only by the purest devotion can it possible be
As with a desireless love alone can one know Me
And truly see Me in essence and element
And in My consciousness be immersed and present.|54|

O *Arjuna,* Surrender to Me, perform My bidding
Become My devotee and an instrument of My working
With an enmity towards none, from desires become free
Accept Me-My way, for such a man shall only come to Me|55|"

(Thus ended the eleventh Canto of the Bhagavad Gita where Sri Krishna blessed Arjuna with the ful vision of the Universal Divine being)

❄ ❄ ❄

अथ द्वादशोऽध्यायः ।
atha dvādaśodhyāyaḥ

अर्जुन उवाच ।
एवं सततयुक्ता ये भक्तास्त्वां पर्युपासते ।
ये चाप्यक्षरमव्यक्तं तेषां के योगवित्तमाः ॥ १२-१॥

arjuna uvāca
evaṃ satatayuktā ye bhaktās tvāṃ paryupāsate
ye cāpy akṣaram avyaktaṃ teṣāṃ ke yogavittamāḥ 12.1

श्रीभगवानुवाच ।
मय्यावेश्य मनो ये मां नित्ययुक्ता उपासते ।
श्रद्धया परयोपेताः ते मे युक्ततमा मताः ॥ १२-२॥

śrībhagavān uvāca
mayy āveśya mano ye māṃ nityayuktā upāsate
śraddhayā parayopetāḥ te me yuktatamā matāḥ 12.2

ये त्वक्षरमनिर्देश्यमव्यक्तं पर्युपासते ।
सर्वत्रगमचिन्त्यञ्च कूटस्थमचलन्ध्रुवम् ॥ १२-३॥

ye tv akṣaram anirdeśyam avyaktaṃ paryupāsate
sarvatragam acintya ṃ ca kūṭasthaṃ acalaṃ dhruvam12.3

सन्नियम्येन्द्रियग्रामं सर्वत्र समबुद्धयः ।
ते प्राप्नुवन्ति मामेव सर्वभूतहिते रताः ॥ १२-४॥

saṃniyamyendriyagrāmaṃ sarvatra samabuddhayāḥ
te prāpnuvanti mām eva sarvabhūtahite ratāḥ 12.4

क्लेशोऽधिकतरस्तेषामव्यक्तासक्तचेतसाम् ॥
अव्यक्ता हि गतिर्दुःखं देहवद्भिरवाप्यते ॥ १२-५॥

kleśodhikataras teṣāṃ avyaktāsaktacetasām
avyaktā hi gatir du ḥkhaṃ dehavadbhir avāpyate 12.5

Canto XII: *The Yoga of the Devotee:*

(Verses 1: *Arjuna*'s query about the formless and formed God; 2-6: *Krishna*'s answer; 7: The deliverance of *Krishna*; 8-13: The way of the devotee; 14-19: The devotees dear to *Krishna*; 20: *Krishna*'s dearest devotee)

Arjuna asked:
"There exist devotees who constantly seek Thee,
But who has the greatest knowledge of *Yoga*, according to Ye,
Those who worship the form of Thy Divine manifestation,
Or those who seek Thee-the formless unmanifest with devo-
tion?|1|"

Sri *Krishna* spoke:
"Those who affix their mind's concentration-
And seek verily only My union
With the most supreme faith, who offer Me their prayers
I hold them to be the best amongst My seekers.|2|

Those who worship the formless- Immutable
And seek the unconceivable-imperishable,
The all-pervading omniscient and supernal,
Who is the equilibrial infinite ethereal and eternal.|3|

With regulation, those who control their senses
With their minds balanced and free from pretenses
Seeking the betterment of all living beings with dedication
In Me they too certainly attain a dissolution.|4|

The difficulties of those seekers are indeed great-
Who are devoted in their quest for the formless un-incarnate
Success is quaint for such individuals trapped in the physical
With sufferings they realize the imperceptible metaphysical|5|

ये तु सर्वाणि कर्माणि मयि संन्यस्य मत्परः ।
अनन्येनैव योगेन मां ध्यायन्त उपासते ॥ १२-६॥

ye tu sarvāṇi karmāṇi mayi saṃnyasya matparaḥ
ananyenaiva yogena māṃ dhyāyanta upāsate 12.6

तेषामहं समुद्धर्ता मृत्युसंसारसागरात् ।
भवामि नचिरात्पार्थ मय्यावेशितचेतसाम् ॥ १२-७॥

teṣāṃ ahaṃ samuddhartā mṛtyusaṃsārasāgarāt
bhavāmi na cirāt pārtha mayy āveśitacetasām 12.7

मय्येव मन आधत्स्व मयि बुद्धिं निवेशय ।
निवसिष्यसि मय्येव अत ऊर्ध्वं न संशयः ॥ १२-८॥

mayy eva mana ādhatsva mayi buddhi ṃ niveśaya
nivasiṣyasi mayy eva ata ūrdhvaṃ na saṃśayaḥ 12.8

अथ चित्तं समाधातुं न शक्नोषि मयि स्थिरम् ।
अभ्यासयोगेन ततो मामिच्छातुं धनञ्जय ॥ १२-९॥

atha cittaṃ samādhātuṃ na śaknoṣi mayi sthiram
abhyāsayogena tato mām ichāptuṃ dhanaṃjaya 12.9

अभ्यासेऽप्यसमर्थोऽसि मत्कर्मपरमो भव ।
मदर्थमपि कर्माणि कुर्वन्सिद्धिमवाप्स्यसि ॥ १२-१०॥

abhyāsepy asamarthosi matkarmaparamo bhava
madartham api karmā ṇi kurvan siddhim avāpsyasi 12.10

अथैतदप्यशक्तोऽसि कर्तुं मद्योगमाश्रितः ।
सर्वकर्मफलत्यागं ततः कुरु यतात्मवान् ॥ १२-११॥

athaitad apy aśaktosi kartuṃ madyogam āśrita ḥ
sarvakarmaphalatyāgaṃ tataḥ kuru yatātmavān 12.11

श्रेयो हि ज्ञानमभ्यासाज्ज्ञानाद्ध्यानं विशिष्यते ।
ध्यानात्कर्मफलत्यागस्त्यागाच्छान्तिरनन्तरम् ॥ १२-१२॥

śreyo hi jñānam abhyāsāj jñānād dhyānaṃ viśiṣyate
dhyānāt karmaphalatyāgas tyāgāc chāntir anantaram 12.12

But those who offer to Me their every action
Possessing within them the highest state of devotion,
They reach Me as they engage in meditation
By seeking to attain the unwavering union|6|

O *Arjuna,* For the soul's evolution
I bring deliverance from death's material ocean
I propel the journey across the eternal sea-
Of all whose consciousness is affixed in Me|7|

Make Me the sole focus of your mind
Your intellect founded in Me alone may you find
Then you shall, without doubt, reside in Me
In a plane beyond the mortal one that you see.|8|

If to dwell in Me O *Arjuna,* you are not capable
And cannot keep your mind firm and stable
Then by practicing *Yoga* make yourself able
And make your awakened consciousness sustainable|9|

And If this *Yoga* too you cannot partake,
Then just perform all your actions for My sake
And let all your works be only Mine
For then you shall attain the perfection Divine.|10|

If constantly thinking of Me is beyond You
There is yet another thing that you can still do
Tame your mind through a spirited self-control-
And renounce the fruits of your actions as a whole|11|

Compared to a practice that is in ignorance performed
Knowing is better than being naïve and uninformed
Better than knowledge is meditation, but best is renunciation
Renouncing the fruits of actions
alone brings peace's satisfaction.|12|

अद्वेष्टा सर्वभूतानां मैत्रः करुण एव च ।
निर्ममो निरहङ्कारः समदुःखसुखः क्षमी ॥ १२-१३॥

adveṣṭā sarvabhūtānāṃ maitraḥ karuṇa eva ca
nirmamo nirahaṃkāraḥ samaduḥkhasukhaḥ kṣamī 12.13

सन्तुष्टः सततं योगी यतात्मा दृढनिश्चयः ।
मय्यर्पितमनोबुद्धिर्यो मद्भक्तः स मे प्रियः ॥ १२-१४॥

saṃtuṣṭaḥ satataṃ yogī yatātmā dṛḍhaniścayaḥ
mayy arpitamanobuddhir yo madbhaktaḥ sa me priyaḥ 12.14

यस्मान्नोद्विजते लोको लोकान्नोद्विजते च यः ।
हर्षामर्षभयोद्वेगैर्मुक्तो यः स च मे प्रियः ॥ १२-१५॥

yasmān nodvijate loko lokān nodvijate ca ya ḥ
harṣāmarṣabhayodvegair mukto ya ḥ sa ca me priyaḥ 12.15

अनपेक्षः शुचिर्दक्ष उदासीनो गतव्यथः ।
सर्वारम्भपरित्यागी यो मद्भक्तः स मे प्रियः ॥ १२-१६॥

anapekṣaḥ śucir dakṣa udāsīno gatavyathaḥ
sarvārambhaparityāgī yo madbhaktaḥ sa me priyaḥ 12.16

यो न हृष्यति न द्वेष्टि न शोचति न काङ्क्षति ।
शुभाशुभपरित्यागी भक्तिमान्यः स मे प्रियः ॥ १२-१७॥

yo na hṛṣyati na dveṣṭi na śocati na kāṅkṣati
śubhāśubhaparityāgī bhaktimān yaḥ sa me priyaḥ 12.17

समः शत्रौ च मित्रे च तथा मानापमानयोः ।
शीतोष्णसुखदुःखेषु समः सङ्गविवर्जितः ॥ १२-१८॥

samaḥ śatrau ca mitre ca tathā mānāpamānayoḥ
śītoṣṇasukhaduḥkheṣu samaḥ saṅgavivarjitaḥ 12.18

तुल्यनिन्दास्तुतिर्मौनी सन्तुष्टो येन केनचित् ।
अनिकेतः स्थिरमतिर्भक्तिमान्मे प्रियो नरः ॥ १२-१९॥

tulyanindāstutir maunī saṃtuṣṭo yena kenacit
aniketaḥ sthiramatir bhaktimān me priyo naraḥ 12.19

Be devoid of envy and hold compassion and friendship,
Experiencing towards all living beings a loving kinship,
Tolerant and poised in both comfort and hardship
And bereft of ego and its feeling of ownership |13|

That soul who remains ever in a contented happiness
Always practicing *Yoga* with a steady firmness,
Who has surrendered to Me his intellect and mind-
Dear to me that devotee you shall find.|14|

He who by the world's chaos remains unperturbed
Nor can the world by him be in any way disturbed
From pleasure, anger, fear and anxiety he who is free
Such a soul, is dear to Me|15|

Expecting nothing, he is pure and perfect in every action
And is free from the pains of worry and agitation
For every work begun, the ownership he forgoes
To Me, Such a devotee is dear and close.|16|

He neither rejoices nor rejects
Neither grieves over nor desires material objects
To whom both the auspicious and inauspicious are same
That devotee as dear to Me, I acclaim.|17|

Friends and foes, he treats as one
In honor or dishonor-nothing is lost nor won
In comfort or sorrow and in heat or cold
In the opposites of nature, a balance he does hold.|18|

In praise or censure, he is poised and peaceful
With whatever that comes naturally, he remains blissful
When from his people, things or home he can detached be
A soul with such devotion and conviction is dear to Me.|19|

ये तु धर्म्यामृतमिदं यथोक्तं पर्युपासते ।
श्रद्दधाना मत्परमा भक्तास्तेऽतीव मे प्रियाः ॥ १२-२०॥
ye tu dharmyāmṛtam idaṃ yathoktaṃ paryupāsate
śraddadhānā matparamā bhaktās tetīva me priyāḥ 12.20

But the dearest of My devotees is he
Whose supreme aim in life is to love only Me
For he emulates My teachings with perfect devotion
And his life is the immortal *Dharma*'s exemplification.|20|"

(Thus ended the twelfth Canto of the Bhagavad Gita where Sri Krishna described to Arjuna the Yoga of the devotion)

❋ ❋ ❋

अथ त्रयोदशोऽध्यायः ।
atha trayodaśodhyāyaḥ

श्रीभगवानुवाच ।
इदं शरीरं कौन्तेय क्षेत्रमित्यभिधीयते ।
एतद्यो वेत्ति तं प्राहुः क्षेत्रज्ञ इति तद्विदः ॥ १३-१॥

śrībhagavān uvāca
idaṃ śarīraṃ kaunteya kṣetram ity abhidhīyate
etad yo vetti taṃ prāhuḥ kṣetrajña iti tadvidaḥ 13.1

क्षेत्रज्ञं चापि मां विद्धि सर्वक्षेत्रेषु भारत ।
क्षेत्रक्षेत्रज्ञयोर्ज्ञानं यत्तज्ज्ञानं मतं मम ॥ १३-२॥

kṣetrajñaṃ cāpi māṃ viddhi sarvakṣetreṣu bhārata
kṣetrakṣetrajñayor jñānaṃ yat taj jñānaṃ mataṃ mama 13.2

तत्क्षेत्रं यच्च यादृक्च यद्विकारि यतश्च यत् ।
स च यो यत्प्रभावश्च तत्समासेन मे शृणु ॥ १३-३॥

tat kṣetraṃ yac ca yādṛk ca yadvikāri yataś ca yat
sa ca yo yatprabhāvaś ca tat samāsena me śṛṇu 13.3

ऋषिभिर्बहुधा गीतं छन्दोभिर्विविधैः पृथक् ।
ब्रह्मसूत्रपदैश्चैव हेतुमद्भिर्विनिश्चितैः ॥ १३-४॥

ṛṣibhir bahudhā gītam chandobhir vividhaiḥ pṛthak
brahmasūtrapadais caiva hetumadbhir viniścitaiḥ 13.4

महाभूतान्यहङ्कारो बुद्धिरव्यक्तमेव च ।
इन्द्रियाणि दशैकं च पञ्च चेन्द्रियगोचराः ॥ १३-५॥

mahābhūtāny ahaṃkāro buddhir avyaktam eva ca
indriyāṇi daśaikaṃ ca pañca cendriyagocarāḥ 13.5

Canto XIII: ***The Knower, The Field and its divisions***

((Verses 1-11: *Krishna* - the supreme Knower describes the fundamentals of existence and their functioning; 12-18: *Krishna* parts the wisdom of the Brahman; 19: She-The Divine Feminine; 20-22: Purusha and Prakriti-The couple Divine; 23-28: The Way of release from Prakriti's dominion; 29-34: The way to mastery over the Field and the Gnosis of Brahman)

Sri *Krishna* answered:
"O *Arjuna*, this physical body that you own
Is the Field that is to be known.
And he who knows in principle its foundation -
Is the knower who knows its mode of operation.|1|

As the Knower supreme, recognize Me
Knower of all the fields that can in existence be.
The knowledge of the knower and the field
Is the ultimate wisdom that a being can wield.|2|

About the Field and its multifarious diversities,
Of its source, nature, and inherent deformities,
And also what it is and what is its influence's sphere
I shall explain them to you, So lend Me your ear.|3|

The sages and ancient seers of old,
Have in their hymns thus extolled,
The *Brahma-sutras* the great scriptures classical
Describe its philosophy and rationale in a way most logical.|4|

The field consists of the ego and the five elements,
The mind, the ten senses, their five sense components-
Of touch, taste, smell, sound and sight-
And also the inextensible and unmanifest light.|5|

इच्छा द्वेषः सुखं दुःखं सङ्घातश्चेतना धृतिः ।
एतत्क्षेत्रं समासेन सविकारमुदाहृतम् ॥ १३-६॥

icchā dveṣaḥ sukham duḥkham samghātaś cetanā dhṛtiḥ
etat kṣetram samāsena savikāram udāhṛtam 13.6

अमानित्वमदम्भित्वमहिंसा क्षान्तिरार्जवम् ।
आचार्योपासनं शौचं स्थैर्यमात्मविनिग्रहः ॥ १३-७॥

amānitvam adambhitvam ahimsā kṣāntir ārjavam
ācāryopāsanam śaucam sthairyam ātmavinigrahaḥ 13.7

इन्द्रियार्थेषु वैराग्यमनहङ्कार एव च ।
जन्ममृत्युजराव्याधिदुःखदोषानुदर्शनम् ॥ १३-८॥

indriyārtheṣu vairāgyam anahamkāra eva ca
janmamṛtyujarāvyādhiduḥkhadoṣānudarśanam 13.8

असक्तिरनभिष्वङ्गः पुत्रदारगृहादिषु ।
नित्यं च समचित्तत्वमिष्टानिष्टोपपत्तिषु ॥ १३-९॥

asaktir anabhiṣvaṅgaḥ putradāragṛhādiṣu
nityam ca samacittatvam iṣṭāniṣṭopapattiṣu 13.9

मयि चानन्ययोगेन भक्तिरव्यभिचारिणी ।
विविक्तदेशसेवित्वमरतिर्जनसंसदि ॥ १३-१०॥

mayi cānanyayogena bhaktir avyabhicāriṇī
viviktadeśasevitvam aratir janasamsadi 13.10

अध्यात्मज्ञाननित्यत्वं तत्त्वज्ञानार्थदर्शनम् ।
एतज्ज्ञानमिति प्रोक्तमज्ञानं यदतोऽन्यथा ॥ १३-११॥

adhyātmajñānanityatvam tattvajñānārthadarśanam
etaj jñānam iti proktam ajñānam yad atonyathā 13.11

ज्ञेयं यत्तत्प्रवक्ष्यामि यज्ज्ञात्वामृतमश्नुते ।
अनादिमत्परं ब्रह्म न सत्तन्नासदुच्यते ॥ १३-१२॥

jñeyam yat tat pravak ṣyāmi yaj jñātvām ṛtam aśnute
anādimat par am brahma na sat tan nāsad ucyate 13.1 2

Desire, dislike, pleasure and pain
Are the Field's principal deformations that reign
And consciousness, differentiation and perpetuation
Are its principle constituents with many a modification.|6|

Devoid of exhibitionism and self-priding arrogance
Replete with non-violence, compassion and a patient tolerance
With purity from within, serving with love the spiritual teacher,
And with the mind firmly in control over its lower nature.|7|

With absolute detachment, devoid of ego's false perceptions
And beyond the pull of nature's sensual attractions,
Knowing the truth of birth, death, old age and illness
Without sorrow, understanding their underlying oneness.|8|

Bereft of anxieties and familial concerns
His children, wife and home with detachment, he discerns
And his mind is ever immersed in truth's tranquil
Irrespective of the happenings for or against his will.|9|

Practicing *Yoga* with the greatest devotion,
Loving the supreme with an unswerving dedication
With the mind directed towards an inner clarity
Away from the crowds and gatherings of outer vanity.|10|

Seeking verily the true knowledge-spiritual
Understanding its principles-philosophical and factual
All these conform to the true knowledge's way
All against this is ignorance- one can assuredly say.|11|

I now reveal the wisdom, wherein
the golden truth is contained
Knowing which the immortal consciousness can be gained
That knowledge of the eternal *Brahman* supreme-
Beyond existence and non-existence's limits one can deem. |12|

सर्वतः पाणिपादं तत्सर्वतोऽक्षिशिरोमुखम् ।
सर्वतः श्रुतिमल्लोके सर्वमावृत्य तिष्ठति ॥ १३-१३॥

sarvataḥ pāṇipādaṃ tat sarvatokṣiśiromukham
sarvataḥ śrutimal loke sarvam āvṛtya tiṣṭhati 13.13

सर्वेन्द्रियगुणाभासं सर्वेन्द्रियविवर्जितम् ।
असक्तं सर्वभृच्चैव निर्गुणं गुणभोक्तृ च ॥ १३-१४॥

sarvendriyaguṇābhāsaṃ sarvendriyavivarjitam
asaktaṃ sarvabhṛc caiva nirguṇaṃ guṇabhoktṛ ca 13.14

बहिरन्तश्च भूतानामचरं चरमेव च ।
सूक्ष्मत्वात्तदविज्ञेयं दूरस्थं चान्तिके च तत् ॥ १३-१५॥

bahir antaś ca bhūtānām acaraṃ caram eva ca
sūkṣmatvāt tad avijñeyaṃ dūrasthaṃ cāntike ca tat 13.15

अविभक्तं च भूतेषु विभक्तमिव च स्थितम् ।
भूतभर्तृ च तज्ज्ञेयं ग्रसिष्णु प्रभविष्णु च ॥ १३-१६॥

avibhaktaṃ ca bhūteṣu vibhaktam iva ca sthitam
bhūtabhartṛ ca taj jñeyaṃ grasiṣṇu prabhaviṣṇu ca 13.16

ज्योतिषामपि तज्ज्योतिस्तमसः परमुच्यते ।
ज्ञानं ज्ञेयं ज्ञानगम्यं हृदि सर्वस्य विष्ठितम् ॥ १३-१७॥

jyotiṣām api taj jyotis tamasaḥ param ucyate
jñānaṃ jñeyaṃ jñānagamyaṃ hṛdi sarvasya viṣṭhitam 13.17

इति क्षेत्रं तथा ज्ञानं ज्ञेयं चोक्तं समासतः ।
मद्भक्त एतद्विज्ञाय मद्भावायोपपद्यते ॥ १३-१८॥

iti kṣetraṃ tathā jñānaṃ jñeyaṃ coktaṃ sanāsataḥ
madbhakta etad vijñāya madbhāvāyopapadyate 13.18

प्रकृतिं पुरुषं चैव विद्ध्यनादी उभावपि ।

विकारांश्च गुणांश्चैव विद्धि प्रकृतिसम्भवान् ॥ १३-१९॥

prakṛtiṃ puruṣaṃ caiva viddhy anādi ubhāv api
vikārāñś ca guṇāṃś caiva viddhi prakṛtisambhavān 13.19

His hands and feet spread in all directions
Everywhere we see only His eyes and faces' reflections
The whole universe by His divinity, He does engulf and pervade
All life-forms are but dwellers in His shelter and shade.|13|

In all qualities and senses, His splendour is there
But none of the sense impulses does He Himself bear
Detached from all, He nourishes all creations-
He enjoys the senses, but they are not his limitations.|14|

Present inside and outside all the living ones
Both mobile and immobile together at once
He is unimaginable, infinitesimally subtler than the subtlest
Beyond understanding, He is nearest and also the farthest.|13|

He is the immutable and indivisible oneness
And yet His creatures appear as life forms of distinctness
All the living beings from Him only emerge
And back to His eternity all of them return to converge.|16|

The light that illumines light is He
Beyond all the forms of darkness that can be
He is the knowledge and He is the wisdom
And in the hearts of all, presides His kingdom.|17|

Thus the realm of the field, I have surmised and shown
And also what is knowledge and what is to be known
When My devotees can know this and realize
Then into their natures, My Divinity they materialize.|18|

Prakriti is the counterpart of the One being supernal,
Like Him, She too is immaculate and eternal.
Within Her only originate all of Nature's qualities-
But also arising from Her are the many deformities.|19|

कार्यकारणकर्तृत्वे हेतुः प्रकृतिरुच्यते ।
पुरुषः सुखदुःखानां भोक्तृत्वे हेतुरुच्यते ॥ १३-२० ॥

kārya kāraṇa kartṛtve hetuḥ prakṛtir ucyate
puruṣaḥ sukhaduḥkhānāṁ bhoktṛtve hetur ucyate 13.20

पुरुषः प्रकृतिस्थो हि भुङ्क्ते प्रकृतिजान्गुणान् ।
कारणं गुणसङ्गोऽस्य सदसद्योनिजन्मसु ॥ १३-२१ ॥

puruṣaḥ prakṛtistho hi bhuṅkte prakṛtijān guṇān
kāraṇaṁ guṇasaṅgosya sadasadyonijanmasu 13.21

उपद्रष्टानुमन्ता च भर्ता भोक्ता महेश्वरः ।
परमात्मेति चाप्युक्तो देहेऽस्मिन्पुरुषः परः ॥ १३-२२ ॥

upadraṣṭānumantā ca bhartā bhoktā maheśvaraḥ
paramātmeti cāpyukto dehesmin puruṣaḥ paraḥ 13.22

य एवं वेत्ति पुरुषं प्रकृतिं च गुणैः सह ।
सर्वथा वर्तमानोऽपि न स भूयोऽभिजायते ॥ १३-२३ ॥

ya evaṁ vetti puruṣaṁ prakṛtim ca guṇaiḥ saha
sarvathā vartamānopi na sa bhūyobhijāyate 13.23

ध्यानेनात्मनि पश्यन्ति केचिदात्मानमात्मना ।
अन्ये साङ्ख्येन योगेन कर्मयोगेन चापरे ॥ १३-२४ ॥

dhyānenātmani paśyanti kecid ātmānam ātmanā
anye sāṁkhyena yogena karmayogena cāpare 13.24

अन्ये त्वेवमजानन्तः श्रुत्वान्येभ्य उपासते ।
तेऽपि चातितरन्त्येव मृत्युं श्रुतिपरायणाः ॥ १३-२५ ॥

anye tv evam ajānantaḥ śrutvānyebhya upāsate
tepi cātitaranty eva mṛtyuṁ śrutiparāyaṇāḥ 13.25

यावत्सञ्जायते किञ्चित्सत्त्वं स्थावरजङ्गमम् ।
क्षेत्रक्षेत्रज्ञसंयोगात्तद्विद्धि भरतर्षभ ॥ १३-२६ ॥

yāvat samjāyate kiṁcit sattvaṁ sthāvarajaṅgamam
kṣetrakṣetrajñasaṁyogāt tad viddhi bharatarṣabha 13.26

The domino of cause and effect is Her procreation
The experiences of individual consciousness, Her creation.
And the one supreme being- The *Purusha* does but enjoy
Experiencing both pleasure and pain with joy.|20|

Immersed in Her qualities, He presides
Experiencing Her nature, He resides
His attachment to *Prakriti* is the sole cause
Of all births in mortal wombs of sin and good that He draws|21|

Situated within this physical envelope mortal
Is the one supreme indwelling Lord immortal
He is the witness, observer and giver of consents
Nature's modes He enjoys, upholds and augments.|22|

He who knows and realizes the duality-
Of the supreme *Purusha* and *Prakriti's* every quality
His way of living or actions notwithstanding-
That being certainly finds release from rebirth's bonding.|23|

By delving deep into the inner realms while meditation
Or Knowing the eternal *Self'* by the soul-nature separation
Or else by the *Yoga* of dynamic action-
One can gain the indwelling Supreme's realization|24|

But those who are ignorant and do not know-
Of the ways of the paths or which path to go
When to the Knower, they listen and
follow with devotion
Whichever of these paths is tread,
immortal is their destination.|25|

O *Arjuna*, every being living on this earth
Moving or non-moving, however, may be their birth.
Are caused by the Field and its Supreme knower's union
As all entities are born in their communion.|26|

समं सर्वेषु भूतेषु तिष्ठन्तं परमेश्वरम् ।
विनश्यत्स्वविनश्यन्तं यः पश्यति स पश्यति ॥ १३-२७॥

samaṃ sarveṣu bhūteṣu tiṣṭhantaṃ parameśvaram
vinaśyatsv avinaśyantaṃ yaḥ paśyati sa paśyati 13.27

समं पश्यन्हि सर्वत्र समवस्थितमीश्वरम् ।
न हिनस्त्यात्मनात्मानं ततो याति परां गतिम् ॥ १३-२८॥

samaṃ paśyan hi sarvatra samavasthitam īśvaram
na hinasty ātmanātmānaṃ tato yāti parāṃ gatim 13.28

प्रकृत्यैव च कर्माणि क्रियमाणानि सर्वशः ।
यः पश्यति तथात्मानमकर्तारं स पश्यति ॥ १३-२९॥

prakṛtyaiva ca karmāṇi kriyamāṇnāni sarvaśaḥ
yaḥ paśyati tathātmānam akartāraṃ sa paśyati 13.29

यदा भूतपृथग्भावमेकस्थमनुपश्यति ।
तत एव च विस्तारं ब्रह्म सम्पद्यते तदा ॥ १३-३०॥

yadā bhūtapṛthagbhāvam ekastham anupaśyati
tata eva ca vistāraṃ brahma saṃpadyate tadā 13.30

अनादित्वान्निर्गुणत्वात्परमात्मायमव्ययः ।
शरीरस्थोऽपि कौन्तेय न करोति न लिप्यते ॥ १३-३१॥

anāditvān nirguṇatvāt paramātmāyam avyayaḥ
śarīrasthopi kaunteya na karoti na lipyate 13.31

यथा सर्वगतं सौक्ष्म्यादाकाशं नोपलिप्यते ।
सर्वत्रावस्थितो देहे तथात्मा नोपलिप्यते ॥ १३-३२॥

yathā sarvagataṃ saukṣmyād ākāśaṃ nopalipyate
sarvatrāvasthito dehe tathātmā nopalipyate 13.32

यथा प्रकाशयत्येकः कृत्स्नं लोकमिमं रविः ।
क्षेत्रं क्षेत्री तथा कृत्स्नं प्रकाशयति भारत ॥ १३-३३॥

yathā prakāśayaty ekaḥ kṛtsnaṃ lokam imaṃ raviḥ
kṣetraṃ kṣetrī tathā kṛtsnaṃ prakāśayati bhārata 13.33

Seated within all life forms is the one Supreme
Residing equally in all beings of the mortal realm
In a perishable frame, the indestructible dwells to be
Whoever can thus see, he is the one who can truly see.|27|

Witnessing the existence of the One Lord in all things
He perceives the supreme's play of forces in all beings
By the flames of passionate desire he is not injured
And for such a being, the supreme status is assured.|28|

It is *Prakriti-* who alone engages and enacts
In all the worlds working, she acts
But the Self remains inactive and silently foresees
Whoever sees this truth of the world, truly sees.|29|

When one realizes the unexpressed and latent eternal
Dwelling within the myriad forms- the one supernal
Because of whom all of existence sustains,
The gnosis of the *Brahman-* he verily attains.|30|

Immaculate and without any boundaries or ends
All of natures qualities, the supreme Self transcends.
O *Arjuna*, The Self is seated within the body unperturbed
And by occurrences of nature, He is not disturbed.|31|

Like the sky that stretches across all of space-
And its subtleness limits not its all pervading embrace
So too is the Self that in all life forms persists
Unaffected within the physical body, the Self exists|32|

O *Arjuna*, Just as the singular Sun's light
Is adequate to make the whole of the earth bright
So too is the Field illumined complete
With Knower of the Field's light, it is replete.|33|

क्षेत्रक्षेत्रज्ञयोरेवमन्तरं ज्ञानचक्षुषा ।

भूतप्रकृतिमोक्षं च ये विदुर्यान्ति ते परम् ॥ १३-३४॥

kṣetrakṣetrajñayor evam antaraṃ jñānacakṣuṣā
bhūtaprakṛtimokṣaṃ ca ye vidur yānti te param 13.34

With the inner eye of knowledge those who perceive
About the Field and its Knower they can conceive
And of the individuals' liberation from *Prakriti's* dominion
They attain with the Supreme- the complete
merger and union.|34|"

(Thus ended the thirteenth Canto of the Bhagavad Gita where Sri Krishna described to Arjuna the liberating knowledge of the Field, The Knower, The Purusha and Prakriti)

अथ चतुर्दशोऽध्यायः ।
atha caturdaśodhyāyaḥ

श्रीभगवानुवाच ।
परं भूयः प्रवक्ष्यामि ज्ञानानां ज्ञानमुत्तमम् ।
यज्ज्ञात्वा मुनयः सर्वे परां सिद्धिमितो गताः ॥ १४-१॥

śrībhagavān uvāca
param bhūyaḥ pravakṣyāmi jñānānāṃ jñānam uttamam
yaj jñātvā munayaḥ sarve parāṃ siddhim ito gatāḥ 14.1

इदं ज्ञानमुपाश्रित्य मम साधर्म्यमागताः ।
सर्गेऽपि नोपजायन्ते प्रलये न व्यथन्ति च ॥ १४-२॥

idaṃ jñānam upāśritya mama sādharmyam āgatāḥ
sargepi nopajāyante pralaye na vyathanti ca 14.2

मम योनिर्महद् ब्रह्म तस्मिन्गर्भं दधाम्यहम् ।
सम्भवः सर्वभूतानां ततो भवति भारत ॥ १४-३॥

mama yonir mahad brahma tasmin garbhaṃ dadhāmy aham
sambhavaḥ sarvabhūtānāṃ tato bhavati bhārata 14.3

सर्वयोनिषु कौन्तेय मूर्तयः सम्भवन्ति याः ।
तासां ब्रह्म महद्योनिरहं बीजप्रदः पिता ॥ १४-४॥

sarvayoniṣu kaunteya mūrtayaḥ sambhavanti yāḥ
tāsāṃ brahma mahad yonir ahaṃ bījapradaḥ pitā 14.4

सत्त्वं रजस्तम इति गुणाः प्रकृतिसम्भवाः ।
निबध्नन्ति महाबाहो देहे देहिनमव्ययम् ॥ १४-५॥

sattvaṃ rajas tama iti guṇāḥ prakṛtisambhavāḥ
nibadhnanti mahābāho dehe dehinam avyayam 14.5

Canto XIV: *<u>The Three modes of Nature:</u>*

(Verse 1,2,19,20,27: The paramount gnosis; 3-18: The triple qualities of material nature; 21-26: The Path of Ascent)

Lord Sri *Krishna* said:-
"Once more to you, I shall declare and lend
What is the peak of knowledge that man can ascend
This paramount gnosis that the liberated sages have reached
By which the boundaries of mortal perfection have been breached.|1|

By taking shelter in this knowledge, they have obtained
The highest wisdom which in My oneness- can be attained
No more are they reborn in the cycle of destruction and creation
Nor are they agitated or confused by the universal extinction.|2|

O Arjuna, The worldly creation is My womb vast
Within which the seed of life I infuse and cast
From which arise the beings of the mortal realm
For all the living creatures- I am the Creator supreme.|3|

For all the wombs in which the living are generated
O *Arjuna,* I am the womb wherein they are created
And all the life forms on earth, I have fathered
From My seed –all their life energies they have gathered.|4|

Rajas, Tamas, and *Sattwa* are the qualities procreated
Threefold in nature they have been created
O *Arjuna,* The immutable Self is by them bound
Governing the body and consciousness they are found.|5|

तत्र सत्त्वं निर्मलत्वात्प्रकाशकमनामयम् ।
सुखसङ्गेन बध्नाति ज्ञानसङ्गेन चानघ ॥ १४-६॥

tatra sattvaṃ nirmalatvāt prakāśakam anāmayam
sukhasaṅgena badhnāti jñānasa ṅgena cānagha 14.6

रजो रागात्मकं विद्धि तृष्णासङ्गसमुद्भवम् ।
तन्निबध्नाति कौन्तेय कर्मसङ्गेन देहिनम् ॥ १४-७॥

rajo rāgātmakaṃ viddhi tṛṣṇāsaṅgasamudbhavam
tan nibadhnāti kaunteya karmasaṅgena dehinam 14.7

तमस्त्वज्ञानजं विद्धि मोहनं सर्वदेहिनाम् ।
प्रमादालस्यनिद्राभिस्तन्निबध्नाति भारत ॥ १४-८॥

tamas tv ajñānajaṃ viddhi mohanaṃ sarvadehinām
pramādālasyanidrābhis tan nibadhnāti bhārata 14.8

सत्त्वं सुखे सञ्जयति रजः कर्मणि भारत ।
ज्ञानमावृत्य तु तमः प्रमादे सञ्जयत्युत ॥ १४-९॥

sattvaṃ sukhe saṃjayati rajaḥ karmaṇi bhārata
jñānam āvṛtya tu tamaḥ pramāde saṃjayaty uta 14.9

रजस्तमश्चाभिभूय सत्त्वं भवति भारत ।
रजः सत्त्वं तमश्चैव तमः सत्त्वं रजस्तथा ॥ १४-१०॥

rajas tamaś cābhibhūya sattvaṃ bhavati bhārata
rajaḥ sattvaṃ tamaś caiva tamaḥ sattvaṃ rajas tathā 14.10

सर्वद्वारेषु देहेऽस्मिन्प्रकाश उपजायते ।
ज्ञानं यदा तदा विद्याद्विवृद्धं सत्त्वमित्युत ॥ १४-११॥

sarvadvāreṣu dehesmin prakāśa upajāyate
jñānaṃ yadā tadā vidyād vivṛddhaṃ sattvam ity uta 14.11

लोभः प्रवृत्तिरारम्भः कर्मणामशमः स्पृहा ।
रजस्येतानि जायन्ते विवृद्धे भरतर्षभ ॥ १४-१२॥

lobhaḥ pravṛttir ārambhaḥ karmaṇām aśamaḥ spṛhā
rajasy etāni jāyante vivṛddhe bharatarṣabha 14.12

Sattwa is the quality that reflects in serenity,
Illumined by virtue and an immaculate purity.
This quality produces in man no disease or affliction,
O Arjuna! It expresses through happiness and knowledge's fas-
cination|6|

Rajas is that which ignites in one a passionate fire
A strong feeling of liking, longing and desire
O *Arjuna* it is borne out of a possession for things
Through attachment to works, it binds the *Self* in all beings|7|

But *Tamas* is the quality that creates a delusion
And traps all beings by ignorance's illusion
O *Arjuna*, the mortals are by it confounded
In laxity, laziness and sleep it is founded|8|

By happiness, nature- *Sattwa*- is bound
And by desires and actions- *Rajas* is ensnared found.
O *Arjuna*, But *Tamas* is attached to negligence
And its cloak of ignorance cages the intelligence |9|

O *Arjuna*, When the *Sattwa* qualities of nature lead
Overpowered, the *Rajas* and *Tamas* components recede
Rajas rises when *Sattwa* and *Tamas* are suppressed
And *Tamas* grows when *Rajas* and *Sattwa* are depressed.|10|

When the light barges open all the doors of the being
Its luminous knowledge brings forth the awakening
Know that whenever there is such an activation
The quality of *Sattwa* is leading in domination|11|

When the *Rajas* quality is in an increasing state
O *Arjuna*, the following tendencies begin to escalate:-
Greed and a restless desire to initiate action,
And the being seeks fruits with an impulsive passion|12|

अप्रकाशोऽप्रवृत्तिश्च प्रमादो मोह एव च ।
तमस्येतानि जायन्ते विवृद्धे कुरुनन्दन ॥ १४-१३॥

aprakāśopravṛttiś ca pramādo moha eva ca
tamasy etāni jāyante vivṛddhe kurunandana 14.13

यदा सत्त्वे प्रवृद्धे तु प्रलयं याति देहभृत् ।
तदोत्तमविदां लोकानमलान्प्रतिपद्यते ॥ १४-१४॥

yadā sattve pravṛddhe tu pralayaṃ yāti dehabhṛt
tadottamavidāṃ lokān amalān pratipadyate 14.14

रजसि प्रलयं गत्वा कर्मसङ्गिषु जायते ।
तथा प्रलीनस्तमसि मूढयोनिषु जायते ॥ १४-१५॥

rajasi pralayaṃ gatvā karmasaṅgiṣu jāyate
tathā pralīnas tamasi mūḍhayoniṣu jāyate 14.15

कर्मणः सुकृतस्याहुः सात्त्विकं निर्मलं फलम् ।
रजसस्तु फलं दुःखमज्ञानं तमसः फलम् ॥ १४-१६॥

karmaṇaḥ sukṛtasyāhuḥ sāttvikaṃ nirmalaṃ phalam
rajasas tu phalaṃ duḥkham ajñānaṃ tamasaḥ phalam 14.16

सत्त्वात्सञ्जायते ज्ञानं रजसो लोभ एव च ।
प्रमादमोहौ तमसो भवतोऽज्ञानमेव च ॥ १४-१७॥

sattvāt saṃjāyate jñānaṃ rajaso lobha eva ca
pramādamohau tamaso bhavatojñānam eva ca 14.17

ऊर्ध्वं गच्छन्ति सत्त्वस्था मध्ये तिष्ठन्ति राजसाः ।
जघन्यगुणवृत्तिस्था अधो गच्छन्ति तामसाः ॥ १४-१८॥

ūrdhvaṃ gacchanti sattvasthā madhye tiṣṭhanti rājasāḥ
jaghanyaguṇavṛttisthā adho gacchhanti tāmasāḥ 14.18

नान्यं गुणेभ्यः कर्तारं यदा द्रष्टानुपश्यति ।
गुणेभ्यश्च परं वेत्ति मद्भावं सोऽधिगच्छति ॥ १४-१९॥

nānyaṃ guṇebhyaḥ kartāraṃ yadā draṣṭānupaśyati
guṇebhyaś ca paraṃ vetti madbhāvaṃ sodhigacchhati 14.19

Darkness, delusion, and an ignorant negligence
And a futile indulgence in actions of impotence.
O *Arjuna*, Whenever *Tamas* is on the rise.
All these nature's deformities in that being arise|13|

At the final moments if *Sattwa* nature is in abundance
During the period of death, dissolution and ascendance,
The being reaches the realm that is most fortunate –
Where dwell the highest knowledgeable souls-immaculate.|14|

If *Rajas* abounds when the embodied being is passing away
The soul is born into the womb that seeks desire's way
And if *Tamas* is the dying soul's nature predominant
The being is reborn in the low womb of a being ignorant.|15|

When the works, are performed in *Sattwa's* light
The fruits are pure, as the mode of action is right
And works done in *Rajas's* state bring only pain
But Ignorance results of *Tamas's* actions vain|16|

From *Sattwa* alone true gnosis comes
While with *Rajas* the being only greedy becomes
But Tamas brings forth ignorance's illusion-
The negligent being dwells in a state of delusion|17|

The embodied ones in *Sattwa* upwards ascend
Those in *Rajas* remain in the middle but do not descend.
While the beings of *Tamas's* inertial negligence
In the soul's journey only sink in further decadence|18|

When the Divine being attains the realization
Of Natures threefold modular operation
And of the Supreme who is beyond nature
Towards Me he turns and attains My stature.|19|

गुणानेतानतीत्य त्रीन्देही देहसमुद्भवान् ।
जन्ममृत्युजरादुःखैर्विमुक्तोऽमृतमश्नुते ॥ १४-२० ॥
guṇān etān atītya trīn dehī dehasamudbhavān
janmamṛtyujarāduḥkhair vimuktomṛtam aśnute 14.20

अर्जुन उवाच ।
कैर्लिङ्गैस्त्रीन्गुणानेतानतीतो भवति प्रभो ।
किमाचारः कथं चैतांस्त्रीन्गुणानतिवर्त्तते ॥ १४-२१ ॥
arjuna uvāca
kair liṅgais trīn guṇān etān atīto bhavati prabho
kimācāraḥ katham caitāṃs trīn guṇān ativartate 14.21

श्रीभगवानुवाच ।
प्रकाशं च प्रवृत्तिं च मोहमेव च पाण्डव ।
न द्वेष्टि सम्प्रवृत्तानि न निवृत्तानि काङ्क्षति ॥ १४-२२ ॥
śrībhagavān uvāca
prakāśaṃ ca pravṛttiṃ ca moham eva ca pāṇḍava
ta dveṣṭi sampravṛttāni na nivṛttāni kāṅkṣati 14.22

उदासीनवदासीनो गुणैर्यो न विचाल्यते ।
गुणा वर्तन्त इत्येवं योऽवतिष्ठति नेङ्गते ॥ १४-२३ ॥
udāsīnavad āsīno guṇair yo na vicālyate
guṇā vartanta ity eva yovatiṣṭhati neṅgate 14.23

समदुःखसुखः स्वस्थः समलोष्टाश्मकाञ्चनः ।
तुल्यप्रियाप्रियो धीरस्तुल्यनिन्दात्मसंस्तुतिः ॥ १४-२४ ॥
samaduḥkhasukhaḥ svasthaḥ samaloṣṭāśmakāñcanaḥ
tulyapriyāpriyo dhīras tulyanindātmasaṃstutiḥ 14.24

मानापमानयोस्तुल्यस्तुल्यो मित्रारिपक्षयोः ।
सर्वारम्भपरित्यागी गुणातीतः स उच्यते ॥ १४-२५ ॥
mānāpamānayos tulyas tulyo mitrāripakṣayoḥ
sarvārambhaparityāgī guṇātītaḥ sa ucyate 14.25

Rising upwards the embodied soul is elevated
When from Nature's triple bondage, it is liberated
From birth, death, old age, and disease; the sufferings mortal
The soul is freed and attains to the immortal.|20|"

Arjuna asked:

"What are the signs that one can see?
And what are the actions of that soul free?
The triple natures, How does one ascend?
O Lord, Answers to these questions- please extend."|21|

Lord *Krishna* replied:

"O *Arjuna, Sattwa*'s enlightened mode of action,
Rajas's work impulsions and *Tamas*'s delusion-
He who neither detests nor shirks away
Nor desires these vehicles of nature in any way|22|

He who remains firm and witnesses quietly
Seated well above the triple modes-nonchalantly
Knowing all occurrences to be in sync with nature's way
Detached and immobile he observes the forces play|23|

Who dwells in the *Self,* poised and still
In both joy and sorrow- he remains tranquil
Stone, mud or gold-all as one he treats
Praise or blame, friends and foes-alike he greets|24|

To him honor and insult are just the same
The factions of foes and friends – another zero sum game
In all his work actions, his desire for initiating has ended
Mortal nature, such a being is said to have transcended.|25|

मां च योऽव्यभिचारेण भक्तियोगेन सेवते ।

स गुणान्समतीत्यैतान्ब्रह्मभूयाय कल्पते ॥ १४-२६॥

māṃ ca yovyabhicāreṇa bhaktiyogena sevate
sa guṇān samatītyaitān brahmabhūyāya kalpate 14.26

ब्रह्मणो हि प्रतिष्ठाहममृतस्याव्ययस्य च ।

शाश्वतस्य च धर्मस्य सुखस्यैकान्तिकस्य च ॥ १४-२७॥

brahmaṇo hi pratiṣṭhāham amṛtasyāvyayasya ca
śāśvatasya ca dharmasya sukhasyaikāntikasya ca 14.27

He who loves and yearns for Me with his heart
He whose devotion for Me has no end or start
Nature's triple modes, he can easily breach
And the supreme state he is said to be ready to reach.|26|

Because I am the eternal foundation-
The imperishable and immortal Lord of the creation
The timeless code of Man, I verily uphold
I am the highest bliss that a mortal can behold |27|"

(Thus ended the fourteenth Canto of the Bhagavad Gita where Sri Krishna described to Arjuna the modes and functionings of the triples natures-Rajas, Tamas and Sattwa)

❋ ❋ ❋

अथ पञ्चदशोऽध्यायः ।

atha pañcadaśodhyāyaḥ

श्रीभगवानुवाचा।

ऊर्ध्वमूलमधःशाखमश्वत्थं प्राहुरव्ययम्।

छन्दांसि यस्य पर्णानि यस्तं वेद स वेदवित्॥१५-१॥

śrībhagavānuvāca
ūrdhvamūlamadhaḥ śākhamaśvattham prāhuravyam
chandāmsi yasya parṇāni yastam veda sa vedavit 15.1

अधश्चोर्ध्वं प्रसृतास्तस्य शाखा गुणप्रवृद्धा विषयप्रवालाः।

अधश्च मूलान्यनुसन्ततानि कर्मानुबन्धीनि मनुष्यलोके॥१५-२॥

adhaścordhvam prasṛtāstasya śākhā guṇapravṛddhā
viṣayapravālāḥ adhaśca mūlānyanusamtatāni karmānubandhīni
manuṣyaloke 15.2

न रूपमस्येह तथोपलभ्यते नान्तो न चादिर्न च सम्प्रतिष्ठा।

अश्वत्थमेनं सुविरूढमूलं असङ्गशस्त्रेण दृढेन छित्त्वा॥१५-३॥

na rūpamasyeha tathopalabhyate nānto na cādirna ca sampratiṣṭhā
aśvatthamenam suvirūḍhamūlam asaṅgaśastreṇa dṛḍhenachittvā
15.3

ततः पदं तत्परिमार्गितव्यं यस्मिन्गता न निवर्तन्ति भूयः।

तमेव चाद्यं पुरुषं प्रपद्ये यतः प्रवृत्तिः प्रसृता पुराणी॥१५-४॥

tataḥ padam tatparimārgitavyam yasmingatā na nivartanti bhūyaḥ
tameva cādyam puruṣam prapadye yataḥ pravṛttiḥ prasṛtā purāṇī
15.4

निर्मानमोहा जितसङ्गदोषा अध्यात्मनित्या विनिवृत्तकामाः।

द्वन्द्वैर्विमुक्ताः सुखदुःखसंज्ञैर्गच्छन्त्यमूढाः पदमव्ययं तत्॥१५-५॥

nirmānamohā jitasaṅgadoṣā adhyātmanityā vinivṛttakāmāḥ
dvandvairvimuktāḥ sukhaduḥkhasamjñaiḥ gacchanty amūḍhāḥ
padamavyayam tat 15.5

Canto XV: *The Eternal Supernal*

(Verse 1-3: Ashwattha- the Tree of life; 4- 6: *Krishna* speaks of the destination that is the origin; 7-20: The etiology of the Divine)

Lord Krishna spoke:

"From its roots above, seeded in eternity
And branching below, is the ethereal *Ashwattha* tree
The many hymns of the *Vedas* are but its leaves
He who knows this, the essence of *Vedas* he perceives.|1|

Above and below, the cosmic tree's branches extend
In the material and supra-physical planes they portend
Raised by nature's qualities and their derivative senses,
Roots of bonded actions into the mortal world it dispenses|2|

This inverted *Ashwattha*'s form on earth is inconceivable
Neither beginning nor end nor foundation is perceivable
With the sharpest saber of detachment alone can one sever
And escape from its roots that entangle the being forever.|3|

Yearn for the one destination that is the goal supreme
From where you return not once more to the mortal realm
Seek refuge in the ancient timeless eternal-
The beginning of every action-the source original.|4|

Bereft of pride and delusion, with a desire-less detachment
Embedded in the *Self*, by conquering the fault of attachment
Having surpassed the dualities of joy and sorrow for good
The enlightened ones progress towards
the status of Godhood.|5|

न तद्भासयते सूर्यो न शशाङ्को न पावकः।
यद्गत्वा न निवर्तन्ते तद्धाम परमं मम॥१५-६॥

na tad bhāsayatesūryonaśaśāṅkonapāvakaḥ
yadgatvānanivartante tad dhāmaparamaṁ mama 15.6

ममैवांशो जीवलोके जीवभूतः सनातनः।
मनःषष्ठानीन्द्रियाणि प्रकृतिस्थानि कर्षति॥१५-७॥

mamaivāṁśo jīvaloke jīvabhūtaḥ sanātanaḥ
manaḥsasthānīndriyāṇi prakṛtisthāni karṣati 15.7

शरीरं यदवाप्नोति यच्चाप्युत्क्रामतीश्वरः।
गृहीत्वैतानि संयाति वायुर्गन्धानिवाशयात्॥१५-८॥

śarīraṁ yadavāpnoti yaccāpyutkrāmatīśvaraḥ
gṛhitvaitāni saṁyāti vāyurgandhānivāśayāt 15.8

श्रोत्रं चक्षुः स्पर्शनं च रसनं घ्राणमेव च।
अधिष्ठाय मनश्चायं विषयानुपसेवते॥१५-९॥

śrotraṁ cakṣuḥ sparśanaṁ ca rasanaṁ ghrāṇameva ca
adhiṣṭhāya manaścāyaṁ viṣayānupasevate 15.9

उत्क्रामन्तं स्थितं वापि भुञ्जानं वा गुणान्वितम्।
विमूढा नानुपश्यन्ति पश्यन्ति ज्ञानचक्षुषः॥१५-१०॥

utkrāmantaṁ sthitaṁ vāpi bhuñjānaṁ vā guṇānvitam
vimūḍhā nānupaśyanti paśyanti jñānacakṣuṣaḥ 15.10

यतन्तो योगिनश्चैनं पश्यन्त्यात्मन्यवस्थितम्।
यतन्तोऽप्यकृतात्मानो नैनं पश्यन्त्यचेतसः॥१५-११॥

yatanto yoginaścainaṁ paśyantyātmanyavasthitam
yatantopyakṛtātmāno nainaṁ paśyantyacetasaḥ 15.11

यदादित्यगतं तेजो जगद्भासयतेऽखिलम्।
यच्चन्द्रमसि यच्चाग्नौ तत्तेजो विद्धि मामकम्॥१५-१२॥

yadādityagataṁ tejo jagadbhāsayatekhilam
yaccandramasi yaccāgnau tattejo viddhi māmakam 15.12

For it is there, the timeless resplendent One comes to their sight
Whose radiance is beyond the fire, the moon or the sun's light
They return not after having journeyed the distance
For they reach the zenith of the status of My existence.|6|

All the bodies of the living manifest only from Mine
For their soul is but a quantum of my energies Divine
As a portion of Me in nature begins to dwell
And powers their mind and the five senses as well|7|

When the Divine assumes the body mortal
For the entry of the six senses he creates the portal
And while leaving the body he takes them away
Like the fragrances dispersed by the wind on its way|8|

Eyesight, touch, taste, smell and hearing
And the mind is utilized by the soul indwelling
All the objects of the mind and senses He embellishes
And their sensations He enjoys and relishes|9|

But the deluded understand not His coming or going
Nor do they perceive within themselves His staying
They know not that for all qualities He is the enjoyer
As this realization comes only to the eye of the knower.|10|

The indwelling Self they recognize and observe
And so the *yogis* and the saints strive to know and serve
But to the ignorant, this truth is not known
For beyond the material they have never really grown|11|

For the entire cosmos it I who am the light
Illumining the creation, I set the world alight
The sun, the moon and the fire – I verily ignite
Know all that is radiant to be only My might.|12|

गामाविश्य च भूतानि धारयाम्यहमोजसा।
पुष्णामि चौषधीः सर्वाः सोमो भूत्वा रसात्मकः॥१५-१३॥

gāmāviśya cabhūtāni dhārayāmyahamojasā
puṣṇāmi cauṣadhīḥ sarvāḥ somo bhūtvā rasātmakaḥ 15.13

अहं वैश्वानरो भूत्वा प्राणिनां देहमाश्रितः।
प्राणापानसमायुक्तः पचाम्यन्नं चतुर्विधम्॥१५-१४॥

aham vaiśvānaro bhūtvā prāṇinām dehamāśritaḥ
prāṇāpānasamāyuktaḥ pacāmyannam caturvidham 15.14

सर्वस्य चाहं हृदि सन्निविष्टो मत्तः स्मृतिर्ज्ञानमपोहनञ्च।
वेदैश्च सर्वैरहमेव वेद्यो वेदान्त कृद्वेदविदेव चाहम्॥१५-१५॥

sarvasya cāham hṛdi samniviṣṭo mattaḥ smṛtirjñānamapohanamca
vedaiśca sarvairahameva vedyo vedānta kṛdvedavideva cāham
15.15

द्वाविमौ पुरुषौ लोके क्षरश्चाक्षर एव च।
क्षरः सर्वाणि भूतानि कूटस्थोऽक्षर उच्यते॥१५-१६॥

dvāvimau puruṣau loke kṣaraścākṣara eva ca
kṣaraḥ sarvāṇi bhūtāni kūṭasthokṣara ucyate 15.16

उत्तमः पुरुषस्त्वन्यः परमात्मेत्युदाहृतः।
यो लोकत्रयमाविश्य बिभर्त्यव्यय ईश्वरः॥१५-१७॥

uttamaḥ puruṣastvanyaḥ paramātmetyudāhṛtaḥ
yo lokatrayamāviśya bibhartyavyaya īśvaraḥ 15.17

यस्मात्क्षरमतीतोऽहमक्षरादपि चोत्तमः।
अतोऽस्मि लोके वेदे च प्रथितः पुरुषोत्तमः॥१५-१८॥

yasmāt kṣaramatītoḥ ahamakṣarādapi cottamaḥ
atosmi loke vede ca prathitaḥ puruṣottamaḥ 15.18

यो मामेवमसम्मूढो जानाति पुरुषोत्तमम्।
स सर्वविद्भजति मां सर्वभावेन भारत॥१५-१९॥

yo māmevamasammūḍho jānāti puruṣottamam
sa sarvavidbhajati mām sarvabhāvena bhārata 15.19

Onto the earth I have descended
And into the material, My spirit has thus extended
Know me to be *Soma*- the immortal lord
And My ambrosia- to the medicines and living I accord.|13|

Life's fire I have instilled and sustained
By which the physical body of every being is maintained
Controlling the inhalation and exhalation of the life energy
The four types of foods, I verily digest in synergy.|14|

In every heart that beats, I verily reside
Over every being's memory and knowledge I preside
I am known by the *Vedas* and am also their knower
And for the gnostic texts-*Vedantas* I am the creator|15|

In the universe, there are two forms of manifestation
One indestructible, while the other attains destruction
In all the living things- is found the form destructible
But seated high above them all is the form imperishable|16|

Apart from these two is the spirit highest
Of all manifestations it is considered greatest
Entering existence this supreme *Self* latent exists
All three worlds, this being Divine uplifts.|17|

As I am beyond the manifestations perishable,
Transcendent and surpassing even the imperishable
The *Vedas* and the world together proclaim-
'I am the Supreme *Self*' they exclaim.|18|

My gnosis complete, he who has attained
Myself-as the Supreme *Self*, he who has ordained-
He loves Me with everything he has in every way
As per his own nature he adores Me every day.|19|

इति गुह्यतमं शास्त्रमिदमुक्तं मयानघ।
एतद्बुद्ध्वा बुद्धिमान्स्यात्कृतकृत्यश्च भारत॥१५-२०॥

iti guhyatamaṃ śāstramidamuktaṃ mayānagha
etatbuddhvā buddhimānsyātkṛtakṛtyaśca bhārata 15.20

The cryptic wisdom, thus I have declared
To you, O *Arjuna*, I have unveiled and shared
This occult secret, by knowing and understanding
One attains the highest enlightenment possible to the living.|20|"

(Thus ended the fifteenth Canto of the Bhagavad Gita where Sri Krishna described to Arjuna the supreme wisdom of the eternal supernal Divine)

❇ ❇ ❇

अथषोडशोऽध्यायः ।

athaṣoḍaśodhyāyaḥ

श्रीभगवानुवाच ।

अभयं सत्त्वसंशुद्धिर्ज्ञानयोगव्यवस्थितिः ।

दानं दमश्च यज्ञश्च स्वाध्यायस्तप आर्जवम् ॥ १६-१॥

śrībhagavānuvāca
abhayaṃ sattvasaṃśuddhirjñānayogavyavasthitiḥ
dānaṃ damaśca yajñaśca svādhyāyas tapa ārjavam 16.1

अहिंसा सत्यमक्रोधस्त्यागः शान्तिरपैशुनम् ।

दया भूतेष्वलोलुप्त्वं मार्दवं ह्रीरचापलम् ॥१६-२॥

ahiṃsā satyamakrodhastyāgaḥ śāntirapaiśunam
dayā bhūteṣvaloluptvam mārdavam hrīr acāpalam 16.2

तेजः क्षमा धृतिः शौचमद्रोहो नातिमानिता ।

भवन्ति सम्पदं दैवीमभिजातस्य भारत ॥१६-३॥

tejaḥ kṣamā dhṛtiḥ śaucamadroho nātimānitā
bhavanti sampadam daivīmabhijātasya bhārata 16.3

दम्भो दर्पोऽभिमानश्च क्रोधः पारुष्यमेव च ।

अज्ञानं चाभिजातस्य पार्थ सम्पदमासुरीम् ॥१६-४॥

dambho darpobhimānaśca krodhaḥ pāruṣyameva ca
ajñānaṃ cābhijātasya pārtha sampadamāsurīm 16.4

दैवी सम्पद्विमोक्षाय निबन्धायासुरी मता ।

मा शुचः सम्पदं दैवीमभिजातोऽसि पाण्डव ॥१६-५॥

daivī sampadvimokṣāya nibandhāyāsurī matā
mā śucah sampadam daivīmabhijātosi pāṇḍava 16.5

द्वौ भूतसर्गौ लोकेऽस्मिन्दैव आसुर एव च ।

दैवो विस्तरशः प्रोक्त आसुरं पार्थ मे शृणु ॥१६-६॥

dvau bhūtasargau lokesmindaiva āsura eva ca
daivo vistaraśaḥ prokta āsuraṃ pārtha me śṛṇu 16.6

Canto XVI: *<u>The Divine and the Demoniac</u>*

(Verse 1-3,5,6,22: The Divine Nature and consequences; 4, 7-23: The Demoniac Nature and consequences; 24- *Krishna*'s instruction to choose the right nature)

Lord Krishna spoke:
"Fearlessly persevering for the inner purification
And engaging in the *Yoga* of knowledge with dedication
Holding all the senses in control and by selflessly giving
Engaging in sacrifice, askesis and scriptural reading|1|

Bereft of anger, practicing non-violence and truthfulness
Self giving, absence of fault-finding and peacefulness
Devoid of greed and holding a global compassion
Modesty, tenderness and an unswerving determination.|2|

Radiating purity, showing forgiveness and valiance
Not having envy or pride and holding a poised balance
O *Arjuna*, these qualities encompass the treasure
Inherited by those born with the Divine nature.|3|

Egoism, false pride and a deceitful arrogance
Anger, harshness and the vice of ignorance
O *Arjuna* these are the qualities that define
Those born with the demoniac nature-undivine.|4|

By these qualities Divine, liberation one can gain
But demoniac-nature ties one to bondage's chain
O *Arjuna*, Be not under any duress
It is the Divine qualities that you possess.|5|

O *Arjuna*, All the living creatures
Belong to one of these two natures
The Divine–I have just surmised and extolled
The demoniac- I will now state for you to behold.|6|

प्रवृत्तिं च निवृत्तिं च जना न विदुरासुराः ।
न शौचं नापि चाचारो न सत्यं तेषु विद्यते ॥१६-७॥

pravṛttiṃ ca nivṛttiṃ ca janā na vidurāsurāḥ
na śaucaṃ nāpi cācāro na satyaṃ teṣu vidyate 16.7

असत्यमप्रतिष्ठं ते जगदाहुरनीश्वरम् ।
अपरस्परसम्भूतं किमन्यत्कामहैतुकम् ॥१६-८॥

asatyamapratiṣṭhaṃ te jagadāhuranīśvaram
aparasparasambhūtaṃ kimanyatkāmahaitukam 16.8

एतां दृष्टिमवष्टभ्य नष्टात्मानोऽल्पबुद्धयः ।
प्रभवन्त्युग्रकर्माणः क्षयाय जगतोऽहिताः ॥१६-९॥

etāṃ dṛṣṭimavaṣṭabhya naṣṭātmānolpabuddhayaḥ
prabhavantyugrakarmāṇaḥ kṣayāya jagatohitāḥ 16.9

काममाश्रित्य दुष्पूरं दम्भमानमदान्विताः ।
मोहाद्गृहीत्वासद्ग्राहान्प्रवर्तन्तेऽशुचिव्रताः ॥१६-१०॥

kāmamāśritya duṣpūraṃ dambhamānamadānvitāḥ
mohādgṛhītvāsadgrāhānpravartanteśucivratāḥ 16.10

चिन्तामपरिमेयां च प्रलयान्तामुपाश्रिताः ।
कामोपभोगपरमा एतावदिति निश्चिताः ॥१६-११॥

cintāmaparimeyāṃ ca pralayāntāmupāśritāḥ
kāmopabhogaparamā etāvaditi niścitāḥ 16.11

आशापाशशतैर्बद्धाः कामक्रोधपरायणाः ।
ईहन्ते कामभोगार्थमन्यायेनार्थसञ्चयान् ॥१६-१२॥

āśāpāśaśatairbaddhāḥ kāmakrodhaparāyaṇāḥ
īhante kāmabhogārthamanyāyenārthasaṃcayān 16.12

इदमद्य मया लब्धमिमं प्राप्स्ये मनोरथम् ।
इदमस्तीदमपि मे भविष्यति पुनर्धनम् ॥१६-१३॥

idamadya mayā labdhamima mprāpsye manoratham
idamastīdamapi me bhaviṣyati punardhanam 16.13

The demoniac beings are ignorant of the right action
Devoid of knowledge and unaware of the path of abstention
There exists no truth in any of these beings
Nor is faithfulness observed in their dealings.|7|

"There is No God"- they jubilantly proclaim
"There is no truth in this world"- so they claim
The origins of the world they dismiss as mere chance
"Only desire is its sole foundation"-Thus is their stance.|8|

And by this falsehood alone, all life they perceive
With their minds polluted, their souls they deceive-
Becoming playthings of the demoniac forces of damnation
With violence and injury they perpetuate only destruction|9|

With arrogance and a lust that is never quenched
Their devious minds in egos are drenched
A philosophy of ignorance fuels their desires
And to grab power, their mind incessantly conspires.|10|

Believing astutely in the pseudo-bliss of unconsciousness
Enjoyment and desire is their only source of happiness.
They are incessantly plagued by worries indefinite
Until their ends, they are consumed by thoughts infinite|11|

By a hundred bonds of desire, they are bound
For inside them a reign of anger and lust is found
They only yearn for material wealth to accumulate
A mountain of possessions they seek to cumulate.|12|

They think- "Today so much I have gained,
But tomorrow so much more has to be obtained
So much wealth, I possess with me now
But tomorrow, I need to amass more somehow.|13|

असौ मया हतः शत्रुर्हनिष्ये चापरानपि ।
ईश्वरोऽहमहं भोगी सिद्धोऽहं बलवान्सुखी ॥१६-१४॥

asau mayāhataḥśatrurhaniṣyecāparānapi
īśvaro.ahamahaṃbhogīsiddhohambalavānsukhī 16.14

आढ्योऽभिजनवानस्मि कोऽन्योऽस्ति सदृशो मया ।
यक्ष्ये दास्यामि मोदिष्य इत्यज्ञानविमोहिताः ॥१६-१५॥

āḍhyobhijanavānasmi konyosti sadṛśo mayā
yakṣye dāsyāmi modiṣya ityajñānavimohitāḥ 16.15

अनेकचित्तविभ्रान्ता मोहजालसमावृताः ।
प्रसक्ताः कामभोगेषु पतन्ति नरकेऽशुचौ ॥१६-१६॥

anekacittavibhrāntā mohajālasamāvṛtāḥ
prasaktāḥ kāmabhogeṣu patanti narakeśucau 16.16

आत्मसम्भाविताः स्तब्धा धनमानमदान्विताः ।
यजन्ते नामयज्ञैस्ते दम्भेनाविधिपूर्वकम् ॥१६-१७॥

ātmasambhāvitāḥ stabdhā dhanamānamadānvitāḥ
yajante nāmayajñaiste dambhenāvidhipūrvakam 16.17

अहङ्कारं बलं दर्पं कामं क्रोधं च संश्रिताः ।
मामात्मपरदेहेषु प्रद्विषन्तोऽभ्यसूयकाः ॥१६-१८॥

ahaṃkāraṃ balaṃ darpaṃ kāmaṃ krodhaṃ ca saṃśritāḥ
māmātmaparadeheṣu pradviṣantobhyasūyakāḥ 16.18

तानहं द्विषतः क्रुरान्संसारेषु नराधमान् ।
क्षिपाम्यजस्रमशुभानासुरीष्वेव योनिषु ॥१६-१९॥

tānahaṃ dviṣataḥ krurānsaṃsāreṣu narādhamān
kṣipāmyajasramaśubhānāsurīṣveva yoniṣu 16.19

आसुरीं योनिमापन्ना मूढा जन्मनि जन्मनि ।
मामप्राप्यैव कौन्तेय ततो यान्त्यधमां गतिम् ॥१६-२०॥

āsurīṃ yonimāpannā mūḍhā janmani janmani
māmaprāpyaiva kaunteya tato yāntyadhamāṃ gatim 16.20

One enemy of mine I have thus exterminated
Soon I will have all of them annihilated
For I am the most supreme amongst men powerful
Enjoyer of desires- Invincible and successful.|14|

I am wealthy and from a family of the rich I hail
In comparison to me, everyone looks poor and pale
I perform sacrifice, I do so much charity
I am the real enjoyer"- thus is their narrow mentality|15|

Their minds which are in many ways deluded
In craving's trap they are ever confounded
Ever restless by their endless desire
They ultimately end in lust's hellish fire.|16|

Even sacrifice they perform with narcissism
Obsessed with wealth in a state of egotism
All their offerings are just namesake
As their vanity they never forsake.|17|

With egoism in their strength, a bloated arrogance
And minds consumed by desire, anger and ignorance
They deride the God, that in all living beings, resides
And also the God that within themselves, presides|18|

These beings to whom both good and God are detestable
Are the vilest of creatures- inhuman and despicable
These beings I send into the lowest wombs of earth
Repeatedly they suffer the pangs of a demoniac birth.|19|

Ever so deluded are those creatures
That are consumed in their own selfish natures
For birth after birth they find Me not
And they sink to the lowest of statures that can be got.|20|

त्रिविधं नरकस्येदं द्वारं नाशनमात्मनः ।
कामः क्रोधस्तथा लोभस्तस्मादेतत्त्रयं त्यजेत् ॥१६-२१॥

trividhaṃ narakasyedam dvāraṃ nāśanamātmanaḥ
kāmaḥ krodhastathā lobhastasmādetattrayaṃ tyajet 16.21

एतैर्विमुक्तः कौन्तेय तमोद्वारैस्त्रिभिर्नरः ।
आचरत्यात्मनः श्रेयस्ततो याति परां गतिम् ॥१६-२२॥

etairvimuktaḥ kaunteya tamodvāraistribhirnaraḥ
ācaratyātmanaḥ śreyastato yāti parāṃ gatim 16.22

यः शास्त्रविधिमुत्सृज्य वर्तते कामकारतः ।
न स सिद्धिमवाप्नोति न सुखं न परां गतिम् ॥१६-२३॥

yaḥ śāstravidhimutsṛjya vartate kāmakārataḥ
na sa siddhimavāpnoti na sukhaṃ na parāṃ gatim 16.23

तस्माच्छास्त्रं प्रमाणं ते कार्याकार्यव्यवस्थितौ ।
ज्ञात्वा शास्त्रविधानोक्तं कर्म कर्तुमिहार्हसि ॥१६-२४॥

tasmācchāstraṃ pramāṇaṃ te kāryākāryavyavasthitau
jñātvā śāstravidhānoktaṃ karma kartumihārhasi 16.24

Threefold too are the gates of darkness and destruction
That sentence a being into Hell's damnation
Desire, rage, and lust are the accursed three
By renouncing them only can man be free.|21|

O *Arjuna*, liberated from the doors of darkness
Man can attain a union in My oneness
For then he can journey on his own alone
Reaching the highest status of the soul that is known|22|

But he who disregards these rules mandatory
That the golden scriptures deem necessary
Follows his desires and reaches the sorry plight
Of imperfection and sorrow that comes in absence of light|23|

Therefore, Let the scriptures be your guide
And by their truths may you always abide
By understanding them, follow their declaration
In all works and actions, bring forth your emancipation.|24|"

(Thus ended the sixteenth Canto of the Bhagavad Gita where Sri Krishna explained the divine and the demoniac natures to Arjuna)

❈ ❈ ❈

अथ सप्तदशोऽध्यायः ।

atha saptadaśodhyāyaḥ

अर्जुन उवाच ।
ये शास्त्रविधिमुत्सृज्य यजन्ते श्रद्धयान्विताः ।
तेषां निष्ठा तु का कृष्ण सत्त्वमाहो रजस्तमः ॥१७-१॥

arjuna uvāca
ye śāstravidhimutsṛjya yajante śraddhayānvitāḥ
teṣāṃ niṣṭhā tu kā kṛṣṇa sattvamāho rajastamaḥ 17.1

श्रीभगवानुवाच।
त्रिविधा भवति श्रद्धा देहिनां सा स्वभावजा ।
सात्त्विकी राजसी चैव तामसी चेति तां शृणु ॥१७-२॥

śrībhagavānuvāca
trividhā bhavati śraddhā dehināṃ sā svabhāvajā
sāttvikī rājasī caiva tāmasī ceti tāṃ śṛṇu 17.2

सत्त्वानुरूपा सर्वस्य श्रद्धा भवति भारत ।
श्रद्धामयोऽयं पुरुषो यो यच्छ्रद्धः स एव सः ॥१७-३॥

sattvānurūpā sarvasya śraddhā bhavati bhārata
śraddhāmayoyaṃ puruṣo yo yacchraddhaḥ sa eva saḥ17.3

यजन्ते सात्त्विका देवान्यक्षरक्षांसि राजसाः ।
प्रेतान्भूतगणांश्चान्ये यजन्ते तामसा जनाः ॥१७-४॥

yajante sāttvikā devānyakṣarakṣāṃsi rājasāḥ
pretānbhūtagaṇānñścānye yajante tāmasā janāḥ 17.4

Canto XVII: *Faith and the Triple Formulae in Nature*

(Verse 1: *Arjuna*'s query; 2-4, 7: *Krishna* speaks of Faith and the triplicate Natures; 5- 6: The signs of perverse egoism; 8,11,14-20: Sattwa- the Nature of goodness; 9,12,18,21: Rajas- the Nature of impulsiveness; 10,13,19,22: Tamas- the Nature of delusion; 23- 27: Om tat Sat- the triple mantra; 28: Asat- falsehood)

Arjuna asked:
"*O Krishna*, What about those who follow not the scripture
And yet perform sacrifices with a faith of the highest stature
What is the underlying nature of their devotion?
Which of the three-*Sattwa, Rajas* or *Tamas*- is their action?|1|"

Sri *Krishna* replied:
"A triple combination of the natures, it may be told
Listen for I shall verily explain their faith-three fold
Whichever of the three qualities is dominant
In that being, that nature of faith is predominant.|2|

O *Arjuna*, The faith in every being is distinct-
Depending purely on the soul's natural instinct
Made up of faith is the inner embodiment living
However his faith is, that way is the being.|3|

The men of *Sattwa* offer their oblations to the Gods
Those of *Rajas* to the brute beings and wealthy demigods
The beings of *Tamas* to the restless spirits offer their prayers
And to the deceased beings roaming in the subtle layers |4|

अशास्त्रविहितं घोरं तप्यन्ते ये तपो जनाः ।
दम्भाहङ्कारसंयुक्ताः कामरागबलान्विताः ॥१७-५॥

aśāstravihitaṃ ghoram tapyante ye tapo janāḥ
dambhāhaṃkārasaṃyuktāḥ kāmarāgabalānvitāḥ 17.5

कर्षयन्तः शरीरस्थं भूतग्राममचेतसः ।
मां चैवान्तःशरीरस्थं तान्विद्ध्यासुरनिश्चयान् ॥१७-६॥

karṣayantaḥ śarīrasthaṃ bhūtagrāmamacetasaḥ
māṃ caivāntaḥ śarīrasthaṃ tānviddhyāsuraniścayān17.6

आहारस्त्वपि सर्वस्य त्रिविधो भवति प्रियः ।
यज्ञस्तपस्तथा दानं तेषां भेदमिमं शृणु ॥१७-७॥

āhārastvapi sarvasyatrividho bhavati priyaḥ
yajñastapastathā dānaṃ teṣāṃ bhedamimaṃ śṛṇu17.7

आयुः सत्त्वबलारोग्यसुखप्रीतिविवर्धनाः ।
रस्याः स्निग्धाः स्थिरा हृद्या आहाराः सात्त्विकप्रियाः ॥१७-८॥

āyuḥ sattvabalārogyasukhaprītivivardhanāḥ
rasyāḥ snigdhāḥ sthirā hṛdyā āhārāḥ sāttvikapriyāḥ17.8

कट्वम्ललवणात्युष्णतीक्ष्णरूक्षविदाहिनः ।
आहारा राजसस्येष्टा दुःखशोकामयप्रदाः ॥१७-९॥

kaṭvamlalavaṇātyuṣṇatīkṣṇarūkṣavidāhinaḥ
āhārā rājasasyeṣṭā duḥkhaśokāmayapradāḥ 17.9

यातयामं गतरसं पूति पर्युषितं च यत् ।
उच्छिष्टमपि चामेध्यं भोजनं तामसप्रियम् ॥१७-१०॥

yātayāmaṃ gatarasaṃ pūti paryuṣitaṃ ca yat
ucchiṣṭamapi cāmedhyaṃ bhojanaṃ tāmasapriyam17.10

अफलाङ्क्षिभिर्यज्ञो विधिदृष्टो य इज्यते ।
यष्टव्यमेवेति मनः समाधाय स सात्त्विकः ॥१७-११॥

aphalāṅkṣibhiryajño vidhidṛṣṭo ya ijyate
yaṣṭavyameveti manaḥ samādhāya sa sāttvikaḥ 17.11

Against the teachings of the scriptures-celestial,
They perform the austerities-violent and bestial
Powered by their egos and propelled by arrogance
With restless desires, they pride themselves in ignorance.|5|

They torment and torture their physical components
Subjecting their bodies to the extreme elements
The crude minds also discomfort the Me seated within
Understand such beings to be demoniac creatures of sin.|6|

Even the foods that are consumed by every creature
Depending on liking are threefold in nature
So too is sacrifice, austerity and charity
Listen to me for I shall explain with clarity.|7|

The men of *Sattwa* prefer the following food-
To them all that nourishes and prolongs their life is good.
A succulent, smooth and firm diet they choose to adhere,
For to their mind and bodies, this type of food is most dear.|8|

The men of *Rajas* very much enjoy consuming
All that is bitter, sour, salty, hot, dry and dehydrating
Borne of anxiety and worry they are affected by ailments
And their health is affected by their temperaments.|9|

The men of *Tamas* derive a pleasure perverted
In consuming food that is cold, stale and rotted
Foods that are foul, tasteless and even decomposing sour
Like animals, even leftovers they choose to devour.|10|

When the sacrifice is performed to
the deities and Divine lords,
Without seeking any personal gains or rewards,
Concentrating and being focused as per scripture
And bereft of desire, it is said to be of *Sattwa* nature.|11|

अभिसन्धाय तु फलं दम्भार्थमपि चैव यत् ।
इज्यते भरतश्रेष्ठ तं यज्ञं विद्धि राजसम् ॥१७-१२॥

abhisaṃdhāya tu phalaṃ dambhārthamapi caiva yat
ijyate bharataśreṣṭha taṃ yajñaṃ viddhi rājasam 17.12

विधिहीनमसृष्टान्नं मन्त्रहीनमदक्षिणम् ।
श्रद्धाविरहितं यज्ञं तामसं परिचक्षते ॥१७-१३॥

vidhihīnamasṛṣṭānnaṃ mantrahīnamadakṣiṇam
śraddhāvirahitaṃ yajñaṃ tāmasaṃ paricakṣate 17.13

देवद्विजगुरुप्राज्ञपूजनं शौचमार्जवम् ।
ब्रह्मचर्यमहिंसा च शारीरं तप उच्यते ॥१७-१४॥

devadvijaguruprājñapūjanaṃ śaucamārjavam
brahmacaryamahiṃsā ca śārīraṃ tapa ucyate 17.14

अनुद्वेगकरं वाक्यं सत्यं प्रियहितं च यत् ।
स्वाध्यायाभ्यसनं चैव वाङ्मयं तप उच्यते ॥१७-१५॥

anudvegakaraṃ vākyaṃ satyaṃ priyahitaṃ ca yat
svādhyāyābhyasanaṃ caiva vāṅmayaṃ tapa ucyate 17.15

मनः प्रसादः सौम्यत्वं मौनमात्मविनिग्रहः ।
भावसंशुद्धिरित्येतत्तपो मानसमुच्यते ॥१७-१६॥

manaḥ prasādaḥ saumyatvaṃ maunamātmavinigrahaḥ
bhāvasaṃśuddhirityetattapo mānasamucyate 17.16

श्रद्धया परया तप्तं तपस्तत्त्रिविधं नरैः ।
अफलाकाङ्क्षिभिर्युक्तैः सात्त्विकं परिचक्षते ॥१७-१७॥

Śraddhayā parayā taptaṃ tapastattrividhaṃ naraiḥ
aphalākāṅkṣibhiryuktaiḥ sāttvikaṃ paricakṣate 17.17

सत्कारमानपूजार्थं तपो दम्भेन चैव यत् ।
क्रियते तदिह प्रोक्तं राजसं चलमध्रुवम् ॥१७-१८॥

satkāramānapūjārthaṃ tapo dambhena caiva yat
kriyate tadiha proktaṃ rājasaṃ calamadhruvam17.18

But those sacrifices that are performed with desires
O, *Arjuna*, when for material benefits when one aspires
Accompanied by a flagrant exhibition and hype
Know such sacrifices to be of the *Rajas* type.|12|

The sacrifices performed against the scripture
Without following any proper procedure
Devoid of faith, *mantras*, offerings of food or charity
Such a sacrifice is said to be *Tamas* in quality|13|

Worshipping the Godhead, the spiritual master
The man of wisdom, the immaculate, the *Brahma*'s seeker
The liberated, the non-violent and the celibate
All as a way of bodily penance, one can postulate|14|

Uttering words that cause others no disturbance
Speaking the truth with kindness and tolerance
Studying the principles that the scriptures ancient preach
All these together constitute – the penance of speech.|15|

With a blissful mind, maintaining a balance
And controlling the mind with a resolute silence
Thus engaging in the inner cleansing when a being you find,
He is said to be performing the penance of the mind |16|

When the three penances are done together
It is a penance in *Sattwa* way altogether-
Performed with a faith that is highest
Holding no fruitive expectations-not even the slightest|17|

But that penance that is performed outwardly
Executed in pride, seeking a glory worldly
Is *Rajas* in nature and is primitive and cursory
Yearning for adulation, it is unstable and temporary.|18|

मूढग्राहेणात्मनो यत्पीडया क्रियते तपः ।
परस्योत्सादनार्थं वा तत्तामसमुदाहृतम् ॥१७-१९॥

mūḍhagrāheṇātmano yatpīḍayā kriyate tapaḥ
parasyotsādanārthaṃ vā tattāmasamudāhṛtam 17.19

दातव्यमिति यद्दानं दीयतेऽनुपकारिणे ।
देशे काले च पात्रे च तद्दानं सात्त्विकं स्मृतम् ॥१७-२०॥

dātavyamiti yaddānaṃ dīyatenupakāriṇe
deśe kāle ca pātre ca taddānaṃ sāttvikaṃ smṛtam 17.20

यत्तु प्रत्युपकारार्थं फलमुद्दिश्य वा पुनः ।
दीयते च परिक्लिष्टं तद्दानं राजसं स्मृतम् ॥१७-२१॥

yattu prattyupakārārthaṃ phalamuddiśya vā punaḥ
dīyate ca parikliṣṭaṃ taddānaṃ rājasaṃ smṛtam 17.21

अदेशकाले यद्दानमपात्रेभ्यश्च दीयते ।
असत्कृतमवज्ञातं तत्तामसमुदाहृतम् ॥१७-२२॥

adeśakāle yaddānamapātrebhyaśca dīyate
asatkṛtamavajñātaṃ tattāmasamudāhṛtam 17.22

ॐ तत्सदिति निर्देशो ब्रह्मणस्त्रिविधः स्मृतः ।
ब्राह्मणास्तेन वेदाश्च यज्ञाश्च विहिताः पुरा ॥१७-२३॥

oṃ tatsaditi nirdeśo brahmaṇastrividhaḥ smṛtaḥ
brāhmaṇāstena vedāśca yajñāśca vihitāḥ purā 17.23

तस्मादोमित्युदाहृत्य यज्ञदानतपःक्रियाः ।
प्रवर्तन्ते विधानोक्ताः सततं ब्रह्मवादिनाम् ॥१७-२४॥

tasmādomityudāhṛtya yajñadānatapaḥ kriyāḥ
pravartante vidhānoktāḥ satataṃ brahmavādinām17.24

The penance that is sought by a person deluded
Who's intellect has by ignorance been clouded
Causing or concentrating with the intention to injure
Either to self or others- is a penance in *Tamas* for sure.|19|

An offering in *Sattwa* is said to be done
Undertaken for the sake of offering,
keeping expectations none
Precisely at the right place and moment,
the offering is successful
To bring forth the betterment of the recipient,
it is bountiful.|20|

A donation in *Rajas* is said to be effected
When unwillingly or with ego it is executed
With hopes of returns is its initiation itself
And causes violence or harm to oneself |21|

A gift of charity in *Tamas* is said to be one
When ignoring the time, place and object it is done
To the receiver's emotions, without showing any empathy
With ill will and despise- such a giving is unworthy.|22|

Many aeons ago, this triple formula was conceived-
By the same sacrifice, the *Vedic* knowledge was received-
The mantra *"Om tat Sat" with-Om* the primordial syllable
Tat the eternal *Brahman, Sat* is the highest truth cognizable.|23|

That is why the knowers of the *Vedic*
sciences chant and meditate
And all their sacrifices, offerings and actions with
'*Om*' they initiate
By the principles of the scriptures they firmly stand.
And the meanings of their procedures they understand|24|

तदित्यनभिसन्धाय फलं यज्ञतपःक्रियाः ।
दानक्रियाश्च विविधाः क्रियन्ते मोक्षकाङ्क्षिभिः ॥१७-२५॥

tadityanabhisaṃdhāya phalaṃ yajñatapaḥkriyāḥ
dānakriyāśca vividhāḥ kriyante mokṣakāṅkṣibhiḥ17.25

सद्भावे साधुभावे च सदित्येतत्प्रयुज्यते ।
प्रशस्ते कर्मणि तथा सच्छब्दः पार्थ युज्यते ॥१७-२६॥

sadbhāve sādhubhāve ca sad ityetatprayujyate
praśaste karmaṇi tathā sacchabdaḥ pārtha yujyate17.26

यज्ञे तपसि दाने च स्थितिः सदिति चोच्यते ।
कर्म चैव तदर्थीयं सदित्येवाभिधीयते ॥१७-२७॥

yajñe tapasi dāne ca sthitiḥ sad iticocyate
karma caiva tadarthīyam sadityevābhidhīyate 17.27

अश्रद्धया हुतं दत्तं तपस्तप्तं कृतं च यत् ।
असदित्युच्यते पार्थ न च तत्प्रेत्य नो इह ॥१७-२८॥

aśraddhayā hutaṃ dattaṃ tapastaptaṃ kṛtaṃ ca yat
asadityucyate pārtha na ca tatprepya no iha 17.28

'*Tat*'- is concentrated upon profusely
Without seeking any fruits, it is pronounced verily
By the awakened seekers of liberation
During penance, offerings and sacrificial action|25|

'*Sat*' is the all pervading goodness in existence
And is the ultimate truth's significance
O *Arjuna*, the word *Sat* is also used to define
The best amongst existences-supremely Divine.|26|

In penance, sacrifice and offering- he who is firm
Such a being's actions are in'*Sat*'- one can thus affirm
Holding a fundamental view in doing the right actions
Performing austerities, sacrificial offerings and oblations|27|

Penance, charity and sacrifices by the beings ill-informed
O *Arjuna*, Without faith when they are performed
They are termed '*Asat*' and detriment the soul's progress
And neither in this nor the next world, do they bring success|28|"

(Thus ended the seventeenth Canto of the Bhagavad Gita where Sri Krishna elucidated to Arjuna the triple phenomena governing all existences in nature's existence)

अथाष्टादशोऽध्यायः ।
athāṣṭādaśodhyāyaḥ

अर्जुन उवाच ।
संन्यासस्य महाबाहो तत्त्वमिच्छामि वेदितुम् ।
त्यागस्य च हृषीकेश पृथक्केशिनिषूदन ॥१८-१॥
arjunauvāca
saṃnyāsasya mahābāhotattvamicchāmi veditum
tyāgasya ca hṛṣīkeśa pṛthakkeśiniṣūdana 18.1

श्रीभगवानुवाच ।
काम्यानां कर्मणां न्यासं संन्यासं कवयो विदुः ।
सर्वकर्मफलत्यागं प्राहुस्त्यागं विचक्षणाः ॥१८-२॥
śrībhagavānuvāca
kāmyānāṃ karmaṇāṃ nyāsaṃ saṃnyāsaṃ kavayo viduh
sarvakarmaphalatyāgaṃ prāhustyāgaṃ vicakṣaṇāḥ 18.2

त्याज्यं दोषवदित्येके कर्म प्राहुर्मनीषिणः ।
यज्ञदानतपःकर्म न त्याज्यमिति चापरे ॥१८-३॥
tyājyaṃ doṣavadityeke karma prāhurmanīṣiṇah
yajñadānatapaḥkarma na tyājyamiti cāpare 18.3

Canto XVIII: *Liberation*

(Verse 1: *Arjuna* seeks the knowledge of renunciation and detachment from *Krishna*; 2-11: *Krishna* explains The True meaning of renunciation; 12-18: The actions, the fruits and the doer; 19-28: The Threefold Gnosis, works and modes of action in nature; 29-32: The Threefold understandings; 33-35: The Threefold States of persistences; 36-39: The Threefold pleasures; 40: The Universal law of triplicate Natures; 41-44: The fourfold Divisional system of the society; 45-48:The need for working as per one's own nature; 49-57: The way to become one with the Brahman; 58: Uniting the Mind and heart-the key to victory; 59-66: The Stairway to Liberation; 67-71: *Krishna*'s message to spread the knowledge Divine for the uplifting of the world's peoples; 72: *Krishna*'s final words in the Gita; 73: *Arjuna*-the awakened warrior; 74-78: Sanjaya's salutation to The Gita, to *Krishna* and to *Arjuna*)

Arjuna said:
"O Mighty armed one, O *Krishna*, O Lord of every being
I wish to verily understand *Sannyasa*'s meaning
And also the fundamentals of *Tyaga*, I need to know
What the underlying principles are, Please show.|1|"

Lord *Krishna* spoke:
"The learned consider *Sannyasa* to be total abstention
From the proscribed duties and actions-an absolute abnegation
But *Tyaga* implies not a complete abstinence
Giving up the fruits of all actions is its key essence.|2|

By some literate men it is thus pronounced
"It is necessary for all actions to be renounced"
By some others, this view is subjected
"Sacrifice, offering and penance alone shouldn't be neglected"|3|

निश्चयं शृणु मे तत्र त्यागे भरतसत्तम ।
त्यागो हि पुरुषव्याघ्र त्रिविधः सम्प्रकीर्तितः ॥१८-४॥

niścayaṃśṛṇu me tatra tyāge bharatasattama
tyāgo hi puruṣavyāghra trividhaḥ samprakīrtitaḥ 18.4

यज्ञदानतपः कर्म न त्याज्यं कार्यमेव तत् ।
यज्ञो दानं तपश्चैव पावनानि मनीषिणाम् ॥१८-५॥

yajñadānatapaḥ karma na tyājyaṃ kāryameva tat
yajño dānaṃ tapaścaiva pāvanāni manīṣiṇām 18.5

एतान्यपि तु कर्माणि सङ्गं त्यक्त्वा फलानि च ।
कर्तव्यानीति मे पार्थ निश्चितं मतमुत्तमम् ॥१८-६॥

etānyapi tu karmāṇi saṅgaṃ tyaktvā phalāni ca
kartavyānīti me pārtha niścitaṃ matamuttamam 18.6

नियतस्य तु संन्यासः कर्मणो नोपपद्यते ।
मोहात्तस्य परित्यागस्तामसः परिकीर्तितः ॥१८-७॥

niyatasya tu saṃnyāsaḥ karmaṇo nopapadyate
mohāttasya parityāgastāmasaḥ parikīrtitaḥ 18.7

दुःखमित्येव यत्कर्म कायक्लेशभयात्त्यजेत् ।
स कृत्वा राजसं त्यागं नैव त्यागफलं लभेत् ॥१८-८॥

duḥkhamityeva yatkarma kāyakleśabhayāttyajet
sa kṛtvā rājasaṃ tyāgaṃ naiva tyāgaphalaṃ labhet 18.8

कार्यमित्येव यत्कर्म नियतं क्रियतेऽर्जुन ।
सङ्गं त्यक्त्वा फलं चैव स त्यागःसात्त्विको मतः ॥१८-९॥

kāryamityeva yatkarma niyataṃ kriyaterjuna
saṅgaṃ tyaktvā phalaṃ caiva sa tyāgaḥ sāttviko mataḥ 18.9

न द्वेष्ट्य कुशलं कर्म कुशले नानुषज्जते ।
त्यागी सत्त्वसमाविष्टो मेधावी छिन्नसंशयः ॥१८-१०॥

na dveṣṭya kuśalaṃ karma kuśale nānuṣajjate
tyāgī sattvasamāviṣṭo medhāvī chinnasaṃśayaḥ 18.10

Listen to Me now as I declare
My conclusions for you to clear the air
O *Arjuna*, O fiercest amongst warriors, Listen to Me
Renunciation too is of modes three|4|

Sacrifice, Penance and Offering- these actions three
Must be verily performed, neglected they shouldn't be
For they bring about in the wise an inner purification
And lead verily in the soul's emancipation.|5|

O *Arjuna*, even while these actions are performed
This following principle must be conformed
"All actions must be done in a state of detachment
Without holding on to any fruitive attachment"|6|

The abnegation of prescribed actions is not proper
As neglecting the right action is deemed improper
Such an approach is a *Tamas* type of renunciation
That has arisen simply out of ignorance's illusion|7|

He who renounces his works due to depression
Or due to bodily discomfort or a troubled apprehension
Such a person engages in a *Rajas* type of abstention
And gains not the entitlements of true renunciation|8|

He who performs regulated and right actions
Detached and without any fruitive attractions
With a sense of duty, he discharges his deeds every day
Such a renunciation is in sync with *Sattwa*'s way|9|

The wise man who has overcome all contradictions
In a state of *Sattwa* are all his renounced actions
Towards difficult actions he holds no indisposition
And pleasing actions to him hold no attraction.|10|

न हि देहभृता शक्यं त्यक्तुं कर्माण्यशेषतः ।
यस्तु कर्मफलत्यागी स त्यागीत्यभिधीयते ॥१८-११॥

na hi dehabhṛtā śakyaṃ tyaktuṃ karmāṇyaśeṣataḥ
yastu karmaphalatyāgī sa tyāgītyabhidhīyate 18.11

अनिष्टमिष्टं मिश्रं च त्रिविधं कर्मणः फलम् ।
भवत्यत्यागिनां प्रेत्य न तु संन्यासिनां क्वचित् ॥१८-१२॥

aniṣṭamiṣṭaṃ miśraṃ ca trividhaṃ karmaṇaḥ phalam
bhavatyatyāginām pretya na tu saṃnyāsināṃ kvacit 18.12

पञ्चैतानि महाबाहो कारणानि निबोध मे ।
साङ्ख्ये कृतान्ते प्रोक्तानि सिद्धये सर्वकर्मणाम् ॥१८-१३॥

pañcaitāni mahābāho kāraṇāni nibodha me
sāṃkhye kṛtānte proktāni siddhaye sarvakarmaṇām 18.13

अधिष्ठानं तथा कर्ता करणं च पृथग्विधम् ।
विविधाश्च पृथक्चेष्टा दैवं चैवात्र पञ्चमम् ॥१८-१४॥

adhiṣṭhānaṃ tathā kartā karaṇaṃ ca pṛthagvidham
vividhāśca pṛthakceṣṭā daivaṃ caivātra pañcamam 18.14

शरीरवाङ्मनोभिर्यत्कर्म प्रारभते नरः ।
न्याय्यं वा विपरीतं वा पञ्चैते तस्य हेतवः ॥१८-१५॥

śarīravāṅmanobhiryatkarma prārabhate naraḥ
nyāyyaṃ vā viparītaṃ vā pañcaite tasya hetavaḥ 18.15

तत्रैवं सति कर्तारमात्मानं केवलं तु यः ।
पश्यत्यकृतबुद्धित्वान्न स पश्यति दुर्मतिः ॥१८-१६॥

tatraivaṃ sati kartāramātmānaṃ kevalaṃ tu yaḥ
paśyatyakṛtabuddhitvānna sa paśyati durmatiḥ 18.16

यस्य नाहङ्कृतो भावो बुद्धिर्यस्य न लिप्यते ।
हत्वापि स इमाँल्लोकान्न हन्ति न निबध्यते ॥१८-१७॥

yasya nāhaṃkṛto bhāvo buddhiryasya na lipyate
hatvā.api sa imāṃllokānna hanti na nibadhyate 18.17

Works cannot be renounced by any embodied being
Such is the nature of works for all creatures living
He who gives up only the fruits of action
He has understood the true meaning of renunciation|11|

All fruits of actions in this world and the next can thus be
Desired or undesired or mixed – only one of the three
Post death too, the beings enslaved to fruits are bound
But those who renounce truly are in all worlds free found.|12|

O *Arjuna*, Learn from Me as I shall reveal
The five main causes to you, I shall unveil
As per the wisdom of the ancient instruction
By which man attains in all his works a perfection|13|

The five comprise the physical body as the base,
The doer whose commands it obeys
The different kinds of efforts, the senses that perpetuate
And finally it is the individual's governing fate|14|

The five elements constitute and interact
To create the governing cause by which all beings act
They chisel and mould man's development and outcome
And define what his deeds of mind,
body and speech become|15|

But those beings who does not comprehend
Due to ignorance nothing they can apprehend
Themselves to be the cause of actions, they believe
The truth, such blinded beings cannot perceive|16|

He who has given up his sense of possession
He whose intelligence is not driven by passion
Even if multiple people, such a being were to slay
He isn't the slayer and not bound to sin in any way|17|

ज्ञानं ज्ञेयं परिज्ञाता त्रिविधा कर्मचोदना ।
करणं कर्म कर्तेति त्रिविधः कर्मसङ्ग्रहः ॥१८-१८॥

jñānaṃ jñeyaṃ parijñātā trividhā karmacodanā
karaṇaṃ karma karteti trividhaḥ karmasaṃgrahaḥ 18.18

ज्ञानं कर्म च कर्ता च त्रिधैव गुणभेदतः ।
प्रोच्यते गुणसङ्ख्याने यथावच्छृणु तान्यपि ॥१८-१९॥

jñānaṃ karma ca kartā ca tridhaiva guṇabhedataḥ
procyate guṇasaṃkhyāne yathāvacchṛṇu tānyapi 18.19

सर्वभूतेषु येनैकं भावमव्ययमीक्षते ।
अविभक्तं विभक्तेषु तज्ज्ञानं विद्धि सात्त्विकम् ॥१८-२०॥

sarvabhūteṣu yenaikaṃ bhāvamavyayamīkṣate
avibhaktaṃ vibhakteṣu tajjñānaṃ viddhi sāttvikam 18.20

पृथक्त्वेन तु यज्ज्ञानं नानाभावान्पृथग्विधान् ।
वेत्ति सर्वेषु भूतेषु तज्ज्ञानं विद्धि राजसम् ॥१८-२१॥

pṛthaktvena tu yajjñānaṃ nānābhāvānpṛthagvidhān
vetti sarveṣu bhūteṣu tajjñānaṃ viddhi rājasam 18.21

यत्तु कृत्स्नवदेकस्मिन्कार्ये सक्तमहैतुकम् ।
अतत्त्वार्थवदल्पं च तत्तामसमुदाहृतम् ॥१८-२२॥

yattu kṛtsnavadekasminkārye saktamahetukam
atattvārthavadalpaṃ ca tattāmasamudāhṛtam 18.22

नियतं सङ्गरहितमरागद्वेषतः कृतम् ।
अफलप्रेप्सुना कर्म यत्तत्सात्त्विकमुच्यते ॥१८-२३॥

niyataṃ saṅgarahitamarāgadveṣataḥ kṛtam
aphalaprepsunā karma yattatsāttvikamucyate 18.23

यत्तु कामेप्सुना कर्म साहङ्कारेण वा पुनः ।
क्रियते बहुलायासं तद्राजसमुदाहृतम् ॥१८-२४॥

yattu kāmepsunā karma sāhaṃkāreṇa vā punaḥ
kriyate bahulāyāsaṃ tadrājasamudāhṛtam 18.24

The knowledge, the objective senses and the knower
These three trigger the mental impulses in the doer
Then again it is the doer, the instrument and the action
All works arise only by the three's combined sanction|18|

Gnosis, the works and the action's mode
As written in the ancient scriptural code
All persist in nature in ways threefold-
Listen to these too as to you-I shall unfold.|19|

The knowledge coming from the inner eye's opening
That which perceives in all the supreme *Self*'s becoming,
Behind all the divisions, those who perceive the one indivisible
In all such beings, *Sattwa*'s light is recognizable|20|

But that knowledge which perceives in all forms a division
That which in the multiplicity of life sees a separation
Devoid of oneness, it sees in all creations a distinction
The knowledge of such beings is powered
by *Rajas*'s passion.|21|

The pseudo-knowledge gives the beings a very narrow view
For their eyes are blind and see nature to be untrue
Limited in perception, they prefer a routine of sameness
And their knowledge is blighted by *Tamas*'s darkness|22|

Any action that is performed in the manner right-
From likings or aversion, by remaining detached,
Regulated and to the fruits of work, by not being attached
Know such actions to be done in *Sattwa*'s light|23|

But the actions initiated by desire's domination
Egoistically seeking a personal and passionate aspiration,
Which require a great strain and effort to fulfil
Know such actions to be as per *Rajas*'s will.|24|

अनुबन्धं क्षयं हिंसामनपेक्ष्य च पौरुषम् ।
मोहादारभ्यते कर्म यत्तत्तामसमुच्यते ॥१८-२५॥

anubandhaṃ kṣayaṃ hiṃsāmanapekṣya ca pauruṣam
mohādārabhyate karma yattattāmasamucyate 18.25

मुक्तसङ्गोऽनहंवादी धृत्युत्साहसमन्वितः ।
सिद्ध्यसिद्ध्योर्निर्विकारः कर्ता सात्त्विक उच्यते ॥१८-२६॥

muktasaṅgonahaṃvādī dhṛtyutsāhasamanvitaḥ
siddhyasiddhyornirvikāraḥ kartā sāttvika ucyate 18.26

रागी कर्मफलप्रेप्सुर्लुब्धो हिंसात्मकोऽशुचिः ।
हर्षशोकान्वितः कर्ता राजसः परिकीर्तितः ॥१८-२७॥

rāgī karmaphalaprepsurlubdho hiṃsātmakośuciḥ
harṣaśokānvitaḥ kartā rājasaḥ parikīrtitaḥ 18.27

अयुक्तः प्राकृतः स्तब्धः शठो नैष्कृतिकोऽलसः ।
विषादी दीर्घसूत्री च कर्ता तामस उच्यते ॥१८-२८॥

ayuktaḥ prākṛtaḥ stabdhaḥ śaṭho naiṣkṛtikolasaḥ
viṣādī dīrghasūtrī ca kartā tāmasa ucyate 18.28

बुद्धेर्भेदं धृतेश्चैव गुणतस्त्रिविधं शृणु ।
प्रोच्यमानमशेषेण पृथक्त्वेन धनञ्जय ॥१८-२९॥

buddherbhedaṃ dhṛteścaiva guṇatastrividhaṃ śṛṇu
procyamānamaśeṣeṇa pṛthaktvena dhanaṃjaya 18.29

प्रवृत्तिं च निवृत्तिं च कार्याकार्ये भयाभये ।
बन्धं मोक्षं च या वेत्ति बुद्धिः सा पार्थ सात्त्विकी ॥१८-३०॥

pravṛttiṃ ca nivṛttiṃ ca kāryākārye bhayābhaye
bandhaṃ mokṣaṃ ca yā vetti buddhiḥ sā pārtha sāttvikī 18.30

यया धर्ममधर्मं च कार्यं चाकार्यमेव च ।
अयथावत्प्रजानाति बुद्धिः सा पार्थ राजसी ॥१८-३१॥

yayā dharmamadharmaṃ ca kāryaṃ cākāryameva ca
ayathāvatprajānāti buddhiḥ sā pārtha rājasī 18.31

Actions that have arisen out of ignorance's illusion
Disproportionately and mechanically in a state of delusion
Disregarding the consequences, by wastage of effort
These actions of *Tamas* inflict only injury and hurt|25|

In success and loss, whose actions are calm and resolute
In a *Sattwa*'s state all his works he is said to execute.
Devoid of attachment, his ego he has forsaken
And bereft of attachment, all his works are undertaken|26|

With passion, indulgence and by holding attachment
Greedily desiring the fruits of work and their fulfillment,
Extremes of emotions in success and loss, spreading violence
Such a doer is said to be *Rajas* in his nature and essence|27|

One who acts without thinking and reacts by default
His every work is obstinate and wrought with fault
Cunning and ignorant, indolent and inexpressive
Such a doer, in a state of *Tamas* is always depressive|28|

O *Arjuna*, even understanding is said to be threefold
About it I shall reveal what is understood and told
Likewise persistence too has three actualities
Hear Me carefully, I shall explain their qualities.|29|

That which sees the Laws of Action and renunciation
Recognizing the differences between right and wrong action
He who understands what is to be feared and what is not
What binds or frees the spirit- *Sattwa*'s understanding he's got|30|

That which is right action and that which is wrong action
His mind has a faulty sense of discrimination
Of what is to be done and avoided- he holds a wrong notion
Such a being is *Rajas* in understanding and perception.|31|

अधर्मं धर्ममिति या मन्यते तमसावृता ।
सर्वार्थान्विपरीतांश्च बुद्धिः सा पार्थ तामसी ॥१८-३२॥

adharmam dharmamiti yā manyate tamasāvṛtā
sarvārthānviparītāñśca buddhiḥ sā pārtha tāmasī 18.32

धृत्या यया धारयते मनः प्राणेन्द्रियक्रियाः ।
योगेनाव्यभिचारिण्या धृतिः सा पार्थ सात्त्विकी ॥१८-३३॥

dhṛtyā yayā dhārayate manaḥ prāṇendriyakriyāḥ
yogenāvyabhicāriṇyā dhṛtiḥ sā pārtha sāttvikī 18.33

यया तु धर्मकामार्थान्धृत्या धारयतेऽर्जुन ।
प्रसङ्गेन फलाकाङ्क्षी धृतिः सा पार्थ राजसी ॥१८-३४॥

yayā tu dharmakāmārthāndhṛtyā dhārayaterjuna
prasaṅgena phalākāṅkṣī dhṛtiḥ sā pārtha rājasī 18.34

यया स्वप्नं भयं शोकं विषादं मदमेव च ।
न विमुञ्चति दुर्मेधा धृतिः सा पार्थ तामसी ॥१८-३५॥

yayā svapnam bhayam śokam viṣādam madameva ca
na vimuñcati durmedhā dhṛtiḥ sā pārtha tāmasī 18.35

सुखं त्विदानीं त्रिविधं शृणु मे भरतर्षभ ।
अभ्यासाद्रमते यत्र दुःखान्तं च निगच्छति ॥१८-३६॥

sukhamtvidānīmtrividhamśṛṇu me bharatarṣabha
abhyāsādramate yatra duḥkhāntam ca nigacchhati 18.36

यत्तदग्रे विषमिव परिणामेऽमृतोपमम् ।
तत्सुखं सात्त्विकं प्रोक्तमात्मबुद्धिप्रसादजम् ॥१८-३७॥

yattadagre viṣamiva pariṇāmemṛtopamam
tatsukham sāttvikam proktamātmabuddhiprasādajam 18.37

विषयेन्द्रियसंयोगाद्यत्तदग्रेऽमृतोपमम् ।
परिणामे विषमिव तत्सुखं राजसं स्मृतम् ॥१८-३८॥

viṣayendriyasañyogādyattadagremṛtopamam
pariṇāme viṣamiva tatsukham rājasam smṛtam 18.38

Those who are veiled by darkness's cloak
Deluded by falsehood, pseudo-interpretations they evoke
Their perception of the world is blurred by their misunderstanding
O *Arjuna*, such beings are said to be
Tamas in their understanding.|32|

When the grit and determination are firm and unwavering
Through *Yoga*'s regulated efforts and conditioning
When there is control over one's mind, senses and existence
This is said be a *Sattwa*'s state of persistence.|33|

O *Arjuna*, when to attachments the beings are firm
Restlessly wealth, righteousness and desire they affirm
Motivated by them, passion is their main feature
And *Rajas* is said to be their persistence in nature|34|

When O *Arjuna*, one is full of ignorance
Biding time in dreams, sleep and indolence
Filled with fear, foolhardiness and depression
Such a proud being is *Tamas* in his determination|35|

And Now O *Arjuna* listen carefully to Me-
For I shall explain the pleasures three
By knowing them –you can be free of distress
And dwell joyously and verily progress.|36|

That which seems like a venom-poisonous initially
But is an ambrosial nectar ultimately
From a satisfaction of the spirit comes that pleasure
And it is said to be of *Sattwa*'s nature.|37|

That which is borne of the sensual attractions
Of senses, objects and their interactions
Seems nectar like first but is a poison, in the end
Such a pleasure as *Rajas* one can comprehend.|38|

यदग्रे चानुबन्धे च सुखं मोहनमात्मनः ।
निद्रालस्यप्रमादोत्थं तत्तामसमुदाहृतम् ॥१८-३९॥

yadagre cānubandhe ca sukhaṃ mohanamātmanaḥ
nidrālasyapramādottham tattāmasamudāhṛtam 18.39

न तदस्ति पृथिव्यां वा दिवि देवेषु वा पुनः ।
सत्त्वं प्रकृतिजैर्मुक्तं यदेभिः स्यात्त्रिभिर्गुणैः ॥१८-४०॥

na tad astipṛthivyāṃ vā divi deveṣu vā punaḥ
sattvaṃ prakṛtijairmuktam yadebhiḥ syāttribhirguṇaiḥ 18.40

ब्राह्मणक्षत्रियविशां शूद्राणां च परन्तप ।
कर्माणि प्रविभक्तानि स्वभावप्रभवैर्गुणैः ॥१८-४१॥

brāhmaṇakṣatriyaviśāṃ śūdrāṇāṃ ca paraṃtapa
karmāṇi pravibhaktāni svabhāvaprabhavairguṇaiḥ 18.41

शमो दमस्तपः शौचं क्षान्तिरार्जवमेव च ।
ज्ञानं विज्ञानमास्तिक्यं ब्रह्मकर्म स्वभावजम् ॥१८-४२॥

śamo damastapaḥ śaucaṃ kṣāntirārjavameva ca
jñānaṃ vijñānamāstikyaṃ brahmakarma svabhāvajam 18.42

शौर्यं तेजो धृतिर्दाक्ष्यं युद्धे चाप्यपलायनम् ।
दानमीश्वरभावश्च क्षात्रं कर्म स्वभावजम् ॥१८-४३॥

śauryaṃ tejo dhṛtirdākṣyaṃ yuddhe cāpyapalāyanam
dānamīśvarabhāvaśca kṣātraṃ karma svabhāvajam 18.43

कृषिगौरक्ष्यवाणिज्यं वैश्यकर्म स्वभावजम् ।
परिचर्यात्मकं कर्म शूद्रस्यापि स्वभावजम् ॥१८-४४॥

kṛṣigaurakṣyavāṇijyaṃ vaiśyakarma svabhāvajam
paricaryātmakam karma śūdrasyāpi svabhāvajam 18.44

स्वे स्वे कर्मण्यभिरतः संसिद्धिं लभते नरः ।
स्वकर्मनिरतः सिद्धिं यथा विन्दति तच्छृणु ॥१८-४५॥

sve sve karmaṇyabhirataḥ saṃsiddhiṃ labhate naraḥ
svakarmaniratah siddhiṃ yathā vindati tacchṛṇu 18.45

The pleasure which is illusionary in essence
In both its beginning and consequence
That stems from sleep, ignorance and a lazy nature
Arising out of *Tamas* is this pleasure.|39|

No being can exist on earth-
Even in the heavens no God has taken birth
Who is not subject to nature's modes three
From its workings, all qualities come to be.|40|

Depending wholly on their birth nature
There are the quadruple divisions of equal stature
Based on the individual's tendencies and innate aspects.
Brahmins, Kshatriyas,
Vaishyas and *Shudras* – the four sects|41|

Performing penance, seeking knowledge with a forbearance
Maintaining self-control with a steadfast perseverance
He is termed a *Brahmin* who is pure, calm and peaceful
For it is in his nature to seek the spirit and be truthful|42|

Heroism, high spiritedness, and strong physical ability
Daring in battle, with determination and gallantry
Benevolence and a skill in leadership
Such, is the *Kshatriya*'s nature that commands lordship.|43|

The *Vaishyas* are the craftsmen,
the agriculturists, the cattle-raisers
The skilled artisans, the businessmen and the traders
But the *Shudras* have only one aim in mind
To perform service for the betterment of mankind.|44|

A man who in his own works of nature perseveres
His skills mature as towards perfection he nears
How perfection is achieved, I shall now say
Listen to Me as I shall reveal the way.|45|

यतः प्रवृत्तिर्भूतानां येन सर्वमिदं ततम् ।
स्वकर्मणा तमभ्यर्च्य सिद्धिं विन्दति मानवः ॥१८-४६॥

yataḥ pravṛttirbhūtānāṃ yena sarvamidam tatam
svakarmaṇā tamabhyarcya siddhim vindati mānavaḥ 18.46

श्रेयान्स्वधर्मो विगुणः परधर्मात्स्वनुष्ठितात् ।
स्वभावनियतं कर्म कुर्वन्नाप्नोति किल्बिषम् ॥१८-४७॥

śreyānsvadharmo viguṇaḥ paradharmotsvanuṣṭhitāt
svabhāvaniyatam karma kurvannāpnoti kilbiṣam 18.47

सहजं कर्म कौन्तेय सदोषमपि न त्यजेत् ।
सर्वारम्भा हि दोषेण धूमेनाग्निरिवावृताः ॥१८-४८॥

sahajam karma kaunteya sadoṣamapi na tyajet
sarvārambhā hi doṣeṇa dhūmenāgnirivāvṛtāḥ 18.48

असक्तबुद्धिः सर्वत्र जितात्मा विगतस्पृहः ।
नैष्कर्म्यसिद्धिं परमां संन्यासेनाधिगच्छति ॥१८-४९॥

asaktabuddhiḥ sarvatra jitātmā vigataspṛhaḥ
naiṣkarmyasiddhim paramām samnyāsenādhigacchati 18.49

सिद्धिं प्राप्तो यथा ब्रह्म तथाप्नोति निबोधमे ।
समासेनैव कौन्तेय निष्ठा ज्ञानस्य या परा ॥१८-५०॥

siddhim prāptoyathā brahma tathāpnoti nibodhame
samāsenaiva kaunteya niṣṭhā jñānasya yā parā 18.50

बुद्ध्या विशुद्ध्या युक्तो धृत्यात्मानं नियम्यच ।
शब्दादीन्विषयांस्त्यक्त्वा रागद्वेषौ व्युदस्य च ॥१८-५१॥

buddhyā viśuddhayā yukto dhṛtyātmānam niyamyaca
śabdādīnviṣayāmstyaktvā rāgadveṣau vyudasya ca 18.51

विविक्तसेवी लघ्वाशी यतवाक्कायमानसः ।
ध्यानयोगपरो नित्यं वैराग्यं समुपाश्रितः ॥१८-५२॥

viviktasevī laghvāśī yatavākkāyamānasaḥ
dhyānayogaparo nityam vairāgyam samupāśritaḥ 18.52

The creator of all the living beings in the creation
The Supernal one who brought forth every manifestation
By worshipping Him through one's own work with devotion
A man can verily attain the zenith of perfection.|46|

It is better to perform one's own work faultily
Than to, under a compulsion of law, perform perfectly
When one follows one's own inner nature
One incurs not any sin of any stature.|47|

The duty towards oneself, O *Arjuna*, one mustn't forsake
Without abandoning works, in the actions one must partake
Even if defectively done, as all actions are cloaked with defect
Just as the fire is masked by its own smoke's effect|48|

When the soul is conquered with detachment
Leaving no room for desire or any attachment
Man transcends regular actions through renunciation
And every action is performed with impeccable perfection.|49|

How is it that the union with *Brahma* is gained,
When is it that perfection is attained?
O Arjuna, listen for I shall now explain
The most supreme knowledge that man can gain.|50|

By cleansing and purifying the inner Self
And holding a firm control over oneself
By renouncing all objects of sounds and senses,
Being bereft of anger and repulsive reflexes|51|

Controlling mind, speech, body and
ignoring materialistic company
Eating moderately for maintaining an inner harmony
Seeking a union with the eternal through regular meditation
Letting go of desires- gaining absolute renunciation.|52|

अहङ्कारं बलं दर्पं कामं क्रोधं परिग्रहम् ।
विमुच्य निर्ममः शान्तो ब्रह्मभूयाय कल्पते ॥१८-५३॥

ahamkāram balam darpam kāmam krodham parigraham
vimucya nirmamaḥ śānto brahmabhūyāya kalpate 18.53

ब्रह्मभूतः प्रसन्नात्मा न शोचति न काङ्क्षति ।
समः सर्वेषु भूतेषु मद्भक्तिं लभते पराम् ॥१८-५४॥

brahmabhūtaḥ prasannātmā na śocati na kāṅkṣati
samaḥ sarveṣu bhūteṣu madbhaktim labhate parām 18.54

भक्त्या मामभिजानाति यावान्यश्चास्मि तत्त्वतः ।
ततो मां तत्त्वतो ज्ञात्वा विशते तदनन्तरम् ॥१८-५५॥

bhaktyā māmabhijānāti yāvānyaścāsmi tattvataḥ
tato mām tattvato jñātvā viśate tadanantaram 18.55

सर्वकर्माण्यपि सदा कुर्वाणो मद्व्यपाश्रयः ।
मत्प्रसादादवाप्नोति शाश्वतं पदमव्ययम् ॥१८-५६॥

sarvakarmāṇyapi sadā kurvāṇo madvyapāśrayaḥ
matprasādādavāpnoti śāśvatam padamavyayam 18.56

चेतसा सर्वकर्माणि मयि संन्यस्य मत्परः ।
बुद्धियोगमुपाश्रित्य मच्चित्तः सततं भव ॥१८-५७॥

cetasā sarvakarmāṇi mayi samnyasya matparaḥ
buddhiyogamupāśritya maccittaḥ satatam bhava 18.57

मच्चित्तः सर्वदुर्गाणि मत्प्रसादात्तरिष्यसि ।
अथ चेत्त्वमहङ्कारान्न श्रोष्यसि विनङ्क्ष्यसि ॥१८-५८॥

maccittaḥ sarvadurgāṇi matprasādattariṣyasi
atha cettvamahamkārānna śroṣyasi vinaṅkṣyasi 18.58

यदहङ्कारमाश्रित्य न योत्स्य इति मन्यसे ।
मिथ्यैष व्यवसायस्ते प्रकृतिस्त्वां नियोक्ष्यति ॥१८-५९॥

yadahamkāramāśritya na yotsya iti manyase
mithyaiṣa vyavasāyaste prakṛtistvām niyokṣyati 18.59

Discarding egoism, anger and arrogance
Desire, possessiveness and violence
Of all feelings of proprietorship, when one is free
To become the *Brahman*, one is fit to be|53|

When one becomes the *Brahman* of the liberated *Self*
By engaging in the purification of oneself
Neither grieving nor desiring and perceiving all to equal be
With a love Supreme and devotion those
souls verily attain Me|54|

He who by devotion evolves to know Me
And about all My vast existences that can be
My reality and principle- he truly understands
Uniting with My consciousness, supreme he stands.|55|

And when in Me, he is situated firmly
All his actions he performs verily
By My grace – he attains the eternal
Thus uniting with the creator supernal|56|

By surrendering oneself completely to Me
When all the actions and thoughts can devoted be
Through *Yoga*, when one incessantly strives
Uniting the heart and mind, in My shelter he arrives.|57|

When the mind and the heart become one
United with Me, All your battles are won
At the times of peril, their safe page I assuage
Only if the self-ego still prevails, one falls into hell's cage.|58|

It is because you are taking refuge in your ego
This battle you are seeking to forego
"I will not fight" you vainly say
But your inner nature will make you spar anyway.|59|

स्वभावजेन कौन्तेय निबद्धः स्वेन कर्मणा ।
कर्तुं नेच्छसि यन्मोहात्करिष्यस्यवशोपि तत् ॥१८-६०॥

svabhāvajen akaunteya nibaddhaḥ svena karmaṇā
kartum necchasi yanmohātkariṣyasyavaśopi tat 18.60

ईश्वरः सर्वभूतानां हृद्देशेऽर्जुन तिष्ठति ।
भ्रामयन्सर्वभूतानि यन्त्रारूढानि मायया ॥१८-६१॥

īśvaraḥ sarvabhūtānām hṛddeśerjuna tiṣṭhati
bhrāmayansarvabhūtāni yantrārūḍhāni māyayā 18.61

तमेव शरणं गच्छ सर्वभावेन भारत ।
तत्प्रसादात्परां शान्तिं स्थानं प्राप्स्यसि शाश्वतम् ॥१८-६२॥

tameva śaraṇam gaccha sarvabhāvena bhārata
tatprasādātparām śāntim sthānam prāpsyasi śāśvatam 18.62

इति ते ज्ञानमाख्यातं गुह्याद्गुह्यतरं मया ।
विमृश्यैतदशेषेण यथेच्छसि तथा कुरु ॥१८-६३॥

iti te jñānamākhyātam guhyādguhyataram mayā
vimṛśyaitadaśeṣeṇa yathecchasi tathā kuru 18.63

सर्वगुह्यतमं भूयःशृणु मे परमं वचः ।
इष्टोऽसि मे दृढमिति ततो वक्ष्यामि ते हितम् ॥१८-६४॥

sarvaguhyatamambhūyaḥśṛṇu me paramamvacaḥ
iṣṭosi me dṛḍhamititatovakṣyāmitehitam 18.64

मन्मना भव मद्भक्तो मद्याजी मां नमस्कुरु ।
मामेवैष्यसि सत्यं ते प्रतिजाने प्रियोऽसि मे ॥१८-६५॥

manmanā bhavamadbhakto madyājī mām namaskuru
māmevaiṣyasi satyam tepratijāne priyosi me 18.65

सर्वधर्मान्परित्यज्य मामेकं शरणं व्रज ।
अहं त्वा सर्वपापेभ्यो मोक्षयिष्यामि मा शुचः ॥१८-६६॥

sarvadharmānparityajya māmekam śaraṇam vraja
aham tvā sarvapāpebhyo mokṣayiṣyāmi mā śucaḥ 18.66

Because of delusion, you do not desire
To fight this battle, you seem not to aspire
O *Arjuna*, In it you will ultimately have to partake
If not on your own, you will be forced
for your nature's sake.|60|

The Lord, that is seated within every living heart
O *Arjuna,* He stirs and initiates everything's start
Like machines all creatures are made to obey
And act as per the will of His *Maya*'s way.|61|

Seek refuge in Him in every way
O *Arjuna*, verily in every single way
For by His grace the supreme peace you can attain
And the eternal status you can obtain.|62|

Thus to you, O *Arjuna*, I've fully revealed
That most secret knowledge I have unveiled
So, Now by taking my cue
Your mode of action you are free to do|63|

And yet another secret, hear Me for I shall explain
As you are My devotee, I hold you main
You are to Me most intimate and dearest
Hence, I shall say to you what is best |64|

Merge into My consciousness, become My lover
Become My sacrifice, be My adorer
Bow to Me and you shall come to Me certainly
My dear One, This is my promise I shall fulfill verily.|65|

Renounce all your Dharmas that you so rigidly own
Surrender to Me and seek My refuge alone
From all your sins and evil, I shall relieve
I shall bring deliverance, do not grieve|66|

इदं ते नातपस्काय नाभक्ताय कदाचन ।
न चाशुश्रूषवे वाच्यं न च मां योऽभ्यसूयति ॥१८-६७॥

idaṁ te nātapaskāya nābhaktāya kadācana
na cāśuśrūṣave vācyaṁ na ca māṁ yobhyasūyati 18.67

य इदं परमं गुह्यं मद्भक्तेष्वभिधास्यति ।
भक्तिं मयि परां कृत्वा मामेवैष्यत्यसंशयः॥१८-६८॥

ya idaṁ paramaṁ guhyaṁ madbhakteṣvabhidhāsyati
bhaktiṁ mayi parāṁ kṛtvā māmevaiṣyatyasaṁśayaḥ 18.68

न च तस्मान्मनुष्येषु कश्चिन्मे प्रियकृत्तमः ।
भविता न च मे तस्मादन्यः प्रियतरो भुवि ॥१८-६९॥

na ca tasmānmanuṣyeṣu kaścinme priyakṛttamaḥ
bhavitā na ca me tasmādanyaḥ priyataro bhuvi 18.69

अध्येष्यते च य इमं धर्म्यं संवादमावयोः ।
ज्ञानयज्ञेन तेनाहमिष्टः स्यामिति मे मतिः ॥१८-७०॥

adhyeṣyate ca ya imaṁ dharmyaṁ saṁvādamāvayoḥ
jñānayajñena tenāhamiṣṭaḥ syāmiti me matiḥ 18.70

श्रद्धावाननसूयश्च शृणुयादपि यो नरः ।
सोऽपि मुक्तः शुभाँल्लोकान्प्राप्नुयात्पुण्यकर्मणाम् ॥१८-७१॥

Śraddhāvānanasūyaśca śṛṇuyādapi yo naraḥ
sopi muktaḥ śubhāṁllokānprāpnuyātpuṇyakarmaṇām 18.71

कच्चिदेतच्छ्रुतं पार्थ त्वयैकाग्रेण चेतसा ।
कच्चिदज्ञानसम्मोहः प्रनष्टस्ते धनञ्जय ॥१८-७२॥

kaccidetacchrutaṁ pārtha tvayaikāgreṇa cetasā
kaccidajñānasammohaḥ pranaṣṭaste dhanaṁjaya 18.72

Speak not this truth to he who performs not penance
Or to he who lacks faith and dwells in ignorance
Also not to he who performs not any service
And to he who causes the
indwelling-God disservice.|67|

He who shall with the most supreme devotion
Pass over to My devotees-this secret declaration
He too shall verily unite and come to Me
About this no doubt can there ever be.|68|

And no other man can be nearer
For none shall I hold dearer
Than he who does this task for Me
Dearer than him none can ever be|69|

And also, He who studies this discourse
Holding our discussion sacred in his life's course
By him too the sacrifice of knowledge will be performed
Becoming My worshipper, he shall be transformed.|70|

Even the man who merely listens intently
Full of faith and devoid of any envy
For himself, the liberation he shall obtain
And the righteous realms of happiness he'll attain.|71|

O Arjuna, All that I said,did you intently hear,
With a concentrated mind, by lending your ear?
Has the delusion's veil been lifted?
O Arjuna, Has your ignorance been obliterated?|72|"

अर्जुन उवाच ।
नष्टो मोहः स्मृतिर्लब्धा त्वत्प्रसादान्मयाच्युत ।
स्थितोऽस्मि गतसन्देहः करिष्ये वचनं तव ॥१८-७३॥

arjuna uvāca
naṣṭo mohaḥ smṛtirlabdhā tvatprasādānmayācyuta
sthitosmi gatasaṃdehaḥ kariṣye vacanaṃ tava 18.73

सञ्जय उवाच ।
इत्यहं वासुदेवस्य पार्थस्य च महात्मनः ।
संवादमिममश्रौषमद्भुतं रोमहर्षणम् ॥१८-७४॥

sañjaya uvāca
ityahaṃ vāsudevasya pārthasya ca mahātmanaḥ
saṃvādamimamaśrauṣamadbhutaṃ romaharṣaṇam 18.74

व्यासप्रसादाच्छ्रुतवानेतद्गुह्यमहं परम् ।
योगंयोगेश्वरात्कृष्णात्साक्षात्कथयतः स्वयम् ॥१८-७५॥

vyāsaprasādācchrutavānetadguhyamaha ṃ param
yogaṃyogeśvarātk ṛṣ ātsāk ṣātkathayataḥ svayam 18.75

राजन्संस्मृत्य संस्मृत्य संवादमिममद्भुतम् ।
केशवार्जुनयोः पुण्यं हृष्यामि च मुहुर्मुहुः ॥१८-७६॥

rājansaṃsmṛtya saṃsmṛtya saṃvādamimamadbhutam
keśavārjunayo ḥ puṇyaṃ hṛṣyāmi ca muhurmuhu ḥ 18.76

तच्च संस्मृत्य संस्मृत्य रूपमत्यद्भुतं हरेः ।
विस्मयो मे महान्राजन्हृष्यामि च पुनःपुनः ॥१८-७७॥

tacca saṃsmṛtya saṃsmṛtya rūpamatyadbhuta ṃ hareḥ
vismayo me mahānrājanh ṛṣyāmi ca punaḥ punaḥ 18.77

यत्र योगेश्वरः कृष्णो यत्र पार्थो धनुर्धरः ।
तत्र श्रीर्विजयो भूतिर्ध्रुवा नीतिर्मतिर्मम ॥१८-७८॥

yatra yogeśvaraḥ kṛṣṇo yatra pārtho dhanurdharaḥ
tatra śrīrvijayo bhūtirdhruvā nītirmatirmama 18.78

Arjuna replied:
"My delusion is destroyed, my memory has returned
O Krishna, By your grace alone things have thus turned
I am now firm in my resolve, with all doubts cleared
I shall now act, as per Thy words golden that I've heard."|73|

Sanjaya said:
"Thus I heard the words of *Krishna*- The Divine lord
And also that of the pious *Arjuna*- His precious ward
So wondrous it was for me to understand
That it has caused my hair at their ends to stand.|74|

Through the grace of *Vyasa* the mystic sage-
This king of secrets, I was able to envisage
From the Lord of *Yoga*- *Krishna* Himself
Who verily declared the secret of *Yoga* itself |75|

O King, This sacred discourse I am reminiscing
Again and again I am ecstatically remembering
O *Krishna* and *Arjuna* I celebrate their conversation
Repeatedly I am rejoicing in jubilation.|76|

I also distinctly remember that marvelous sight
Of Lord *Krishna* bathed in the Divine light
As He displayed His form resplendent
I again rejoice for witnessing that vision transcendent.|77|

Wherever there is the lord of *Yoga*- *Krishna*,
Wherever there is the master archer- *Arjuna*
There exists the seal of Divine victory and prosperity
And glory for righteousness-Thus, I proclaim with certainty.|78|

(Thus ended the Eighteenth and final Canto of the Bhagavad Gita where Sri Krishna parted to Arjuna the divine knowledge of liberation that can liberate and uplift the world's peoples)

❈ ❈ ❈

Afterword

I conclude with a poetic rendition of the 191st Hymn of the 10th *Mandala* of *Rig Veda*, composed in the by the sages *Aangiras* and *Sanvananah*. Verse 1 is dedicated to *Agni* and Verses 2-4 to *Sangnyanam*- The Knowledge of Oneness in all beings.

Om
We invoke *Agni*, Mighty Lord of Fire, to come-
May the flames of the spirit kindled become.
For Thy comrade- The God within every being,
Shower His grace upon all-the living and non-living
United we – the world peoples stand and pour the libations
May the earth be nourished by our sacrificial oblations |1|

Together, May we progress, prosper and grow
The same knowledge, May we all know
May the language that we speak be one
United may all the minds assemble under the Sun.
May all the Gods their due shares-receive,
Satisfied, Their blessings-May the mortals achieve.|2|

May all offerings, chants and minds echo a sameness
May all of us become One in consciousness.
Becoming one in mantras and mind
All of us chanting and offering, may you find
May the sounds Divine chanted together resonate
The spirit of Oneness may we all impersonate.|3|

From an inner intuition may all utterances start
May the same oneness originate from every heart.
Make us together in our complete union
May all beings agree and live in a joyous communion.|4|

Om

सं-समिद युवसे वर्षन्नग्ने विश्वान्यर्य आ |

इळस पदेसमिधयसे स नो वसून्या भर ||

सं गच्छध्वं सं वदध्वं सं वो मनांसि जानताम् |

देवा भागं यथा पूर्वे संजानाना उपासते ||

समानो मन्त्रः समितिः समानी समानं मनः सह चित्तमेषाम् |

समानं मन्त्रमभि मण्त्रये वः समानेन वोहविषा जुहोमि ||

समानी व आकूतिः समाना हर्दयानि वः |

समानमस्तु वोमनो यथा वः सुसहासति ||

sam-samid yuvase vṛṣannaghne viśvānyarya ā |
iḷas padesamidhyase sa no vasūnyā bhara ||1||
sam ghachadhvam sam vadadhvam sam vo manāmsi jānatām |
devā bhāgham yathā pūrve samjānānā upāsate ||2||
samāno mantraḥ samitiḥ samānī samānam manaḥ saha cittameṣām |
samānam mantramabhi mantraye vaḥ samānena vohaviṣā juhomi ||3||
samānī va ākūtiḥ samānā hṛdayāni vaḥ |
samānamastu vomano yathā vaḥ susahāsati ||4||

Glossary of Important Characters and Sanksrit Terms:

Abhimanyu: The martyr son of *Arjuna*, who fought alongside his father in the mighty battle at *Kurukshetra*. The young lad is remembered for his valiant act of single-handedly penetrating the *Chakravyuh* -a formidable battle formation designed by the *Kauravan* army to obliterate the *Pandavas*.

Acharya Kripa: Described as one among the Seven-*Chiranjeevis* or Immortals. He was the preceptor of both the *Pandavas* and *Kauravas* and was respected for his dedication to impartially fulfilling all his duties towards his way of life as per the *Manusmriti-*the ancient code of ethics.

Acharya: A *Sanskrit* title that is affixed or prefixed to a mentor's name as a mark of respect.

Adityas: In the *Rig Veda*, the *Adityas* refer to the seven celestial suns namely *Varuna, Mitra, Bhaga, Ansha, Dhatri, Indra and Aryaman.*

Airvata: The mystic white elephant and vehicle of the lord of Gods- *Indra* who is considered to be the lord of elephants who roams in the clouds and is the symbolic link between the skies and the waters of the nether worlds.

Ananta: The celestial serpent also called as the hooded *Ananta* Nag or *Shesha* - upon whom *Vishnu* rests in the ethereal sea. *Vishnu* is often depicted in different scriptures as resting upon the uncoiled thousand headed *Shesha* upon whose hoods rest the different planets.

Anantavijaya: The name of the *Shankha* – or divine conch blown by *Yudhishthira*- the crown prince of the *Pandavas*. The conch is a sacred emblem that was used in ancient times as a war trumpet.

Anjaneya: The great *Rudra* who is known by many names is also one of the seven immortals and is worshipped as a God for his role in the *Sanskrit* epic *Ramayana*. *Arjuna* had received a blessing from *Anjaneya* that his presence shall be felt atop *Arjuna's* chariot during the mighty battle of *Kurukshetra*.

Arjuna: The hero of the *Bhagawad Gita* through whom the incarnation Divine-*Sri Krishna* parted the metaphysical, spiritual and practical secrets of life in the form of *The Gita*.

Aryaman: One of the early *Vedic* deities often invoked in conjunction with *Varuna, Mitra* and is considered as one of the main deities of the stature of *Indra* and *Brihaspati*. The path of *Aryaman* is the Milky way (*Aryaman Pantaah*).

Asana: The ancient sages of India had evolved *yogic* postures with the aim of uniting the mind and the body as a whole. These postures were inspired from nature and each posture was a sort of unique physical exercise that aimed at enhancing the physical and mental abilities of the individual. For instance: *Markatasana-* which is the monkey posture, was developed after being inspired by the flexibility of the monkey and this posture has been proven to improve the flexibility of the performer. The *Asanas* form an important feature of the *Hatha Yoga* traditions and sages used to remain immersed for many hours in a particular posture that suited their union of mind and body. Nowadays *Asanas* are gaining much popularity today in most developed countries and are loosely termed *Yoga* poses.

Asat: The *Sanskrit* word literally means all that is not the truth.

Ashwattha: The *Sanskrit* name for the Peepal tree (*ficus religiosa*) which has great symbolic references and may be compared to the sacred tree of life that finds its mention in the most prominent world religions like Islam, Christianity and Hinduism.

Ashwatthama: The son of the Chief mentor of the *Kauravas* and *Pandavas-Dronacharya, Ashwatthama* is also one to the seven immortals. He was cursed for his misdeeds to roam the face of the earth until the next incarnation of *Vishnu* takes birth and lifts his curse.

Ashwini Kumars / Ashwini twins: The *Vedic* twin Gods also referred jointly as the *Ashwins*. They are the healing Gods and divine horsemen. They have their symbolic importance as the twin doctors who parted the knowledge of the *Ayurvedic* medicines to the sages of the *Vedic* times.

Asita: *Asita* was one of the liberated sages. As per the commentary of *Kesava Kashmiri*, the sage *Asita* had described and declared the *Avatar* of *Krishna* to be all pervading with the sky as his head, the earth his chest and his stomach representing the three *Lokas*-or the three worldly realms of existence.

Atma: A *Sanskrit* word for the indwelling 'Self' or Soul. The *Gita* describes the *Atma* as the all knowing, imperishable and immutable portion of the supreme lord that exists and dwells in all living beings.

Avatar: The embodiment of the Divine in the human realm. As per the ancient Indian scriptures, in the present age of *Kaliyuga, Vishnu*- the Perseverer shall manifest in his tenth *Avatar*- as *Kalki*.

Bhagavad Gita: A combination of the two *Sanskrit* words-*Bhagavad*- words uttered by the Divine and *Gita*- that which is sung.

Bhagavad: A *Sanskrit* word meaning words uttered by the Lord or *Bhagwaan*

Bharat/ Bharata: A *Sanskrit* word which is a combination of

Bha- light and *rath-* chariot. Since ancient times, the Indian sub-continent was often referred to as *Bharat* and in the *Gita, Sri Krishna* tries to invoke a confidence in the distraught *Arjuna* by repeatedly referring to him as *Bharat*.

Bheeshma: The legendary elder who was invincible and revered by both the *Pandavas* and the *Kauravas*. He was known to be the backbone of the *Karuavan* defense and offence and had the power to single-handedly change the course of any war. He was blessed with the boon that even death would not touch him without his consent.

Bhima: The juggernaut *Pandava* with a voracious appetite. He was without doubt the most physically powerful amongst the five *Pandava* princes.

Bhrigu: One of the Seven Sages- the *Saptarishis, Bhrigu* was the first compiler of the scripture on Vedic Astrology-named as *Bhrigu Samhita.* The descendents of his school of science were said to belong to the *Bharagava Sampardaya.*

Brahma- sutras: The *Brahma-sutra* is a *Vedantic* text that is a composition of the *Upanishads* and is an exposition and systemic summary of the *Upanishads* as per the *Vedanta* school of thought.

Brahma/ Brahman: The *Sanskrit* word used to depict the supreme creator of the universe. *Brahma* belongs to the trinity of the supreme deities and was responsible for thrusting the seed of creation of life on earth.

Brahmin: *Krishna* describes a system of four-fold castes based upon the aptitude, capacity and quality of the individual – The *Brahmins,* the *Kshatriyas,* the *Vasihyas* and the *Shudras.* A seeker of *Brahma* is called a Brahmin. The warrior was the *Kshatriya,* the merchant – the *Vaishya* and those who served for the betterment of others were the *Shudras.* However, the teachings of *Sri Krishna,* the caste system which was flexible became rigid and castes were enforced upon children based upon birth.

Brihaspati: Worshipped by all the sages and the gods alike, *Brihaspati* is considered as their supreme teacher and is identified with the planet *Guru* or Jupiter.

Brihat Sama: The mantra of great reverence in the *Sama Veda* hymns. Sage *Bharadwaja* was credited with bringing out the *Brihat Sama* mantra out of *Agni*.

Chekitan: The son of King *Dhrishtaketu* and ruler of *Kekayas*, the brave *Vrshini* warrior who fought alongside the Pandavas at *Kurukshetra*.

Chitraratha: The King of the *Gandharvas* who parted the knowledge of the *Gandharva* wisdom to Arjuna and was considered the amongst the Gandharvas.

Darshana: A blessing of vision of God conferred upon to a mortal.

Devadatta: The war conch that was gifted to *Arjuna* by *Varuna*-the Vedic deity who is the lord of the skies and the celestial oceans

Devala: One of the high seers mentioned in the *Bhagawad Gita* of the stature of *Narada* and *Vyasa*.

Devas: The *Sanskrit* collective word for the confederation of Gods.

Dharma: The *Sanskrit* word has multiple meanings in the Hindu, Buddhist and Jain traditions that vary as per the context, *Dharma* is synonymous with the word 'duty' and can be collectively looked at as a way of living that leads to the overall progress of an individual, a group or a nation at large.

Dhritarashtra: The Emperor and blind father of the *Kauravas* who had ascended the throne on the demise of the incumbent king and brother- *Pandu* whose children later came to be called the *Pandavas*.

Drishtadyumna: *Dhrishtadyumna* – the son of King *Drupada* and brother of *Draupadi* and *Shikhandi*, was a commander of the Pandava army during the war.

Dronacharya/ Drona: Dronacharya was the royal guru to *Kauravas* and *Pandavas*. He was considered invincible because of his mastery over the advanced battle techniques as well as the *Divya astras* or divine nuclear weapons. His attachment to his son-*Ashwatthama* brought about his downfall in the great battle of *Kurukshetra*.

Drupada: The King of *Panchala* who had eleven children *Satyajit, Shikhandi Uttamauja, Kumar, Yudhamanyu, Vrika, Panchalya, Suratha, Shatrunjaya and Janamejaya,* fought the battle of *Kurukshetra* alongside the *Pandavas*.

Duryodhana: The chief antagonist of the epic, *Duryodhana* is the eldest of the hundred sons of the blind Emperor *Dhritarashtra*.

Gandharvas: The messengers between the humans and the Gods, the *Gandharvas* are the male counterparts of the beautiful *Apsaras-* the angelic female beings and are known for their musical and dancing abilities.

Gandiva: The divine bow wielded by *Arjuna* who used it in the Great War. It was considered sacred and was studded with gold bosses and was believed to have been handed over the *Arjuna* by the Vedic deity *Varuna*.

Garuda: The mystic king eagle found in both The Hindu and The Buddist Mythology and is the vehicle of Lord *Vishnu-* (The Preserver). The *Garuda* is worshipped in most south-east Asian countries mainly in India, Mongolia, Thialand and Indonesia. The *Garuda* is the national emblem of Thailand and Indonesia.

Gayatri: One of the most popular amongst the many *Chandas* poetic metres of the *Sanskrit* languages. Some other metres are *Anushtubh, Trishtubh etc.*

Gopikas: The cowherd girls who were known for their utmost devotion to *Krishna* who had experienced the greatest joys of watching the divine Krishna grow from his early childhood days.

Ikshvaku: The first King of the *Vedic* times who was the first *Suryavanshi* or descendent of the Sun.

Indra: The post of the leader of *Devas* or Gods in the *Swargaloka* or heavens. Wielder of the *Vajra* or thunderbolt, riding the *Airavata* or the white elephant- he is one of the most important deities invoked in the Rig *Vedic* hymns. He is also known in the Buddhist traditions as the *Dharmapala* or the defender and upholder of the *Dharma*.

Janaka: The great philosopher king of *Videha* (Modern day Nepal) who was a patron of the Vedic sciences and was also known to be an enlightened ruler.

Japa: The act of silent repetition of a *Sanskrit mantra* is called *Japa*. The practice of *Japa* and meditation together are associated with emotional and cognitive well-being.

Jayadrata: The son of king *Vridhaksatra*, he was the king of *Sindhu* kingdom. He was a brother in law of the *Pandavas* and fought against them by joining the side of the *Kauravas*.

Kaliyuga: The Age of Darkness or the Age of '*Kali*'- wherein mankind is farthest away from God. As per the Hindu, Sikh, Buddhist and Jain traditions, the world goes through four cyclic stages of periods – *Satyayuga, Tretayuga, Dwaparayuga and Kaliyuga*. At present as per the ancient Indian scriptures- the world is going through the phase of *Kaliyuga*.

Kamadhenu: The divine cow goddess, *Kamadhenu* or *Surabhi* is described as the mother of all cows and is the divine wish yielding cow that grants the owner with whatever wish he desires.

Kandarpa: The God of human love, desire and attraction who is responsible for planting the seed of desire for procreation in all mortals.

Kapila muni: One of the prominent *Vedic* sages who founded the *Sankhya* school of philosophy and is described in some texts as a descendent of *Manu.*

Karma: A *Sanskrit* word that means action, work or deed and is widely used by the proponents of Hinduism, Buddhism, Sikkhism, Taoism and Shintoism. Good *Karma* is gathered by performing good deeds and brings happiness and prosperity for the future whereas bad *Karma* is gathered by wrong deeds and brings sorrow and misery for the future. The *Gita* speaks of transcending both good and bad karma so that one can be truly liberated.

Karma-Yoga: *Sanskrit* word referring to *Yoga* of Action. See *Yoga.*

Karna: He was the King of *Anga*, was also a *Pandava* who fought alongside his friend *Duryodhana.* He was considered one of the greatest martial warriors in the battle and was admired even by *Krishna* and *Bheeshma.*

Kauravas: The hundred sons of *Dhritarashtra* and *Gandhaari* who fought against their cousins- *Pandavas.* Though both the *Pandavas* and *Kauravas* belonged to the same *Kuru* Dynasty- the sons of *Pandu* created a niche for themselves and were called *Pandavas.*

Krishna: The Lord of The *Bhagavad Gita* is known by several names for his different roles. *Krishna* has many meanings in *Sanskrit* – the dark skinned one, one who attracts etc.

Kshatriyas: The Class of warriors, kings and leaders. See *Brahmin.*

Kunti: The wife of the deceased Emperor *Pandu* and mother of the *Pandava* princes

Kuntibhoj: The adoptive father and cousin of Queen *Kunti* the mother of the *Pandavas*.

Kurukshetra: The battlefield where the mighty battle of *Mahabharata* between the princes of the Kuru dynasty took place.

Kusha: *Kusha* grass or *desmostachiya bipinnata* is a sacred and medicinal grass as per Ayurveda texts and has its spiritual significance as well. A mat made of *Kusha* grass was deemed fit for the high sages and the Gods in the *Vedic* texts and as per the Buddist tradtions, *Buddha* received his enlightenment while meditating on a seat of *Kusha* grass.

Mahabharata: *Vyasa* composed the epic "*Mahabharata*" while meditating upon the great battle of *Kurukshetra.*

Manipushapaka: The divine conch that was used by the *Pandava* prince *Sahadeva.*

Manu/ Manus: According to the Vedic traditions, *Manu* is the title for the progenitor of humanity. A Manu is the created by *Brahma* and the *Manu* creates the different species during his lifetime which is called the *Manvantara* or the Age of *Manu.* At the end of the *Manvantara*; *Brahma* creates a new *Manu* to replace the deceased *Manu* and the cycle of creation continues, *Vishnu* takes a new *Avatar* and a new *Indra* and new *Saptarishis* are appointed.

Marichi: The son of *Brahma*- the cosmic creator, *Marichi* is one of the Seven Sages or *Saptarishis.*

Maruts: The *Vedic* Gods and fierce roaring deities of the storms armed with thunderbolts and golden weapons and often identified with the *Rudras* or the deities of destruction. They are said to be twenty-three in number.

Maya: A *Sanskrit* word denoting the veil of outer-worldy illusion that prevents a being from attaining the true knowledge of the indwelling Supreme Self or the "*Atman*".

Meru/ Mahameru: The sacred mountain of the Hindu, Buddhist and Jain traditions is the holy mountain of five peaks that is the locus of both the physical and the metaphysical universes.

Moksha: A *Sanskrit* word that can be equated to the English terms of liberation or salvation of the soul.

Mrigashirsha: The fifth constellation or *Nakshatra* as per the Vedic astrological calculations. In English, the constellation of *Mrigashirsha* is called *Orion*.

Naga: The race of the Serpent peoples-attributed to play many positive and negative roles in different traditions viz. the Hindu, Buddhist, Sikh and the Jain traditions.

Nakul: The twin brother of *Sahadeva* – the fourth of the Five *Pandava prince*s of the *Mahabharata*.

Narada/ Narada muni: The ancient Vedic sage and worshipper of Narayana who was revered in all three *lokas* or realms. He had the power to travel at will to any location and he functioned as a messenger of the Divine.

Nirvana: A *Sanskrit* word that has been widely used in Hindu and Buddhist traditions. It is a state of complete dissolution or as Sri Aurobindo has described, an extinction into the infinite

Om tat sat: The triple mantra that is often prescribed in the texts for *japa* or repetition By concentrating at the centre between the eyebrows and by repetition of this mantra- one can experience an ascent in consciousness.

Panchajanya: The Divine conch that was used by *Sri Krishna*.

Pandavas: The sons of the deceased Emperor *Pandu* and Kunti. The descendents of the Pandu came to be called Pandavas.

Poundra: The divine conch that was used by the *Pandava* prince *Bhima*.

Prahalada: The pious king of the *Daityas* and the son of the demoniac natured *Hiranyakashyapu* known for his ardent and unswerving devotion to *Vishnu*.

Prakriti: Nature is defined as the feminine counterpart of the Supernal Divine and is called *Prakriti*. All the modes of nature, their qualities and deformities of existences are part of *Prakriti*.

Puranas: The texts containing tales of the creation and destruction of the universe and also narratives and genealogies of the different kings, heroes, demi-Gods and Gods of the *Hindu* mythologies. They also contained spiritual, metaphysical references and discussions.

Purujit: The brother of *Kunti* and maternal uncle of the *Pandavas* who participated in the battle.

Purusha: The all-pervading, imperishable and faultless cosmic Divine is referred to as the *Purusha*.

Rajas: It is one of the threefold *gunas* or qualities that govern all living beings in nature.

Rama: The Seventh Avatar of *Vishnu* and the King of *Ayodhya* who was called the ideal and best amongst all men. He is the protagonist of the great epic *Ramayana*.

Rudras: They are the fierce beings of destruction and are the embodiments of *Shiva*- See *Shankara*). In total, the *Rudras* are eleven in number.

Sadhyas: The twelve *Vedic* Gods who are the sons of *Daksha* and *Sadhya* whose responsibility is to guard the prayers and oblations during a *Yagnya.*

Sahadeva: He was the youngest of the five *Pandavas* princes and the twin of *Nakul. Nakul* and *Sahadeva* were born by invoking the *Ashwini Kumars* – the Vedic deities and twin horsement who parted the Knowledge of *Ayurveda.*

Sama Veda: The third *Veda, Sama Veda* is a collection of melodious hymns in *Vedic Sanskrit* and is considered a core or seed scripture of the *Vedic* traditions.

Samadhi: It is the final meditative state of absorption into the Divine as per the Hindu, Sikh, Jain and Buddhist traditions. The *Gita* shows the way of attaining *Samadhi* while in the midst of all actions.

Sanjay: He was blessed with *Divya Drishti* or Divine sight. With this gift of foresight, he narrated the events taking place at the *Kurukshetra* as and when they unfolded to the blind Emperor *Dhritarashtra.*

Sanyasa/ Sanyasin: He who has attained-*Sanyasa*- the state of complete renunciation of all desires and ambitions.

Saptarishi: The Seven Sages who were appointed with the responsibility to further the creation of the human race, namely *Marichi, Atri, Angiras, Pulaha, Kratu, Pulatsya* and *Vashishta.*

Sarawasti: The *Vedic* deity considered to be the Goddess of thought, word, inspiration and knowledge.

Sattwa: One of the three *gunas* or qualities that persist in nature. Sattwa denotes all that is pure and good.

Shaivya: The father in law of *Yudhishthira, Shaivya* was the king who was an expert archer who fought alongside the *Pandavas* in the *Kurukshetra* war.

Shankara: *Shankara* or *Shiva* is the supreme deity who facilitates new creation and is the Destroyer among the holy Trinity of Gods. He is the God of Gods and is also known as *Mahadeva.* He is worshipped in the symbolic form of the *Lingam.*

Shikhandi: The child of *Drupad* who played a vital role in the death of *Bheeshma.*

Shudras: The class of men who believe in dedicating their lives in the service of mankind. Also See **Brahmin.**

Skanda: *Skanda* also known as *Karthikeya* or *Subramaniyam* or *Kumaran* is the God of war and is the commander of the armies of the *devas.*

Soma: *Soma* is the name of a *Vedic God,* a medicinal herb and also an ambrosial drink that grants immortality. Soma also finds many references as *Sauma* in the *Zorastrian* traditions.

Somadatta: The father of *Bhuvisravas,* the prince of *Bahlikan* who fought alongside the *Kauravas*

Sri Krishna: The Lord of The *Bhagwat Gita* is known by several names for his different roles. *Krishna* literally means in *Sanskrit* – the dark skinned one. *Sri* is a title that is prefixed as a mark of reverence.

Subhadra: The wife of *Arjuna* and mother of the brave *Abhimanyu.*

Sughosha: The war conch that belonged to the Pandava prince *Nakul.*

Tamas: One of the three *gunas* or qualities that persist in nature. Tamas is the darkness of ignorance that is associated with inertia, dullness, lethargy and delusion.

Tyaga: The *Sanskrit* word for sacrifice. Throughout the *Gita, Krishna* encourages *Arjuna* to sacrifice the fruits of actions and perform his *karma* dutifully with a state of detachment.

Ucchaisravas: The seven-headed flying horse that arose out of the milk-sea during the *Samudra manthanam* or churning of the ocean that took place during the fight for the immortal nectar between the *Devas* and the *Asuras*.

Ushanas: The son of *Kavyamata* or *Ushana* is *Vedic* sage *Ushanas* and is revered as the best amongst the seers and is also known as Shukra, identified with the planet Venus.

Ushmapas: The class of ancestors who receive the oblations and are said to dwell in *Pitru loka*- the realm of the deified ancestors.

Uttamauja: The valiant son of King *Drupad* who fought along-side the *Pandavas*.

Vaishnava/ Vaishnavism: The followers of *Vishnu* are called *Vaishnavites* and their religion is called *Vaishnavism* which is one of the many offshoots of the Hindu traditions. *Krishna* is considered to be an incarnation of the Divine *Vishnu*- whose role is to look after the sustenance of the Universe.

Vaishyas: The class of businessmen, artisans, traders and agriculturists. See **Brahmin**.

Vajra: The thunderbolt of *Indra,* the *Vajra* was a terrible weapon of destruction and was the highest amongst the weapons that could be obtained through penance.

Varuna: The Vedic God of the waters and of the celestial oceans. He is the upholder of the laws of the world below the seas much like *Poseidon* of the Greeks and *Neptune* of the Romans.

Vasuki: The snake of *Shiva*- the Destroyer is called *Vasuki. Vasuki* is one of the most formidable amongst the *Naga*-Serpent kings and is revered in both Hindu and Buddhist traditions. Even amongst the Chinese and Japanese mythologies- *Vasuki* is one amongst the eight great *Naga* kings.

Vasus: These are the eight elemental deities who are the attendants of *Vishnu* and they represent the cosmic powers manifesting in nature.

Vedantas: The *Vedantas* comprise all the philosophical inter-pretations of the *Brahma-sutras* and the *Upanishads.* There are many schools of *Vedantas.* Some examples are *Dvaita, Advaita, Vishisht-advait, Bheda, Achintya-Bheda etc.*

Vedas: Composed in *Vedic Sanskrit,* they are amongst the oldest scriptures of the world dating before 1500 BC.

Vikarna: The son of *Dhritarashtra* and brother of crown prince *Duryodhana* who fought alongside the *Karuravas. Vikarna* was the only *Kaurava* who questioned the humiliation of *Draupadi,* the wife of his cousin *Pandavas* after they lost her in a game of dice to *Duryodhana.*

Virata: The king in whose court the *Pandavas* spent a year in concealment during their exile. Virata participated in the war and fought alongside the *Pandavas.*

Vishnu: One of the Supreme Trinity of the Creator, the Perserver and the Destroyer. *Vishnu* is also known as *Narayana* or *Hari* and the scriptures describe a thousand different names of *Vishnu* as per his manifestations. *Vishnu* is responsible for the perpetuation of the Creation and has been described to have taken nine different *Avatars* to facilitate evolution namely- *Matsya, Kurmah, Varaha, Narasimha, Vamana, Parashuram, Ram, Krishna* and *Buddha.* It has been prophesized that the tenth manifestation- *Kalki* would be the final manifestation that would lead to the greatest ascension of the human race.

Vishwaroopam: A combination of two *Sanskrit* words, *Vishwa-* world and *roopam-* form. *Vishwaroopam* refers to the vision of the all-pervading universal form of the Divine.

Vrishni: The *Vrishni* Clan was an ancient clan of warriors of the lunar race and *Krishna* belonged to this race.

Vyasa: The composer of *Mahabharata,* mystic and sage and first master whose greatest contribution to the universe was the splitting of the Vedas into the four primordial texts- *Rig Veda, Yajur Veda, Sama Veda* and *Atharva Veda*. The *Atharva Veda* was added later on and many time the Vedas are referred as three in number – The Rig, the Yajur and the Sama.

Yadava: The *Yaduvamsha* or descendents of King *Yadu* and *Mathura* was their principle bastion. A number of dynasties originated from the *Yadavas* namely the *Vrishnis*, the Bhojas, the *Haihayas*, the *Chedis*, the *Vidharbhas*, the *Satvatas*, the *Andhakas*, the *Kukuras* and the *Shainyas*.

Yagnya: *Yagnya* which means sacrifice- can imply both the ritual sacrifices that are performed since the *Vedic* times and also the inner sacrifices.

Yakshas: They appear in the Hindu, Buddhist and Jain traditions and are the friendly sentient spirits and beings who are caretakers of nature's wealth.

Yama: Death is often portrayed in most Indian scriptures as Lord *Yama-* blue skinned,wearing red clothes with a noose in hand and his vehicle is the water buffalo. With his noose- he pulls the soul out of the corpse and initiates the soul journey.

Yoga: A *Sanskrit* word that can be interpreted in English as the way of union with the divine. The threefold paths of Union with the Divine are defined in the *Gita-* The *Yoga* of Knowledge, The *Yoga* of *Bhakti* or Devotion and The *Yoga* of works wherein man can attain a union with the cosmic divine through three modes -knowledge, works and right action. The Integral *Yoga* of *Sri Aurobindo* which embraces all three *Yogas* of knowledge, devotion and works considers perfection in work to be the means of attaining the zenith of spiritual realizations. *Sri Aurobindo's Yoga* describes perfection in work as true spirituality- emphasizing the need for embarking on the triple paths.

Yogi: He who devotes his life to the practice of *Yoga* i.e. He who dedicates his life to attain a union with the Divine.

Yudhamanyu: The valiant son of *Drupada* who fought alongside the *Pandavas* in the battle of *Kurukshetra*

Yudhishthira: The eldest of the *Pandava* kings and the leader of the *Pandavas*, He was also known as *Dharmaraj* who staunchly followed his *Dharma* and waged war as per his moral code of conduct.

Yuyudhana: He was a valiant warrior who fought alongside the *Pandavas*. He was known for his devotion to *Krishna* and was a student of *Arjuna*. He is also known as the unconquerable *Satyaki*.

Vowels and codas

Devanāgarī	Transcription		Category
अ	a	A	
आ	ā	Ā	
इ	i	I	
ई	ī	Ī	
उ	u	U	monophthongs
ऊ	ū	Ū	& syllabic liquids
ऋ	r̥	R	
ॠ	r̥̄	R̥	
ऌ	l̥	L	
ॡ	l̥̄	L̥	
ए	e	E	
ऐ	ai	Ai	
ओ	o	O	diphthongs
औ	au	Au	
अं	m̥	M	anusvara
अः	ḥ	H	visarga
अऽ	'		avagraha

International Alphabet of Sanskrit Transliteration

IAST is based on a standard established by the International Congress of Orientalists at Geneva in 1894.

It represents not only the phonemes of Sanskrit, but allows essentially phonetic transcription, e.g., visarga ḥ is an allophone of word-final r and s

This table has been provided to enable the readers to pronounce the Sanskrit words in the right phonetic sense from the transliteration.

Source:http://en.wikipedia.org/wiki/International_Alphabet_of_Sanskrit_Transliteration)

Consonants

velars	palatals	retroflexes	dentals	labials	
क k K	च c C	ट ṭ Ṭ	त t T	प p P	tenuis stops
ख kh Kh	छ ch Ch	ठ ṭh Ṭh	थ th Th	फ ph Ph	aspirated stops
ग g G	ज j J	ड ḍ Ḍ	द d D	ब b B	voiced stops
घ gh Gh	झ jh Jh	ढ ḍh Ḍh	ध dh Dh	भ bh Bh	breathy-voiced stops
ङ ṅ Ṅ	ञ ñ Ñ	ण ṇ Ṇ	न n N	म m M	nasal stops
ह h H	य y Y	र r R	ल l L	व v V	approximants
	श ś Ś	ष ṣ Ṣ	स s S		sibilants

About the Author:

The author is a poet and resident of Pondicherry who lives with his teacher- Sri. M.R. Damle *(in pic)* who was a former founder trustee of the Auro Service Trust and is the Proprietor of KVM Research Laboratories an SSI unit that has been manufacturing Ayurvedic Medicines and Health & Beauty products since 1988 in Pondicherry and exporting since 1990. Inspired by the principles of the Integral Yoga of Sri Aurobindo, he joined his teacher after graduating in Mechanical Engineering in 2011.

As a researcher at Midam Charitable Trust – an NGO founded by Sri. M.R. Damle, he collaborated with the Dept. of Genetics, Madras University to implement a **Vedic Chants Intervention Program**- a free group therapy for children with Autism. Their therapy was awarded the Best therapeutics presentation at the 29th International Conference on Human Genetics (ISHG), in Ahmedabad, Gujarat in January 2014. His first book "Rhythm of the Spirit" - was well received by connoisseurs of poetry beyond Indian boundaries and his second e-book Voice of Krishna: Secrets of the Self set a record in December 2014 in the India Book of Records as the **"First Rhyme Book based on Bhagavad Gita"**. The author also writes articles in Sri Aurobindo's Action- the journal of India's Resurgence which was set up in 1970 by The Mother of Sri Aurobindo Ashram, Pondicherry.

The Midam Symbol

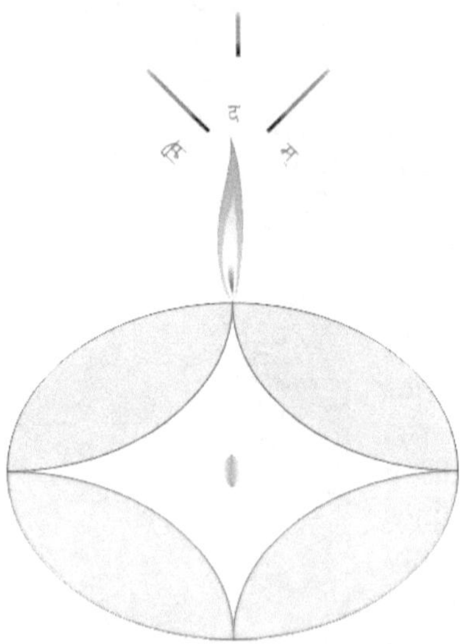

The sphere represents the earth that we live on. The blue color (upper hemisphere) depicts the skies and green (lower hemisphere) the flora and fauna.

The yellow arched diamond represents man who is always in communion with the five elements. Inside man is a tiny flame - the flame of aspiration which represents the chaitya purusha -"the psychic being". Man's aspiration takes him higher and higher to meet the Supreme light represented by Agni- the flame.

This higher knowledge descends in man and he then embraces the earth having received this light- the knowledge, and he uses it for the betterment of all life on earth.

Midam Charitable Trust's -Krishna's Butter Project (For Kids & Adults)

In 2015 Krishna's Butter Project was started by Midam Charitable Trust, Pondicherry under the direction of its founder Sri Madhusudan Damle which led to the development of a Free teaching module and course book published by Midam titled, "Krishna's Butter For Champion Students" authored by senior Pathologist and ex.HOD, Dr.Bhawana Badhe and student of Sri Madhusudan Damle. This was later translated into Hindi and Marathi language by Sri Arvind Chandorkar, a retired banker and student of Damelji and the same was also published by the trust.

Dr.Bhawana Badhe took it to the school class rooms of the students of Class 8 of Vidhyaniketan School, Puducherry and this became a regular feature at their institute. During her free time especially in the weekend, she conducted more classes and connected with various parents and kids who enjoyed the classes. In 2018, one parent, Mrs.Chitra Torvi, a homemaker, was so happy after observing the positive changes in her 2 daughters that she began to learn the methodology of the Krishna's Butter Project and began teaching to interested persons.

In 2020, Once the lockdown started all schools were closed and Mrs.Chitra Torvi came up with the idea of taking it to the digital classrooms. And the module was adopted to suit the Digital platforms and online batches for children 8 and above were launched for children of all countries and backgrounds. **No fee is charged for these sessions** and all children are accommodated on First Come First Serve Basis. Avanti Badhe and Sushrut Badhe, also students of Sri Madhsudan Damle began conducting separate batches for kids and adults respectively after receiving the training to meet the demand for the classes.

So Far, 20 Batches have been launched including 4 batches for adults with over 600 enrolments from participants in India, USA, UK, Canada, Australia, Singapore and Dubai. Due to popularity through word of recommendation, waiting lists have been launched and parents who saw positive changes in their children have enrolled for teacher training sessions to conduct similar free sessions from their respective cities as per the Krishna's Butter Module. Approx 6 New batches are launched every month and more are expected once new teachers are ready.

KRISHNA'S BUTTER MODULE:
Taking the Practical principles of the Gita to children, a strong foundation of value education is laid on the basis on select 99 verses from Bhagavad Gita from all 18 chapters of the Gita over a period of 19 sessions on weekdays, with each session lasting for 45 minutes. Audio's of Sanskrit verses are provided and each day a cartoon illustration is shared matching the Lesson of the day and the shlokas are explained as English rhymes taken from "Bhagavad Gita : Rhythm of Krishna" written by Sushrut Badhe. Weekends are Off where participants share their questions which are answered by the Krishna's Butter core team. For the Adults, most of the verses of the Gita are covered with relevant day to day examples.

FEEDBACK RECEIVED:
We have received several feedbacks from parents that their kids have shown significant and positive behavioural changes. Improvements in creativity, reduction in shyness, improvement in confidence, anger control and overall happiness during the current period are a common theme in the feedback. Due to demand from happy parents asking for advanced courses, follow up batches called Krishna's Delight also have been started for a monthly meeting to revise on the practical principles of the Gita which children can practise in everyday lives.

The teachers were most impressed with children sharing their everyday experiences where they utilized the Concepts like Karma Yoga , doing things happily with detachment, asking for help from elders when in trouble like Arjuna and also how they grasped the nutritional concepts of food on the basis of Satvik-

Rajasic –Tamasic Foods from the Gita.

Niharika Khanna, a participant from the Adults batch wrote to us "Insightful discussions, practical examples, new learnings that too, in the form of Rhythmic explanations, have strengthened the sense of our own duties, knowledge, ability, to discriminate between righteousness and wrong, value of dedication, true form of Dharma and list goes on and on". To know more about the classes, visit here: www.facebook.com/midamtrust

Hi,

My sister, Avanti and I are working under our teacher- Sri Madhusudan R Damle at his unit, KVM Research Laboratories sharing the responsibilities as GM and CEO respectively. Together we manufacture and export 100% Natural Ayurvedic health and beauty products at our unit in Midam Ashram at Kothapurinatham Village.

To find out more, Check out our online store: www.amazon.in/herbomineral or scan this QR code on your smartphone.

- Sushrut Badhe

Om tat Sat

<u>NOTES</u>